IT'S NOT OVER

Books by Michelangelo Signorile

QUEER IN AMERICA

OUTING YOURSELF

LIFE OUTSIDE

HITTING HARD

IT'S NOT OVER

IT'S NOT OVER

GETTING BEYOND TOLERANCE, DEFEATING HOMOPHOBIA, AND WINNING TRUE EQUALITY

Michelangelo Signorile

Houghton Mifflin Harcourt

BOSTON   NEW YORK

2015

For information about permission to reproduce selections from this book,
write to Permissions, Houghton Mifflin Harcourt Publishing Company,
215 Park Avenue South, New York, New York 10003.

www.hmhco.com

Library of Congress Cataloging-in-Publication Data is available.
ISBN 978-0-544-38100-1

Book design by Patrick Barry

Printed in the United States of America
DOC 10 9 8 7 6 5 4 3 2 1

In memory of Sarah Pettit

CONTENTS

AUTHOR'S NOTE

IT'S NOT OVER LOOKS AT dramatic, ongoing transformations in politics, society, and culture whose effects are focused on lesbian, gay, bisexual, and transgender Americans. Those terms — *lesbian, gay, bisexual,* and *transgender* — describe distinct groups and identities that have intersected as a people, though each group has its own unique history. The acronym *LGBT* is useful as an umbrella term in that it encompasses all the groups without negating the important differences among them. The challenge that anyone writing about these groups faces is to balance keeping them visible both separately and together, all without being repetitive. My hope is that readers appreciate and understand the inherent challenges in writing about these groups and their intersections, as well as the spirit of my undertaking. I have done my best to represent everyone I'm writing about by alternating among the historical, all-encompassing use of the word *gay,* the term *LGBT,* and more specific combinations of the words that acronym comprises.

In a similar way, this book often uses the word *homophobia* to encompass *biphobia, lesbophobia,* and *transphobia.* Again, it would be challenging and cumbersome to use all of these words in every instance. I use certain words, such as *transphobia,* throughout the book when they are relevant and appropriately specific, but I rely primarily on the term *homophobia* to draw together several different but inter-related phenomena.

When I write about "the closet" in *It's Not Over,* I discuss it as it relates to sexual orientation, not gender identity. There is long-standing agreement — among mental-health professionals as well as gay activists — that closeting one's sexual orientation exerts psychological costs and causes harm. For transgender people, the idea of the closet, and publicly acknowledging being transgender, takes on a much different meaning. It's been a topic of discussion for some time among transgender activists and writers, whose work should be read to help people become more informed of the ongoing conversation.

It's Not Over often quotes listeners to my radio program, as well as interviews from the show. For context, *The Michelangelo Signorile Show* is a news, commentary, and call-in show covering progressive and LGBT political and cultural issues. The show began on SiriusXM's OutQ channel (the first national LGBT radio channel) and, after ten years, moved to SiriusXM Progress, in July 2013. It airs three hours each weekday afternoon all across the United States and Canada. On Progress, the show has a larger, diverse mix of LGBT and heterosexual listeners. Most are progressives, but many, I'm happy to say, are conservatives who call in to challenge — and be challenged — and to spark discussion. The listeners are diverse in many other ways as well. They come from every geographic region, for example, as the show is heard from big cities to small towns and even in the most remote rural areas of the United States and Canada.

I also often refer to — and use passages from — my opinion pieces, interviews, and analysis on *Huffington Post* in this book. Serving as editor at large of *Huffington Post*'s Gay Voices vertical since November 2011 has been a dynamic experience, and much of the input I have received from the large and diverse readership there is also reflected in this book.

IT'S NOT OVER

1

VICTORY BLINDNESS

THE DANGEROUS ILLUSION THAT WE'VE ALMOST WON

IMAGINE A GROUP OF PEOPLE who have spent decades — generations, centuries — in fear, invisibility, struggle, and silence. Imagine they find their voice, only to be decimated by an era of death and unthinkable loss made more bitter by crushing societal indifference to their predicament.

Now imagine that, in a matter of a few short years, everything seems to change. At what feels like light speed, they make momentous gains. The world begins to open its arms to them in ways they had never thought possible. The experience is powerful, exhilarating, spellbinding even. It feels like they are living in a dream. But behind that dream is a reality more treacherous than many of them may vaguely imagine.

Over the past few years, lesbian, gay, bisexual, and transgender Americans have been living in that dream. In 2011 the onerous "don't ask, don't tell" law banning gays and lesbians from serving openly in the military was repealed. The destructive force of the Defense of Marriage Act disintegrated in 2013 when a thunderous Supreme Court ruling in *U.S. v. Windsor* struck it down. In rapid succession, state after state, from the coasts well into the heartland, transformed into what appeared to be bastions of full equality as thousands of gay and lesbian couples marched down the aisle. Even deep in Mormon Utah and in Oklahoma, the "buckle of the Bible Belt," federal judges threw out hateful bans on gay marriage, and the issue worked its way back up to an apparently sympathetic Supreme Court.

We saw LGBT people represented in movies, in music, and on TV in ways we'd not experienced before. Not only were gay and transgender characters more visible than ever, but also openly gay, lesbian, bisexual, and transgender actors were more and more often invited to play these roles. A mass wedding occurred at the Grammy Awards. Ellen DeGeneres, a lesbian comedian, made an enormous comeback after her sitcom was canceled the year following her coming out in the 1990s, to become a daytime television sensation. Rosie O'Donnell was back on *The View* and more outspoken than ever. A transgender actress, Laverne Cox, stood tall on the cover of *Time* magazine. Apple's Tim Cook made a huge impact in the business world, becoming the most high-profile CEO — and the only one among the Fortune 500 companies — to come out, proclaiming he is "proud to be gay."

Since the mid-'90s many people with HIV were no longer suffering and dying; they were increasingly thriving and the picture of good health because of life-saving drug treatments. Gay–straight alliance groups were formed in schools across the country, and LGBT people began to come out of the closet at ever-younger ages. Even in the world of sports, visibility arrived in unprecedented ways. A midcareer NBA player, Jason Collins, came out as gay, and even the barrier of the macho world of football broke when Michael Sam became the first openly gay player drafted to the NFL and shared his happiness by expressing his love, kissing his boyfriend for all of America to see.

In seductive ways, it started to feel as if we had almost finally "made it," that we were just about equal in the eyes of most of the American people. The media reported on dizzying poll results that seemed to point to acceptance. We heard cheering and huge sighs of relief as many soaked up the success that now seemed so evident. Like many people, I even noticed my Facebook feed regularly erupting with posts expressing congratulations or disbelief about seeing these great strides in our lifetime.

Yet it was — and is — a dangerous moment. It's a moment in which all of us, LGBT and straight, who support equality risk falling prey to what I've come to call victory blindness. We're overcome by the heady whirl of a narrative of victory, a kind of bedtime story that tells us we've reached the promised land, that can make everything else seem like a blur. Even with the enormously positive developments — and, as this book will show, sometimes perhaps as a reaction to them — homophobia rages on in America, as sports stars are practically rewarded after spouting hate, as TV sitcoms still make gay and transgender people the insulting punch line, as the media respects and airs bigoted views of the "other side," as businesses now brazenly flaunt a "no gays allowed" policy, as many workers fear coming out on the job more than ever, as federal civil rights protections seem further away than before, and as we are often not well served by a gay establishment that apologizes for and lauds political leaders rather than demanding action. Maybe it's time to get rid of the bedtime story and wake up from the dream.

I say it's a "dangerous" moment because at the same time that all the great strides have occurred, discrimination, violence, and tragic horror stories — in addition to the daily slights that all of us who are gay, lesbian, bisexual, or transgender have experienced for years — have not only continued, they've sometimes become more blatant. Rather than dissipating, reports of violence against LGBT people have surged, even in the most liberal, gay-accepting cities, spiking 27% in New York City alone from 2013 to 2014, according to the Anti-Violence Project. In Seattle, where an increase in hate crimes had also been seen since 2013, a man pleaded guilty in 2014 to setting a gay bar on fire on New Year's Eve, saying in a statement that homosexuals should be "exterminated." And nationally, homicides motivated by hatred against gay, lesbian, and bisexual people are themselves outnumbered by hate-motivated killings of transgender women by a factor of almost 3 to 1. These attacks, the vast majority of which have been perpetrated against transgender women of color, have reached what one advocate called "epidemic" levels.

In Philadelphia, in September 2014, onlookers were stunned

when, according to several reports, a group of between eight and twelve "well-dressed" men and women in their twenties hurled what witnesses described as homophobic slurs — "dirty faggot" and "fucking faggot" — at a gay male couple walking by. One of the gay men was knocked unconscious, sustaining severe damage to his face, requiring surgery and the wiring of his jaw. Three people were later arrested and charged with assault, but, outrageously, they couldn't be charged with a hate crime because Pennsylvania lacked a hate-crimes law protecting LGBT people. In Georgia a twenty-year-old man captured video on his phone of a scene that could have taken place in the '80s or '90s: his family tried to perform an "intervention" to take him to an "ex-gay" program. The video shows family members beating him and his father calling him a "queer." This took place in August 2014.

Wrenching reports about suicides of gay and transgender teens, which exploded in the media beginning several years ago, only escalated. It could be that these stories are being reported more rather than actually rising in number. Perhaps it's both. Either way, LGBT teens, who are believed to make up fewer than 10% of all teens, still account for between 30% and 40% of teen suicides, according to several studies. As shocking as they are, these statistics fail to capture the very real pain and suffering. In December 2014, an Ohio transgender teen, Leelah Alcorn, took her own life after posting a suicide note online in which she described torment and despair because her parents and "Christian therapists" refused to accept her. In August 2014, another story came to light of a bullied gay teen, Alexander Betts Jr. in Iowa, who'd taken his own life; even after his death, he was bullied by our federal health establishment. The sixteen-year-old's eyes were rejected for donation to a fourteen-year-old boy, because the Food and Drug Administration (FDA), in a policy that harks back to the '80s and AIDS hysteria, banned for life "men who have sex with men" from donating blood and certain organs. After thirty-one years, in December 2014 the FDA announced a partial change, to allow those who've been sexually abstinent for a full year to donate (a rule to which heterosexuals aren't held). Given advanced testing, the policy should be based on science and sexual risk no matter an individual's sexual orientation. Why was this kind of double standard still evident if we were almost near victory?

Every day we read stories of people losing their jobs, or being tossed out of a restaurant or a shop, or losing their homes. A Texas gay couple I interviewed in the spring of 2014 were denied parental rights of their own biological twin boys, born with the help of a surrogate. Only the surrogate's name appeared on the birth certificate, though she has no biological connection to the children — all because judges in Texas have had the discretion to deny parental rights in such cases. (I was proud to help attract media attention to the couple's case when an interview I conducted with them about this injustice went viral. They finally got parental rights to their own children after re-petitioning.) Again, perhaps these stories are being reported more often and not necessarily increasing in occurrence. But the fact that they are happening in such great number at all reveals that we're far from true victory.

And these kinds of stories are just the clearest points in a much larger constellation of homophobia, transphobia, and bigotry that continues to permeate this country, and that every gay or transgender person recognizes intuitively. It's that daily slog of slights and injustices I mentioned — a bigoted joke by a comedian, an insulting comment by a stranger on the street, an invitation not sent by a relative — that can seem small and banal when looked at individually but that, together, add up to a lifetime's worth of assault and self-doubt. It's easy to become blind to this persistent physical and psychological violence, focusing on the big wins, telling ourselves it's getting better — it's gotten better — almost as a salve to that daily, cumulative barrage of continued injustice.

But while this salve might feel soothing in the moment, it also has some real, long-term consequences. Ironically, it actually makes us fearful of further and bigger wins, and of taking on that deeply embedded homophobia, because it makes us think we've achieved so much and that we shouldn't rock the boat. We feel we're asking for too much, when actually we've not gotten nearly enough. It makes us lose our gumption, fearful of taking risks when really we've got nothing to lose. Worst of all, it not only keeps us back, it also allows our enemies to advance a backlash, which could then chip away at rights already won.

This landscape, in fact, resembles the one laid out by Susan Faludi in her 1991 classic, *Backlash: The Undeclared War Against American Women,* in which she argued that the victories for women's rights in the '80s were undermined by a powerful backlash against equality — a backlash that has led to setbacks on abortion rights and on many other gains right up to this day. The backlash to gender equality, Faludi noted in the 2006 edition of her book, benefited from apathy among "much of female America," reflecting the postfeminist belief that the battle was over. And what is the title of one of the prominent recent histories of the gay rights movement? *Victory: The Triumphant Gay Revolution,* for which author Linda Hirshman received a great deal of media attention in 2012, perhaps the most blatant example of how victory blindness began taking hold.

A Story of Victory Blindness

This was the mood in the spring of 2014 when a remarkable story out of Silicon Valley revealed the tensions inherent in the victory narrative in spectacular fashion. Over a series of days that grew into weeks, we saw, with crystalline focus, how much LGBT people had yet to win in this country and how fierce the opposition would be. We saw that the way forward was paved with an unabashed grassroots conviction, among progressive gays and straights alike, that nothing short of full equality was acceptable. And we saw that the greatest obstacle standing in our way would be our own complacency and a timidity that made us reluctant to fight.

In March 2014, a man named Brendan Eich was appointed CEO

of Mozilla, the Internet company that developed the free and open-source web browser Firefox, which is used by five hundred million people worldwide. In some respects, Eich seemed a natural fit for the role. Exceptionally talented, he had created the widely used programming language JavaScript and was a cofounder of Mozilla itself. In 2008 Eich donated $1,000 to the campaign supporting Proposition 8, the ballot measure that wrote a same-sex-marriage ban into California's state constitution and, famously, sparked a legal battle that led all the way to the Supreme Court. This fact ignited a firestorm on Twitter when it came to light, in 2012, but the controversy soon died down, and two years later it didn't stop Mozilla's board of directors from naming Eich CEO of the company.

The events that followed were distorted in later tellings, so it's worth examining them in detail. Upon Eich's promotion, as some employees and Mozilla users again began to speak out on social media about their concern regarding Eich's 2008 donation, three Mozilla board members resigned. Reportedly, this wasn't an act of protest against Eich's having supported Prop 8; the *Wall Street Journal* quoted sources saying that the board members wanted someone from outside the company brought in to run it. Still, their stepping down focused more attention on Eich's Prop 8 donation and the discontent it inspired. Journalists covering the tech industry began to take notice of criticisms coming from Mozilla employees, users, and outside developers who worked with the company. In another company this discontent might have remained at the level of grumbling, but Mozilla's particular structure and qualities amplified and intensified the effects. As *The New Yorker*'s James Surowiecki explained it, Mozilla is a subsidiary of the nonprofit Mozilla Foundation, which encompasses a global community of open-source software developers and others who volunteer their time. These people are vital to Mozilla. They do much of the hard work behind the products, donating their knowledge and skills, because they endorse Mozilla's commitment to keeping the web transparent and open. In this values-driven environment, dissatisfaction with the company's social and political philosophies

— or even with one of its executives' beliefs — could inspire many volunteers to stop donating their efforts. In progressive Silicon Valley, with a company answerable to a network of socially liberal (and even libertarian) programmers, an apparently antigay political record couldn't just be swept under the rug.

And then the marketplace, as economists like to say, responded. The high-tech company Rarebit, founded by two married gay men, removed its app from the Firefox Marketplace. One of Rarebit's founders, Hampton Catlin, said in a blog post that he had met with Eich and asked him to apologize for the discrimination he'd supported, but Eich refused. "People think we were upset about his past vote," Catlin wrote. "Instead we were more upset with his current and continued unwillingness to discuss the issue with empathy. Seriously, we assumed that he would reconsider his thoughts on the impact of the law (not his personal beliefs), issue an apology, and then he'd go on to be a great CEO."

Next, CREDO Mobile, a nonprofit mobile-phone company that uses its politically active customer base to advocate for change, launched a petition urging Eich to resign. And then people navigating to the dating site OkCupid via the Firefox browser found themselves greeted with a message they hadn't seen before: "Mozilla's new CEO, Brendan Eich, is an opponent of equal rights for gay couples. We would therefore prefer that our users not use Mozilla software to access OkCupid." The company's stand brought further media attention to the story.

At first Mozilla defended the decision by clarifying the company's "official support of equality and inclusion for LGBT people" as well as its history in supporting equality. It was true that there had not been reports in the past that Eich was hostile to gay people in the company. In the media, Eich was adamant that he would stay on as CEO and called OkCupid's actions "rash." "I don't want to talk about my personal beliefs because I kept them out of Mozilla all these 15 years we've been going," he told *The Guardian* in an interview published on April 2, 2014. "I don't believe they're relevant." Yet in the same interview Eich implied that opposing LGBT equality might be justifiable for business reasons. Mozilla is a global company, he said, operating in countries such as Indonesia that have "different opinions" on homosexuality. Gay marriage was "not considered universal human rights yet, and maybe they will be, but that's in the future, right now we're in a world where we have to be global to have effect." Eich implied that any antigay opinions he might have were a personal matter and were irrelevant to his life as a businessman — except, obviously, when they aligned with his company's strategic goal of making inroads into antigay countries.

The comments were certainly not reassuring. And later that day the same reporter cowrote and published another article for *The Guardian* that seemed to shake both Mozilla's and Eich's confidence. As James Ball and his colleague Alex Hern reported, Eich's record of donations to antigay candidates went back decades. Between 1991 and 1992, he donated $1,000 to Pat Buchanan, who was then running for president. Buchanan, of course, was a fixture of right-wing politics who, as a pundit and as a communications director for the Reagan White House, had been among the most antigay politicians of our time. In 1983 he said of AIDS, "The poor homosexuals. They declared war upon nature, and now nature is extracting an awful retribution." He reiterated that sentiment in a column in 2006.

This donation of Eich's was followed, in 1996 and 1998, by a total of $2,500 in donations to GOP politician Ron Paul's congressional campaigns in Texas's Fourteenth District. In 2008 it was revealed in the *New Republic* that newsletters Paul had published during the '90s included unbylined columns with racist and homophobic passages, including the claim that "homosexuals, not to speak of the rest of society, were far better off when social pressure forced them to hide their activities." (Paul repudiated the comments in 2008, saying he didn't know who wrote them and that the newsletter had many contributors.)

The Guardian's list went on. In 1998, Eich donated to Washington State U.S. Senate candidate Linda Smith, a Republican and Pentecostalist who publicly called homosexuality a "morally unfit inclination." And in 2008, the same year he gave money to support Prop 8, Eich contributed to then California GOP state senator Tom McClintock's successful U.S. House bid. During that race, McClintock, a Prop 8 supporter, said, "Lincoln asked, 'If you call a tail a leg, how many legs has a dog? The answer is four. Calling a tail a leg doesn't make it one.' And calling a homosexual partnership a marriage doesn't make it one." It was clear that Eich's pro–Prop 8 donation was not an anomaly but part of a long-standing pattern. Given the opportunity to respond and distance himself from the bigoted views of candidates he had favored, Eich declined to comment.

Less than twenty-four hours after *The Guardian*'s report, Brendan Eich, the CEO of Mozilla, resigned.

Giving Ammunition to the Enemy

On my radio show, the resignation sparked passionate responses from people who'd been following the events and had perhaps expected, once again, that homophobia would be brushed aside. "I think it's an amazing thing and a wonderful thing that, all of a sudden, being against equality [for LGBT people] is becoming something in society that can be toxic for someone," said Alison from Georgia. "At least at the corporate level, at this company, they realized they were damaging their brand by having someone at the helm driving their company who had that level of hate." The majority of my callers, both straight- and gay-identified, agreed: what had happened at Mozilla was strictly a business decision, and it signaled something new. "The money talked here, and that's what took him down," Jen from Indiana said. "It made sense for him to resign or [otherwise to] ruin the company. And I have to tell you, it gives me some hope."

These words — "amazing," "hope" — were typical of the reactions to Eich's resignation that many LGBT people and progressives expressed on Facebook, on Twitter, and in other forums. Imagine what would happen if a Silicon Valley CEO were exposed for donating to openly racist or anti-Semitic politicians and years later still refused to apologize for it. Here was evidence that homophobia, too, was beginning to join that kind of bigotry exiled from acceptable discourse. It was enough to make Mozilla executive chairwoman Mitchell Baker apologize in a statement: "Mozilla prides itself on being held to a different standard and, this past week, we didn't live up to it. We didn't act like you'd expect Mozilla to act. We didn't move fast enough to engage with people once the controversy started. We're sorry. We must do better."

Religious-conservative leaders, such as Tony Perkins of the Family Research Council and Bryan Fischer at the American Family Association, were predictably incensed by these events. Stranger, though, was the response from free-market conservatives, who might have accepted Eich's downfall on a purely philosophical level. As prominent blogger Markos Moulitsas put it in a headline on the progressive website he founded, Daily Kos, BRENDAN EICH WAS A VICTIM OF MARKET FORCES, CONSERVATIVES SHOULD APPLAUD. "Brendan Eich is a tech legend, the inventor of JavaScript — a programming language that powers much of what's cool on the web," Moulitsas wrote. "The problem with Eich is that, well, he's a bigot. And worse than that, he hasn't 'evolved' since 2008, like so much of America. He held steadfast to his beliefs, out-of-step with the world his product serves. So the Mozilla community erupted in anger, and after a half-assed effort to hang on, Eich resigned the position . . . Of course this is intolerance . . . We are allowed to be intolerant of people who operate outside the bounds of civil decency. This wasn't governmental action infringing on any Constitutional rights . . . In short, it was the free market expressing itself."

But Republicans weren't about to back down so easily. Eich's resignation struck at the core of what the GOP has become. It is a pro-business party, increasingly putting corporations above people, that draws significant revenue from individuals and companies seeking decreased corporate regulation. At the same time, most Republican members of Congress (either to court religious voters or because they are zealots themselves) vote antigay and publicly espouse antigay positions, even as the country is changing dramatically. The legislators who push those pro-business policies — and who now, through super PACs that take in unlimited cash from corporations and wealthy donors and spend unlimited amounts advocating for or against candidates — are thus often the same ones expressing opposition to everything from marriage equality to antidiscrimination laws. There are only four Republican U.S. senators, for example, who support marriage equality. Only fifteen Republican House members voted to repeal "don't ask, don't tell." Republicans in the House have stalled a narrow employment-antidiscrimination bill that would offer some protections for gay and transgender people. It took two decades to pass in the Senate, where only ten Republicans joined all fifty-two Democrats and two independents to vote for it in 2013.

It wasn't hard for forward-thinking Republicans to see the gathering tension embedded in all of this. If CEOs were seen to court scandal by giving money to antigay candidates or causes, donations to the GOP by corporate leaders could be jeopardized. The change wouldn't come right away, of course. With its unconventional structure and Silicon Valley values, Mozilla was an extreme case. By contrast, it wasn't until mid-2014, when President Obama signed an executive order barring anti-LGBT discrimination among companies receiving lucrative federal contracts, that the oil giant Exxon Mobil said it would "abide by the law" and comply with the order. Each year, Exxon Mobil's board had voted down adding an LGBT antidiscrimination policy despite consistent pressure from LGBT activists and groups like the Human Rights Campaign. With Mozilla, on the other hand, no self-proclaimed activists or LGBT groups were involved in Eich's resignation; it was the result of a natural groundswell from the company's employees and business partners. Mozilla could, in the distant or not-so-distant future, be a bellwether. Republicans needed someone to blame.

The gay blogger and self-described small-*c* conservative Andrew Sullivan supplied the right with a convenient target. "The guy who had the gall to express his First Amendment rights and favor Prop 8 in California by donating $1,000," Sullivan wrote on his website, *The Dish*, "has just been scalped by some gay activists." Sullivan offered no names of gay activists or groups — because there were none to name. "Will [Eich] now be forced to walk through the streets in shame?" Sullivan asked. "Why not the stocks? The whole episode disgusts me — as it should disgust anyone interested in a tolerant and diverse society. If this is the gay rights movement today — hounding our opponents with a fanaticism more like the religious right than anyone else — then count me out. If we are about intimidating the free speech of others, we are no better than the anti-gay bullies who came before us." In a later post, Sullivan again attacked the "ugly intolerance of parts of the gay movement."

Under what he himself would describe as a torrent of criticism from his readers (with only a "small percentage" agreeing with him), Sullivan later backtracked, agreeing with a reader who said the criticism of Eich and calls for his resignation were not driven by gay activists (though Sullivan then claimed the matter was "broader" than that). But the damage was done. The meme, a falsehood, traveled through the right-wing blogosphere and conservative media. In that fact-checking vacuum, mention of Sullivan's "gay activists" morphed into finger pointing at LGBT "groups" that had supposedly called for Eich's resignation. In reality, not one LGBT group had commented on the story in any way. Nevertheless, on Breitbart.com, the highly trafficked bible of the far right, one headline blared, ANDREW SULLIVAN: BRENDAN EICH'S OUSTER AS MOZILLA CEO "DISGUSTS ME." "Gay advocacy groups," the article began, "have been attacking tech company Mozilla for appointing a new CEO who once donated $1,000 to a 2008 campaign for traditional marriage in California." The conservative website Daily Caller also captured the basic tenor: "Gay journalist Andrew Sullivan 'disgusted' by gay rights 'fanaticism' after

Mozilla CEO resigns." On ABC's *This Week* the following Sunday, former House Speaker and GOP presidential candidate Newt Gingrich
said Eich was the victim of "the new fascism" and that if "you have
the wrong views, meaning conservative, you have no career." Rush
Limbaugh spoke for many right-wing pundits when he went ballistic
against what he called "effeminazis" — a queer spin on his infamous
"feminazis" label for feminists — and "leftist fascists" who supposedly
took down Brendan Eich. "It seems to me that [Eich is] the victim
of intolerance here," radio host Sean Hannity declared. "Look, the
gay community has fought for — and I think the right word is tolerance — for many years. There is this intolerance out there because
of maybe their religious faith." Sullivan's scurrilous charge even bled
into liberal and pro-gay media outlets. On his HBO show *Real Time,*
Bill Maher, a supporter of gay rights, attacked "the gay mafia" for
taking down Eich, saying, "If you cross them, you do get whacked."
Conor Friedersdorf at *The Atlantic* called Eich's resignation "an ugly,
illiberal footnote, appended by the winners." Invited onto *The Colbert
Report,* Sullivan gladly paraded his message around well into the next
week.

Of course, the right would have attacked gays and progressives for
Eich's resignation no matter what; it's par for the course. But without
the specter of organized groups of "gay activists" invented by Sullivan,
anything the conservative media asserted would have quickly faded.
That's because the right couldn't cry victimization without a victimizer — and the marketplace, especially to right-wingers, simply can't
be a victimizer. To conservatives, the market is a product of natural economic forces that they assume are aligned with conservative
ideology, so Eich's resignation was certainly a challenge to them. To
look at it another way, in this case no longer was there a delineation
between gay activists and responsible consumers in the marketplace.
Mozilla employees, business partners, and users became de facto activists, just as any and all consumers are by dint of their buying power.
Gay activists didn't need to lead the developments at Mozilla, and that
was a good thing.

Gay Opinion Leaders Run for Cover

If only LGBT and progressive commentators and opinion leaders could all have seen this, rather than, as some did, fear it and run away. If thought leaders in the LGBT community — those with the megaphones, including the pundits and bloggers — had been united in support of Eich's departure, seeing it as a positive societal shift, as many callers to my show and so many everyday LGBT people on Facebook, Twitter, and elsewhere did, we might have been able to combat the conservative backlash more effectively. But, in one of the most unexpected turns this story took, many gay commentators hedged, pulling back and becoming fearful. Otherwise confident, pioneering voices now worried that the event could reflect badly on gay people and possibly set back the movement. Some gay and liberal pundits even took Sullivan's accusations at face value, blaming gay activists when (it can't be repeated enough) no major LGBT group ever called for Eich to resign. This disunity helped the controversy go on for days when it was already dying down. It allowed the right, and the mainstream media, to frame the incident as one in which gays went too far, overreached, and silenced people.

The respected gay blogger Jim Burroway, who has done a great service over the years by exposing homophobia in Uganda and elsewhere around the world through his website, BoxTurtleBulletin.com, asked, "What is the statute of limitations for donating to support Prop 8 before that individual can no longer be fired from his job?" And David Mixner, one of the great gay civil rights activists and authors and someone I'm proud to call a friend, asked on his Facebook page in capital letters, QUICK QUESTION: AM I THE ONLY ONE THAT IS CONCERNED THAT WE DEMAND PEOPLE LOSE THEIR JOBS IF THEY DISAGREE WITH US ON MARRIAGE EQUALITY? This from a man who fought against the war in Vietnam and ended his friendship with Bill Clinton over Clinton's signing of the "don't ask, don't tell" law. Peter Staley, the prominent AIDS activist and another friend and comrade of mine from ACT UP in years past, chimed in with a comment on Mixner's Facebook status: "I've been taking a shellacking [on my Facebook page] since last night for having the same concerns." And if the response to Burroway, Mixner, and Staley on social media was any guide, it was true that the grass roots — people who were well informed about this controversy and who follow these opinion leaders — wasn't buying it. Again, even Sullivan admitted that e-mails from readers overwhelmingly disagreed with his point of view.

To their credit, many LGBT pundits and activists spoke out against Eich and the claims he made in the defense of his job. *Re/code*'s Kara Swisher, perhaps the most prominent lesbian in high-tech journalism, noted that Eich "dragged in a truly bizarre point about people in Indonesia not liking gays marrying to justify his continued leadership." She then added, "Hey Brendan, does that mean we need to just say bygones about some of the virulent anti-women sentiments and laws in some countries, since it's a Firefox world after all? No, I did not think so." Younger gay commentators also seemed to agree Eich should go. John Becker, the editor of the LGBT site *The Bilerico Project,* wrote his own open letter to Andrew Sullivan, condemning Sullivan's rationale for supporting Eich. Mark Joseph Stern at *Slate* noted, "When we talk about Eich's anti-gay stance, we aren't just talking about abstract beliefs. We're talking about concrete actions that harmed thousands of gay families and informed innumerable gay Americans that they were sinful, corrupted predators." Many longtime LGBT journalists and bloggers, too, like veteran syndicated reporter Rex Wockner, John Aravosis at *AMERICAblog*, and transgender writer and activist Rebecca Juro, also thought it right that Eich had resigned.

Yet even the fierce, smart activist and writer Dan Savage, also a friend, sounded a cautious note. "I would watch *Firing Line* with my dad," he recalled in his weekly podcast, *Savage Lovecast*. "I have distinct memories of watching the show and hearing respected media figures, political figures, business leaders, defend segregation, bans on interracial marriage, advocate for . . . racist shit that you can no longer

go on TV and advocate, and talk up, and defend, and expect to be employed the next morning." Then he explained that, when it comes to
"LGBT civil rights in this country . . . we're sort of pre- that moment."
He continued: "You can still go on TV and say shitty, antigay things,
advocate for just the most homophobic, transphobic bullshit, and be
a respected member of the community, run for Congress, get elected
to office, and run for president the next day without anyone getting in
your face about it."

In regard to race, Savage said, "We seemed to reach some cultural
tipping point . . . where you couldn't say that shit on TV. We reached
this point of cultural, political consensus." But, he said, "we haven't
reached that point on LGBT civil rights yet. You can still go on TV
and be Rick Santorum." He added: "When you're a tiny and vulner-
able minority, and we are, you don't want to be in the business of scaring people. We want to be in the business of persuading people and
changing their minds."

This viewpoint seemed to contrast sharply with some of Savage's
past activism. Six months earlier, for example, he had called for a
boycott of Stolichnaya vodka to protest antigay legislation in Russia.
He was criticized by some American business writers and political
progressives, as well as by many in the LGBT community — not to
mention the company's CEO, who came on my show — because Stolichnaya no longer considered itself a Russian brand, has partnered
with LGBT media, groups, and businesses in the United States, and
has reiterated its opposition to the Russian antigay law. (Its expatri-
ate billionaire owner had battled with Vladimir Putin and taken the
word *Russian* off the vodka's label, moving much of the company's
production to Latvia.) Critics saw Savage's boycott as misguided and
unfair, charging that rather than persuading opponents, the boycott
scared them with the threat that the gay community, at any moment,
could unfairly shut down their business. Savage and others, including
me, persevered. As a protest against Russia, the boycott was valid;
Stolichnaya still harvested grain and distilled much of its product in
Russia before sending it to Latvia for bottling, packaging, and distri-

bution. More important, though, were videos on television and online of LGBT bar patrons pouring vodka into the streets. It was a brilliant way to bring attention to Russia's antigay laws prior to the 2014 Winter Olympics. It didn't appear to hurt the company's sales at all (according to Stolichnaya itself) and was worth the criticisms, which the LGBT community will always get during any action or protest.

But now, Savage's fighting spirit seemed muted. What had changed? Savage told me in an online chat that he was "in the middle" on Eich's resignation. He didn't believe a "gay mafia" (Bill Maher's term) had taken the CEO down. But he pointed out that, because of the way the story played out in the media among high-profile straight supporters of gay rights, "the optics were terrible for us" and that therefore it was "a political defeat." He told me he was concerned about "backlash" and that he believed "we should be magnanimous in victory."

It wasn't the first time I'd heard the word *magnanimous*. In his blog post, Burroway posed a question: "We've had a banner two years. Isn't it time we were more magnanimous?" And the gay *New York Times* columnist Frank Bruni expressed a similar feeling (and borrowed some of Sullivan's overblown and inaccurate stockades imagery) when he wrote on the *Times*'s op-ed page, "Sullivan is right to raise concerns about the public flogging of someone like Eich. Such vilification won't accelerate the timetable of victory, which is certain. And it doesn't reflect well on the victors." Bruni wrote about the tactics he believed got us to this supposed near-victory. Citing *Forcing the Spring: The Fight for Marriage Equality,* a then upcoming book by his *New York Times* colleague Jo Becker, Bruni wrote, "Becker mentioned what she called a rebranding of the movement over the last five years, with two important components. First, gay marriage was framed in terms of family values. Second, advocates didn't shame opponents and instead made sympathetic public acknowledgment of the journey that many Americans needed to complete in order to be comfortable with marriage equality."

This ignored the rich history of protest and demonstrations in LGBT activism from the Stonewall riots onward. And the gay rights

struggle has always been framed around love and family and connection with everyday Americans. There was no "rebranding" to appeal
to "family values" (though there was definitely a defining of marriage equality in a way that sought to captivate the public imagination, which I'll discuss in a later chapter); we have always included
our families in marches and protests, and appealed to other families.
True, there was more emphasis on that strategy with the fight for
marriage equality. But Bruni's column — and Becker's book, which
upon publication was almost universally discredited by gay writers
and pundits, including both Andrew Sullivan and me — ignored the
fact that vigorous protests and shaming of opponents for their bigotry continued well into the battle against Prop 8 and beyond. There
were massive protests in New York, Los Angeles, Salt Lake City, and
elsewhere against the Church of Jesus Christ of Latter-Day Saints (the
Mormons), which raised millions among its faithful to pass Prop 8,
and against other antigay supporters of that campaign. Gay and lesbian activists have staged sit-ins — and have been arrested — at marriage bureaus in state after state, some of which eventually won gay
marriage.

This brings us back to the word *optics*. The truth is that we have
not achieved victory; we are not even close. And our history tells us
that LGBT people have always needed to be confrontational in order
to make great strides forward. Surely there were many who felt the
optics weren't right when the Stonewall riots occurred and lesbians,
transgender people, and gay men fought back against the police, but
that protest sent a message to those in authority that the community
would not be contained. Many felt the optics weren't right when ACT
UP held "die-ins" on Wall Street and at Food and Drug Administration offices, or blocked traffic in numerous cities, to demand development of new drugs to treat HIV and AIDS, but these actions sent
a message to the government and business that they had to act. The
optics didn't look good to some when GetEQUAL activists disrupted
President Obama's speeches, or chained themselves to the White
House fence, demanding "don't ask, don't tell" repeal. Whenever

you stand up in protest, some group will think the optics aren't right. There's always a backlash — sometimes from the general public, including some of your would-be or current supporters who just don't like conflict.

"Move Forward by Looking Back"

The Brendan Eich story came up continually weeks after he'd resigned, defining itself as a crystallizing moment. The following month, a group consisting mostly of conservatives, most but not all of them gay, launched a petition to support Eich. The group included Rich Tafel, the former executive director of the gay GOP group the Log Cabin Republicans; Peter Thiel, the gay billionaire cofounder of PayPal, who has supported Tea Party–aligned super PACSs and candidates such as Tea Party standard-bearer senator Ted Cruz of Texas, who opposes gay marriage and voted against a bill that would have banned discrimination against gay and transgender people in employment; former Republican National Committee chairman and George W. Bush campaign manager Ken Mehlman, who'd come out as gay in 2010 and has since worked on behalf of marriage equality; and, yet again, Andrew Sullivan. The group also included some straight conservatives, including Charles Murray, the author of the controversial book *The Bell Curve: Intelligence and Class Structure in American Life,* which posited that there are racial differences in intelligence, and whose inclusion on the letter certainly raised eyebrows. The signers said they were "concerned" that the events surrounding Eich's resignation "signal an eagerness by some supporters of same-sex marriage to punish rather than to criticize or to persuade those who disagree" and that they affirmed their "unwavering commitment to the values of the open society and to vigorous public debate — the values that have brought us to the brink of victory."

One of the signers, Jonathan Rauch of the Brookings Institution, a gay writer who'd authored articles and books making the case for gay marriage, wrote a piece on *The Daily Beast* defending the petition. "After almost 20 years of standing on a soapbox for gay marriage," Rauch wrote, "I am standing on another soapbox making the case for tolerating people who oppose same-sex marriage." In essence, he argued that homophobic positions should be more tolerated than racist positions, because the former are based on religious beliefs. He claimed that Eich's religious views needed to be respected because, "to their discredit, all three of the Abrahamic faith traditions condemn homosexual love, and all of them have theologies that see marriage as intrinsically heterosexual." Rauch wrote that this differed from racism because "defenders of anti-miscegenation laws in the 1960s claimed to have God on their side, but it was evident that they were distorting and abusing the tenets of their faith, not exercising them." Of course, many would argue that antigay Christians are distorting modern Christian faith, and that racist actions and beliefs can be found in the Bible alongside homophobic passages. Also troubling was Rauch's claim that gay marriage and discrimination against LGBT people aren't a "political emergency," as if the persistent thread of violence and bigotry that continues to weave through our lives might be anything less than urgent.

These strange reactions to the Eich controversy left me considering an uncomfortable but necessary question: What could drive this group of gay men of my generation across the political spectrum, from Dan Savage and Frank Bruni to Andrew Sullivan and Jonathan Rauch, to speak against Eich's resignation in ways that seemed like odd, uncharacteristic rationalizations and that were often in direct contradiction to their positions in other, similar controversies? They all seemed to have bought the victory narrative, believing we were nearly on even footing with straight Americans and that behaving inappropriately, or in a less than "magnanimous" way, could jeopardize what we've already won, or the supposedly small list of goals we yet needed to achieve, or both. And they seemed to represent an increasing complacency in the way the LGBT equality struggle was being discussed, as if victory was now a sure thing. This was the essence of victory blindness.

As I wrestled with these questions, I found myself turning to a book titled *Covering: The Hidden Assault on Our Civil Rights,* which was ahead of its time when published in 2006, but which I believe contains vital lessons for us today. I interviewed its author, New York University School of Law professor Kenji Yoshino, when it was published, and I'll discuss its findings in greater depth throughout this book.

Yoshino's brilliant critique is more relevant now than ever. Writing as a gay Asian American, Yoshino defines "covering" as an attempt to downplay difference, making it palatable or at least inoffensive. Prevalent among women, members of sexual and racial minorities, and disabled people, covering becomes particularly strong, Yoshino argues, when people believe they've achieved the rights and recognition they've sought, and begin to fear losing them. It's an attempt to fit in and be "team players" under the assumption that the playing field is now even. Yoshino distinguishes covering from "conversion" (trying to become straight) and "passing" (staying in the closet), and points out that even after gay people come out, society exerts a "covering demand" on its minority members. I would argue that, by pleading for more magnanimous treatment of our opponents, gay thought leaders were unconsciously applying the covering demand to the LGBT equality movement as a whole.

Covering, Yoshino says, is "morally complex. Many [gay people] who accept that conversion and passing are severe harms do not feel the same way about covering. They often perceive the covering demand to be morally appropriate." Actually, in attaining some kinds of rights, covering can be successful — though it does have a cost, and it certainly has a limit. And, I would argue, we've reached that limit.

To take the Eich controversy as one example that will stand in for many, what is covering if not giving up when the battle is just beginning, seduced by the idea that all is almost won, that somehow we weren't being team players when we allowed Brendan Eich to resign? We deserve a marketplace that rejects homophobic bigotry, and covering means accepting something less than that. It means settling for mere tolerance without getting beyond it, without demanding full acceptance of homosexuality and transgender identity as natural and healthy. It means telling ourselves that bedtime story, a victory narrative relating how our rights are almost won, and, as echoed by Bruni and Savage and others, how we've now got to be "magnanimous" and not "sore winners," as the prominent conservative columnist George Will put it in his criticism of the mythical gay activists who supposedly took down Eich.

Yoshino sees covering as a particular stage of assimilation, fitting in, being nice, and not scaring people. I view it more as an impulse, often driven by fear, rather than the description of a type of person or group. In that way, we all can be drawn to covering at different times, seeing some benefits in it. But, as Yoshino says, "Gays should not rest now but move forward by looking back."

That's what this book is about: looking back at key moments of our recent history to see how we chart a course for the future based on what has actually worked, and not based on newfound fears of risk, a trap that allows equality's enemies to foment a backlash. It's about revealing the discrimination and bigotry we experience — that which is blatant, but also that which is hidden and which defies all of the breathless polls we see — and providing a path forward by resisting the covering demand.

It's about refusing to keep silent about the suppressed current of homophobia that still courses through our culture. It's about revealing new and insidious strategies our enemies are developing for stymying LGBT equality. The Eich story was just a small and quickly produced taste of that homophobia, but the right is engaged in a much more organized effort to pose as victims whose religious liberties are being infringed upon. This book is about exposing that strategy, calling it out, and going on the offensive, rather than running away or staying quiet and allowing the right to gain ground.

In that way this book is about dismantling the victory narrative and helping us all get over our victory blindness. It's about what we can do, here and now, in our communities, in our schools, in Washington, in the media, and in popular culture, to win the battle for full equality.

2

"WE DON'T SERVE FAGS HERE"

THE CYCLE OF BIGOTRY AND
DISCRIMINATION ACROSS AMERICA

ONE SUMMER DAY IN EARLY July 2011, Jennifer Tipton of Knoxville and her wife, Olivier Odom, offered to take their friends' two daughters, ages five and eight, to Dollywood, a Dolly Parton–themed amusement park in Pigeon Forge, Tennessee. "I'd never been there before, and I heard it was fun," Odom recalled when she and Tipton came on my show the following month. "The girls really wanted to go. Jen doesn't like waterslides, but she was appeasing me, treating me like I was five for a day." That day, Odom happened to be wearing a T-shirt that read MARRIAGE IS SO GAY. "I wear that T-shirt like I wear any other T-shirt. It was a nice T-shirt and it was clean." But apparently it wasn't clean enough for the guard at the gate, who told the women they couldn't enter the park.

"I had to look down at my shirt first to realize what was going on," Odom told me. "I was definitely in shock. I looked at the guy with a curious look on my face. And he said, 'This is a family park.' And at that point, I became very upset. I mean, visibly, I would think. But the two girls were with me. I didn't want to cause a scene in front of them. I didn't want them to not have a good day. I didn't want to not be able to go. I figured I could comply with this request." She turned her T-shirt inside out.

Odom's story is one of many that illustrate a fact this chapter will vividly show: discrimination of all kinds is happening every day across the country, in big cities and small, in conservative outposts and liberal bastions, where LGBT people are turned away from public accommodations or thrown out of jobs and longtime professions. Homophobia hasn't simply persisted, it has become more public and more violent in response to the increased visibility of gay and transgender people that wins such as marriage equality have brought. The realities of the lives of many LGBT people, from grappling with HIV to the presence of anti-LGBT violence, are unconsciously covered up as the victory narrative consumes us and as we allow it to happen at our own peril. This chapter will expose the blatant as well as the more subtle continuing biases, not just through examples from all over the country but also through new social science research that defies the victory narrative and underscores why LGBT people and our allies must get past victory blindness if we're to attain full equality.

The Cycle of Bigotry

Later that day in July 2011, Jennifer Tipton and Olivier Odom sat down and talked to the children, to try to explain the ugliness they had encountered at the gate. "I had said to Sophia [the eight-year-old] that I needed to change my shirt inside out," Odom said. "And she asked me why. And I said, 'Well, it seems that the man at the gate must be slightly homophobic.' So, then she tried to repeat the word: 'ho-mo-fo-bic.' And I explained that gay people would be able to get married one day and that my shirt promotes that."

Thanks to public pressure that Tipton and Odom applied in the weeks after the incident, with the help of a gay rights group, the Campaign for Southern Equality, the amusement park (and its namesake and part owner, Dolly Parton herself) later apologized and changed its policy. But at the time, the guards and the park were fully within their rights to make this demand. Not only could Dollywood refuse Odom entrance because her shirt expressed something pro-gay, they also had the right to prevent her from entering the park simply because she is a lesbian. Businesses in much of Tennessee had been do-ing so for years and still can today, even while millions of Americans live in states with marriage equality. This is because Tennessee, like twenty-eight other states at this writing, has no statewide law ban-ning discrimination on the basis of sexual orientation in public ac-commodations — or housing, or employment, or credit and lending. The Equal Employment Opportunity Commission (EEOC) ruled in a landmark case in 2012 that, in employment, transgender people are now protected nationally under the Civil Rights Act's prohibition of sex discrimination. But thirty-two states do not protect transgender people specifically by law in employment, nor in housing, education, and credit, and thirty-four do not protect them in public accommoda-tions. And there is still no federal law banning discrimination against LGBT Americans in employment, housing, public accommodations, education, and credit, as well as in federal lending and jury service.

Looking back on Tipton and Odom's story now — a story of an insensitive but nonviolent act that occurred in a southern state sev-eral years ago — it might be easy to diminish it. Perhaps we think so much has changed since then. At the time, Odom herself was ready to just brush it off, as she had done many times before, she explained to me. But in some ways, the most important aspect of the story, perhaps more than the discrimination itself, was the telegraphing of homophobia to the two children. In fact, that was the only reason, Odom told me, that she did finally stand up and do something: the little girl, Sophia, asked her days later if she would fight against it and lodge a complaint. Experiencing homophobic incidents regularly, Odom had tried to let them pass, as frustrating as that was. But now she saw that doing nothing might teach a child to tolerate the bigotry of others, and that realization broke the cycle.

That cycle of pain and resignation, however, continues today among millions of other Americans, even in the most pro-gay places. We may think that, given the statements of a prominent celebrity or the change in a law here or there, homophobia has been eradicated or is on the wane. But it is passed down, in ways overt and subtle, every day as we attempt to brush off slights or even more blatant forms of discrimination.

After my interview with Tipton and Odom, calls came flooding in to my show from people who had experienced similar discrimination, people from all over the country who had been told to leave restaurants, clothing stores, or other establishments, or who were told they couldn't even come in because they were perceived to be gay or transgender. One woman described being called a "dyke" when she entered a shop in Ohio, and being told there was "nothing here" for her. A transgender woman in Florida said she was asked to leave a beauty salon, told that it was for "women only." A gay man said he and his partner were turned away from a hotel in North Carolina, though he knew there were vacancies there; the owner said they could get separate rooms if they liked.

No call-in show can provide a representative sample from which to draw scientific conclusions. But I believe it's significant that every time I report on a case of antigay discrimination in public accommodations, housing, or employment, the phones light up with people sharing similar stories. It's only increased in the years since Tipton and Odom went to Dollywood.

A lesbian couple were denied a pool pass in July 2014 for themselves and their children in Galion, Ohio, because a town ordinance defines a family as having a mother and a father. In May 2014, a gay male couple paying their check after a nice dinner at Big Earl's Bait House in Pittsburgh, Texas, were ordered not to come back. "We don't serve fags here," the cashier, a daughter of the owner, told the men to their faces. "Here at Big Earl's we like for men to act like men and for ladies to act like ladies, so we want you to never return." A transgender businesswoman visiting Centreville, Virginia, in February 2013 said she was told to leave a health club because she "looked different" and five people in the spa had complained about her. She went to the Better Business Bureau, which elicited a response from the spa's owner stating, "It is our policy to not accept any kinds of abnormal sexual oriented customers to our facility such as homosexuals, or transgender."

Many of these incidents happened even in nominally progressive cities and states where antidiscrimination protections do exist. Many business owners either don't know the law or don't care, and we lack the force of a federal law to put them and the American public on notice. A transgender man filed a lawsuit in June 2014 against the City of New York after he was told to leave the changing room of a Staten Island pool. A transgender woman filed a lawsuit in June 2014 in Washington, D.C., after she and some friends left a restaurant and saw "gay bitches" written on their receipt.

Since 2011, the expansion of marriage rights to same-sex couples in many states has been a catalyst for latent homophobia, and reports of these kinds of incidents have actually increased. Bakeries, florists, reception halls, and catering companies have turned away lesbian and gay couples. In Pennsylvania a bridal shop refused service to a lesbian couple in August 2014, claiming it would be breaking "God's law" if it sold dresses to the women. In October 2014 some for-profit wedding chapels in Las Vegas turned away gay couples even after marriage equality came to Nevada, including a chapel where an Elvis impersonator performs the unions. In 2013 a florist who refused to provide flowers for a gay wedding because of her religious beliefs was hit with a lawsuit from the Washington State attorney general. In one of the most well-known cases, which became a national rallying cry for antigay evangelical religious leaders, the Bureau of Labor and Industries in Oregon determined in January 2014 that Sweet Cakes by Melissa, a Portland bakery, violated the civil rights of a lesbian couple when it refused to sell them a wedding cake. Co-owner Aaron Klein said this was an attack on Christian businesses and vowed to fight. "We still stand by what we believe[d] from the beginning," Klein told KATU-TV.

Later in 2014, Sweet Cakes by Melissa co-owners Melissa and Aaron Klein were celebrated at the annual Values Voter Summit in

September, which I attended, covering it for my show, and where I witnessed Melissa Klein being paraded around as a celebrity victim. Major GOP presidential hopefuls speak before this convention of religious-conservative political activists each year. At the 2014 gathering, Republican senators Ted Cruz of Texas, Rand Paul of Kentucky, former GOP Pennsylvania senator Rick Santorum, former Arkansas GOP governor Mike Huckabee, and others spoke to the crowd about what they saw as an attack on "religious liberties" in the country, epitomized by the Kleins' case. This is a newer, more refined version of a strategy the right has employed before, and I'll discuss it in more depth later in this book. At the convention, Melissa Klein sat on a panel, where she wept over shutting down her bakery—a choice she made, given that she wouldn't serve gay and lesbian couples—while the audience cheered her as a hero for the cause.

After a similar ruling by the Colorado Civil Rights Commission against a bakery in Lakewood in May 2014, the owner vowed to stop selling wedding cakes entirely. In standing their ground on hate and refusing to follow the law, these business owners are expressing a backlash to marriage equality that shines a light on whole areas of discrimination that might have remained hidden.

The "Inappropriate Behavior" Double Standard

Owners of businesses often use "decorum" or "inappropriate behavior" as an excuse to boot out gay couples for the kinds of public display of affection that we see heterosexual people engaging in every day in public spaces. In 2013 a lesbian couple in Portland, Oregon, said a cabdriver hurled antigay slurs at them and dumped them and a friend out of his cab on the side of a busy highway after midnight, all because the couple were holding hands and had kissed; in March 2014 the Oregon Bureau of Labor and Industries, after an investigation, found "substantial evidence of discrimination." That same year, in October, two men were allegedly thrown out of a cab on their way into Chicago from O'Hare International Airport after their driver became incensed when they exchanged what the men described as a quick kiss; they filed a lawsuit in 2014. An Iraq war veteran and his boyfriend were tossed out of a cab in Tacoma, Washington, on Independence Day 2014. Eric Williams, who had served two tours of duty in Iraq, left a bar and got in a cab with his boyfriend and exchanged what the two described as a "peck." "[The driver] said, 'You're two men, why are you kissing?'" Williams told Q13FOX TV in Seattle. "We said that's my boyfriend, I'm gay. That's when the cabby started to get really hostile with us. He pulled off the road and told us to get out of the car, he wasn't going to serve us."

Such stories of people turned away from businesses seem to be reported at least every week, and those are only the ones we know about, the ones in which the individuals come forward or the stories are reported in the media. Each time I have reported them on my radio program, not only do calls come in from gay, lesbian, bisexual, and transgender listeners, or their friends and family, telling similar stories, but I also hear from straight, gay-supportive people who express shock that such discrimination is happening and cannot believe that it is often legal and that there are no federal protections against it.

The calls from the opposing side are just as revealing. I hear from listeners who, though they claim not to hold such beliefs themselves, say a business owner should have the right to ban LGBT customers. Others proudly say they believe LGBT people can or should be banned from certain kinds of businesses, or all of them; and I've fielded calls from business people, from shopkeepers to real estate brokers, who've said they should have the right not to serve gay or lesbian couples. Business owners do have a great deal of freedom to turn away anyone they want, for a variety of reasons, such as rude or loud behavior or failure to abide by a dress code enforced equally for all. But people cannot be turned away based on race, gender, religion, or any other protected class, such as disability. In the majority of states, however, this protection does not extend to sexual orientation or gender identity. Why should LGBT people live with and accept the

idea that a shop can at any time put up a sign saying NO GAYS AL-
LOWED — or even NO GAY WEDDINGS SERVED — even if there is another shop down the street that will happily serve them? (Of course,
in many small towns there isn't another shop down the street and
not one for many miles.) Beyond the humiliation and degradation of
such actions, allowing this discrimination opens the door, legally and
morally, to larger acts of discrimination against LGBT people — and
other people — for purported religious reasons. Whether based in religion or not, such behavior is bigotry and simply can't be tolerated.
We must not allow victory blindness to keep us from seeing that.

Radio is an intimate medium in which people can freely speak
their minds anonymously, so they have less fear of speaking out. They
express themselves emotionally, the inflections of their voices revealing what a pseudonymous Internet comment would not. When I ask
them whether the same logic should apply to race or other charac-
teristics, these callers say the difference matters. "Homosexuality is
different from race," said a man who called my show from Illinois. "I
should not, as a business owner, have your sexual or personal agenda
rammed down my face and insulting my religious sensibilities and
those of my customers." Some callers have been honest enough to say,
alarmingly, that they believe even laws banning racial discrimination
are unconstitutional and that they should be able to turn away anyone
they want. Comments like these underscore the vital need for this
legislation. Only in a handful of states do LGBT people who decide to
fight back have recourse to do so, and even these people would benefit greatly from a federal law. Nationwide legislation, Ian Thompson
of the American Civil Liberties Union (ACLU) told me, would give
"federal agencies explicit enforcement powers and LGBT people access to federal courts." A federal law would send a great threat and
warning to businesses, particularly in areas where local law enforcement may be lax or homophobic, even within the most liberal states
and sometimes big cities, too. A federal law would provide another
layer of protection, bringing more attention and more enforcement.

No Freedom to Work

In most states where you can turn gays, lesbians, and bisexuals away from a business, you can also fire them from a job. As I have noted, transgender people won employment protection nationwide in 2012 with the important EEOC ruling. Still, most people, including employers and transgender people themselves, don't know about that ruling, and advocates agree that, especially without a Supreme Court ruling on the issue, it's vital to get both statewide protections and protections under federal law in employment for transgender people. Gay, lesbian, bisexual, and transgender people have been discriminated against in employment for decades: turned away from jobs, sometimes fired once they've been found out, often forced to leave because of psychological or even physical harassment. A Pew Research survey in 2013 found that 21% of LGBT respondents had been treated unfairly by an employer in hiring, pay, or promotions. The Williams Institute at UCLA conducted an extensive study in 2011, which included the largest survey of transgender people to date, showing that 78% of transgender respondents reported harassment or mistreatment at work because of their gender identity.

"One minute I was a trusted, reliable employee on the management promotion shortlist, the next I was an unwanted problem who had to be fired for insubordination," transgender writer, radio host, and activist Rebecca Juro wrote in *The Advocate* in 2014, describing what happened when she told her boss she was transitioning. Over the next few years, it was nearly impossible to find a job and keep it, she wrote. She got a job in a pet store only to have one assistant manager harass her about using the women's room and then fire her when she finally spoke up to him about his harassment. Over the next few years, she'd get jobs in retail that wouldn't last or that hid her in the back, off the selling floor. "When transphobic customers complained that they felt threatened or unsafe in my presence, I would be 'written up,'" she explained, "a disciplinary notice placed in my file as if I had actually done something other than simply be present and visibly trans to cause these customers to complain." Transgender as well as gender-atypical gay, lesbian, and bisexual people — those who cannot convincingly pass — experience a heightened degree of discrimination.

While many Fortune 500 companies have policies that ban workplace discrimination against LGBT people, the Williams Institute, as the *Los Angeles Times* reported in July 2013, found that "between 15% to 43% of lesbian, gay, bisexual and transgender workers have experienced being fired, denied promotion, or harassed." Stories of people being fired because of their LGBT status have only continued to proliferate in the media over the past several years. This may reflect a real rise in discrimination, as employers become more aware of gay and transgender people in general, or it may be because people are more willing to report incidents they used to silently accept and some of the media are covering them more. Either way, it speaks to the persistence of this particular expression of homophobia. After the Great Recession and the stubbornly sluggish economy, when it was difficult for so many people, especially older workers, to find jobs, the stories have been disturbing and angering.

An NCAA-championship-winning track coach at the University of Texas alleged she was forced out of her job in 2013 after it was revealed she'd once had a lesbian relationship. An openly gay 7-Eleven employee in Virginia Beach was assaulted on the job by a man who came into the store and forcibly kissed him in 2013; as the employee later explained to a local TV station, when he reported the incident he was fired because, he believed, management thought "somebody would come in and do it again." The list goes on: a gym teacher in Columbus, Ohio, said she was fired in 2013 from a Catholic high school after nineteen years on the job when an administrator read her mother's obituary and it mentioned the teacher's female partner (she later reached a settlement with the Diocese of Columbus, though she was not given her job back); an eighteen-year veteran Catholic schoolteacher in Minnesota was fired in September 2013 after she told other faculty, "I'm gay, I'm in a relationship with a woman, and I'm happy," while at a conference; and a transgender man, a theology professor in California, was fired that same month from a California Christian university after he announced he was transgender. And there was the heartbreaking story in July 2014 of a Lubbock, Texas, man who worked in a children's home where he cared for and mentored kids from broken homes who were often abused, hoping they could be adopted and helping them find homes. After introducing his fiancé — a man — to some of the kids while on a field trip, he was fired, because, as the president of the home put it, "as a faith-based, church-related outreach providing welfare services . . . when you are implementing life training and so forth — particularly with children — to put a confused message out there is counterproductive."

The backlash against marriage equality also manifests itself as retaliation by employers against lesbian and gay people who exercise the new right to marry. A vice principal at a Catholic high school in the Seattle area was fired in December 2013 after getting married. (The state of Washington has both marriage equality and an antidiscrimination law protecting LGBT people.) The school had been able to tolerate him as long as he'd kept his homosexuality private, but, officials said, by marrying he made his sexuality a matter of public record, going against the teachings of the Catholic Church. The school believed it had to let him go and that in doing so it was exercising its First Amendment rights. Students held protests to support the vice principal and defended him on social media. The principal, a Catholic nun, also resigned in protest. But it was all to no avail. (The case is the subject of a pending lawsuit the vice principal filed in 2014.)

Michael Griffin a Pennsylvania teacher, experienced similar discrimination when he was fired from Holy Ghost Preparatory School in December 2013 after he went to New Jersey (which had marriage equality, while Pennsylvania still did not) and married his longtime partner. "I applied for a marriage license since NJ now has marriage equality," Griffin wrote on his Facebook page. "After 12 years together I was excited to finally be able to marry my partner. Because of that, I was fired from Holy Ghost Preparatory School today. I am an alumnus of the school and have taught there for 12 years. I feel hurt, saddened, betrayed and except for this post, am at a loss for words." Pennsylvania would see its marriage ban struck down in 2014, but as of this writing it remains a state with no antidiscrimination laws for LGBT people, so gay and lesbian couples can conceivably be married there one day and, as a result, fired from their job the next.

I've heard from dozens of people who've called my show who explained how they, too, were penalized for exercising this hard-fought right. Some went to a state where there is marriage equality, planning to return to their home state having at least secured federal benefits (filing a joint tax return, for instance), only to be fired from their jobs when their employers found out, or denied other rights of marriage. Some even got married in their own state, only to find that it was a state where that legal record of their relationship could get them fired.

The only federal antidiscrimination protections that LGBT advocates in Washington have ever worked with members of Congress to introduce in the past twenty years is the woefully inadequate Employment Non-Discrimination Act (ENDA), which would ban employment discrimination solely and, in each version introduced, has included a broad exemption that allows discrimination by any "corporation, association, educational institution or institution of learning, or society" owned by a religious institution — basically excusing the kinds of businesses most likely to discriminate. "ENDA's religious exemption could provide religiously affiliated organizations — far beyond houses of worship — with a blank check to engage in employment discrimination against LGBT people," the ACLU warned. "ENDA's religious exemption essentially says that LGBT discrimination is different — more legitimate — than discrimination against individuals based on their race or sex." That's because ENDA's religious exemption is much broader than that of the 1964 Civil Rights Act's Title VII, which is the gold standard for protection. In just about all of the cases I have described in which gay people were fired from religious schools or institutions, ENDA would have offered no protection from workplace discrimination. Later on, I'll look at why LGBT groups in Washington have asked for so little for so many years — and gotten nothing — and why and how we must change that and demand full equality.

Chronic Conditions

As in public accommodations and in the workplace, LGBT people face discrimination and neglect in the medical profession. Often this can drive them away from getting care, creating adverse health effects. The first federal health survey to include gay, lesbian, and bisexual people, in 2014, confirmed other studies showing higher obesity rates among lesbian and bisexual women than straight women, higher rates of psychological stress among bisexuals, and higher rates of smoking and binge drinking among all three groups than among heterosexuals. Psychologist Carmen Cruz, director of training at Texas Woman's University, analyzed the data, noting in her syndicated column that the "impact of social stigma for LGBT people to come out to others, including their providers, can be a deterrent for health care" and that "some LGBT people feel so stigmatized that they are reluctant to visit a physician or health care provider who may have implicit bias toward their sexual orientation or gender identity." There have been countless stories over the years of discrimination; too many of those stories proliferate today, even in the most unlikely places. In one example from 2014, a Southern California man filed suit against his doctor for diagnosing him with "chronic homosexual behavior," assigning a reference code that hasn't been used to denote homosexuality since it was removed from the American Psychiatric

Association's list of mental disorders, in 1973. The man alleges that when he challenged the doctor, she said the medical profession goes "back and forth" on whether homosexuality is a disease. That's untrue, and medical guidelines are unequivocal on this point, but some doctors continue to flout standards of care that have been in place for decades.

Fears of discrimination from medical professionals are most acute among transgender people. The term *transgender* encompasses a wide array of experiences regarding gender, and not all transgender people experience gender dysphoria. But many do, and the American Medical Association deems it a "serious medical condition" that may require hormone therapy, surgery, or both. The Affordable Care Act holds that transgender people can't be discriminated against. Insurance companies can no longer reject applicants based on pre-existing conditions, including being transgender. Five states and the District of Columbia have made their Medicaid programs inclusive (New York at this writing was moving to become the sixth state), so many low-income transgender people in those few jurisdictions can, in theory, get the cost of hormones and surgery covered. Medicare now covers transition-related medical costs, and nine states and the District of Columbia at this writing have compelled private insurers to do so as well. Yet despite these wins, many transgender people struggle to get medically necessary treatment.

I interviewed Naya Taylor, a transgender woman living in Mattoon, Illinois, whose doctor refused to start hormone replacement therapy as part of her medically necessary, transition-related health care to treat her gender dysphoria. First the doctor claimed that she was not experienced in providing hormones to transgender people. Whether or not that was true, it's no excuse; hormone therapy is regularly provided to nontransgender patients in a variety of settings every day. Later the clinic allegedly told Taylor that it "does not have to treat people like you," prompting Taylor to file a lawsuit with the help of the advocacy group Lambda Legal.

"The End of AIDS"?

A snapshot of the fear many LGBT people experience among medical professionals may be seen in a Kaiser Family Foundation report in September 2014 that found that 47% of gay men have not told their doctors their sexual orientation. And 56% of gay men say their doctors have never suggested an HIV test. This has alarming implications for efforts to stem HIV infections, which have remained constant at roughly fifty thousand new infections per year among gay and bisexual men and transgender women. Getting treatment not only preserves the health of those with HIV but virtually ends transmission, as drugs to treat HIV bring viral loads to undetectable levels. Yet a large percentage of those with HIV don't know their status and aren't on drug therapy; among young people ages thirteen to twenty-four, a majority of those with HIV are unaware of their status. A 2013 report from the Centers for Disease Control (CDC) noted that 27% of transgender women are HIV positive. A 2014 report showed that even as the rate of HIV diagnoses dropped in the American population in general, there was an alarming 132% rise among young gay and bisexual men ages thirteen to twenty-four, from 2003 to 2011, and most dramatically among young African American men.

The CDC has cut its HIV-prevention budget over the years to gay men as diagnosis rates have risen among young gay and bisexual men and transgender women. The epidemiological category "men who have sex with men" (MSM) includes gay and bisexual men and transgender women, all of whom make up nearly two-thirds of new infections. (That transgender women are categorized as men who have sex with men is not only offensive, it's also counterproductive to doing important prevention-outreach work.) On the HIV-prevention front, there have been heated debates among gay men about pre-exposure prophylaxis, or PrEP — the two-drug combination therapy otherwise known by the brand name Truvada — a once-a-day pill that is intended to provide added protection. It's been shown to reduce the risk of HIV infection among gay and bisexual men and transgender women by 92% or more if taken daily. Some have criticized PrEP, saying it will inspire complacency and inhibit condom use (though early research showed it doesn't inhibit condom use). Many AIDS activists counter that many gay men already clearly aren't using condoms and that PrEP, which is covered by most private health insurance companies and by Medicaid, should be promoted to them and made available. PrEP use for affected communities has been endorsed by the CDC, the World Health Organization, and Gay Men's Health Crisis, among many governmental agencies and AIDS groups. French researchers reported a "significant breakthrough" in November 2014 in preliminary results of a study that showed PrEP could be used "on demand," with a double dose taken from two to twenty-four hours before sexual activity and then a single dose taken for two days after the sexual activity.

As Chris Beyrer, director of the Johns Hopkins Training Program in HIV Epidemiology and Prevention Science, has noted, PrEP, if used as prescribed, is an "extraordinarily effective intervention." However, at a lecture he gave in May 2014 in New York, he explained, using a mathematical model, that to bring infections down even by a modest 35% over a five-year period would require enormous commitment from medical authorities: at least 50% of the best candidates for PrEP — right now, that means lower-income, mostly black gay men and transgender women, the hardest-hit group and the group most often excluded from access to or eductaion about PrEP — would need to be on this exorbitantly priced drug, which can cost up to $14,000 per year; a much higher percentage of HIV-positive people would have to be in treatment to bring their viral loads to an undetectable level; enhanced testing, perhaps every three months, among groups most at risk would have to occur; and beyond that we'd *still* need to increase condom use by 15% among all gay and bisexual men and transgender women. That's a heavy lift, and it means we need to stop arguing and channel that energy into enormous pressure on the CDC to do the kind of sex-positive, explicit prevention campaigns (promoting condom use, PrEP, and post-exposure prophylaxis [PEP] as prevention) that we've not seen it do in the history of the epidemic. And of course we need to continue to fight for both a cure and a vaccine. "This epidemic in MSM [men who have sex with men] right now is the expanding part of global HIV, and it is not in control," Beyrer said. "So this rhetoric that you hear about 'the end of AIDS,' and 'controlling AIDS,' and 'it's coming to an end,' and 'we're winning,' and 'victory' —yeah, but. Not yet."

There's a paradox about the life-saving treatment advances and our rightly heralding the hard-fought victory of getting those treatments: while many people with HIV are now thriving, no longer visibly ill while still managing a lifelong illness, HIV is out of sight and out of mind, particularly for younger LGBT people, many of whom are at risk. The victory narrative indeed blinds us all to a lot of the realities of HIV. AIDS activist Peter Staley rightly noted in 2013, "We're so caught up in the giddiness of the marriage-equality movement that we've abandoned the collective fight against HIV and AIDS." The stigma against HIV-positive people helped lead to the passing of HIV-criminalization laws in more than thirty states across the country through the '80s and '90s and beyond, and these only hamper prevention efforts. Hundreds of people have been charged under these laws. The laws vary, but many penalize HIV-positive people for having sex even with a condom but supposedly not disclosing their status — a claim that often can't be verified — even when transmission hasn't taken place. Nick Rhodes, an HIV-positive Iowa man with undetectable viral load, was given a twenty-five-year sentence for a one-time sexual encounter in 2008 during which a condom was used and no transmission occurred, after his sexual partner went to the police. Though his sentence was suspended, he was put on a sex-offender list, was forced to wear an electronic-monitoring bracelet on his ankle, and was not allowed unsupervised contact with his nieces, nephews, and other young children. In 2014, after a long legal battle, the Iowa Supreme Court set aside his conviction, but the ruling didn't affect the law or the cases of others. Activists, working with the legislature, were able to make the law in Iowa less onerous in 2014, but across the country draconian HIV-criminalization laws persist, driven by homophobia and an impulse to criminalize gay sex.

America's Deep and Enduring Closet

Many discussions of bigotry rely on the stories of individuals like Jennifer Tipton and Olivier Odom, or Michael Griffin, or Naya Taylor. These human stories affect us deeply. Yet, for some observers, it is easy to view these incidents as sad but isolated flare-ups of bias that otherwise seems to be dwindling. And indeed, it has been difficult to capture an accurate snapshot of how widespread this discrimination is, and where it lives. Recently, though, I spoke with a young researcher whose work casts this question in an intriguing new light by looking at a phenomenon that thrives in direct proportion to the prevalence of homophobia: the closet, which he shows is much bigger, still, than most of us might imagine, further exposing the myth of the victory narrative.

One of the paradoxes of the Internet is that, even as people say they value their privacy, they are putting much more of their lives out there to be studied. Seth Stephens-Davidowitz is a Google data scientist who writes a regular column for the *New York Times,* and he became interested in measuring the size of the gay male population, which then led him to see just how much of it appears to be closeted, something that shocked him. "I've been spending the last two years using these new data sources to answer a lot of difficult research questions where the traditional sources tend not to work," he told me, explaining how he began researching this subject. "To be honest, it wasn't a passionate topic of mine, although in doing the research I kind of developed a fair deal of anger and stronger political opinions than I had previously." As a straight man who attended Harvard, lived in liberal enclaves all his life, and supported gay rights, Stephens-Davidowitz believed we'd come much further than we actually had. His research revealed how far we are from victory. "One of the things that was so clear and was a little bit surprising to me, though maybe it wouldn't be to you and many of your listeners," he explained in an interview on my radio program, "was the clear effect of intolerance on causing tons of suffering in this country."

Stephens-Davidowitz used a number of data sets: Gallup surveys, which have amassed a lot of information over a period of years on sexual orientation in each state (though Gallup acknowledges that the closet skews these numbers); U.S. census data of the recent past, which offers information on gay couples; Facebook profiles; Craigslist ads for sexual encounters; Google searches (including searches, presumably by gay and bisexual men, for gay male porn); and dating and relationship sites such as Match.com. Although no one data set was perfect, by using several of them he was able to gather an enormous amount of data and to see consistent patterns. Stephens-Davidowitz concluded that roughly 5% of men are gay or predominantly attracted to men, but only 3.6% of men (that is, around 72% of gay men) will say so even anonymously in a survey. These numbers of self-identified gay men correspond, more or less, with figures that the noted demographer Gary Gates, research director of the UCLA Williams Institute, reported in a 2011 study tracking the number of self-identified gay, lesbian, bisexual, and transgender people as a percentage of total population. Gates showed the percentage of self-reported gay, lesbian, and bisexual people, combined, to be roughly between 3.5% and 4% of the American population, and transgender people to be 0.3%. The fact that Stephens-Davidowitz was looking only at gay men as a portion of all American men accounts for some variation in the numbers, but the point is that he was able to capture the roughly 28% of gay or bisexual men who won't state their sexual orientation even in an anonymous survey.

Stephens-Davidowitz's research challenged conventional wisdom in other ways, too. For example, he found that migration to big cities doesn't really create a substantial population shift of gay men from one region to another. "I was able to look at Facebook to see where gay men were born and where they live now," Stephens-Davidowitz said. He saw that, though there is some movement from less accepting places to places with vibrant and open gay communities, like New York and San Francisco, there isn't as much as many of us may have thought. "It's a relatively small number, particularly if you look at some of the other data searches I used," he explained. "You see consistent evidence that throughout the country [there is] a roughly similar [percentage] of gay men everywhere. There definitely is mobility — some people do move toward certain places that are popular in the gay community. But it turned out to be a pretty small factor. Overall, all states have fairly similar gay populations — truly gay populations. But the openly gay populations are very, very different.

"There's no perfect data set," he said. "You have to put together a whole bunch of data to get a consistent picture. Rates of pornographic searches are very similar in all parts of the country. Even closeted men in the privacy of their own homes" are looking at gay porn. In New York and Mississippi, there are relatively similar rates of searches for gay pornography, for example, in contrast to the percentage of the openly gay population, which is so much larger in New York than in Mississippi.

"How Do I Know If My Husband Is Gay?"

After determining that the percentage of men attracted primarily to men is equivalent in states throughout the country, Stephens-Davidowitz was able to draw some preliminary conclusions. The barriers preventing men from building openly gay lives in certain parts of the country are reflected in the fact that the rate of Craigslist searches by men seeking casual encounters with men is higher in Mississippi than in New York, while there's a higher rate of gay men seeking dates and relationships on Match.com in New York than in Mississippi.

"The closet doesn't just mean you don't announce your sexuality on Facebook," Stephens-Davidowitz commented. "It's influencing people's lives in a big way." For a closeted gay or bisexual man in Mississippi or someplace like it, in other words, a relationship with a man may seem impossible. Many men in this situation are married to women or are trying to pass as heterosexual while seeking secretive, casual encounters on the side. Regardless of geography, of course, not everyone is looking for a relationship, nor should they be expected to be in one. Many people who are openly gay, lesbian, or bisexual, too, enjoy being single or constructing varying kinds of relationships. But Stephens-Davidowitz's research points to one horribly confining and terribly sad effect of homophobia in conservative parts of the country and even in conservative areas of more liberal regions: it allows gay and bisexual men in these regions to seek only furtive, often dangerous sexual encounters with other men rather than making free choices about their sexual and emotional interactions and enjoying the rites of passage of dating and relationships just as heterosexuals do.

Looking at Google searches, Stephens-Davidowitz also found that the question "How do I know if my husband is gay?" is far more common than "How do I know if my husband is cheating?" or "How do I know if my husband is depressed?" Moreover, the highest percentage per capita of "How do I know if my husband is gay?" searches come from conservative parts of the country, with South Carolina at number 1, followed by Kentucky and Louisiana.

Stephens-Davidowitz noted that a woman's asking Google this question doesn't mean her husband is necessarily gay or bisexual. Again, it's the consistent patterns among various data sets that permit him to offer the conclusions. The fact that he saw more men searching for casual encounters with men in these places, fewer men looking for long-term relationships with men, and more women searching for answers about whether their husbands are gay added up to something. Stephens-Davidowitz determined that, on Facebook (which is not anonymous, and where users can identify their sexual orientation), about half of gay men nationally do not identify publicly as gay or bisexual. In more conservative places, again using Mississippi as an example, that figure goes up to 80%.

The fascinating demographics of gay men in Stephens-Davidowitz's research point to a broader fact: far fewer people are openly gay (or, we can assume, openly lesbian or bisexual) than we have come to think, even in perhaps the most liberal places, and it's extremely difficult to be out in many parts of the country. The victory narrative whitewashes the hardship of millions of Americans — not just lesbians and gays themselves but also the spouses and children of people living in the closet.

Some of these phenomena may be partly generational. "In Gallup polls, among people under the age of 30, more than 6 percent of adults tell pollsters they're gay," Gary Gates told the *Chicago Sun-Times* in 2013, discussing Stephens-Davidowitz's findings. That's double the rate for adults over 30. "Is that really because young people are gayer?" Gates asked. "I think a large piece of that is younger people are growing up in an environment where this is acceptable, so they're willing to identify themselves as gay."

But this shouldn't lead us to believe we can sit back and assume that, given time, homophobia will simply phase itself out regardless of other underlying factors. In Canada's most recent national survey, for example, fully 5% of Canadians identified as gay, lesbian, bisexual, or transgender, and for those under thirty-four years of age, a whopping 10% identified as LGBT. It's unlikely that there's a higher percentage of LGBT people in Canada than the United States. What is true is that Canada has had nationwide full equality, including marriage, for a number of years and, perhaps more important, has no significant religious-right movement per se. Canada's percentage of evangelical Protestants numbers in the single digits, while in the United States the percentage is more than a quarter of the population. Comparing the two, it's clear that even younger people in the United States are still far less likely to be open about their sexual orientation or gender identity than Canadians. And with many growing up in evangelical

Christian homes across large parts of the country, that may be true for some time to come.

There's also reason to believe that progress on LGBT rights may, ironically, be resulting in harsher treatment for children in such homes, even forcing more of them onto the streets. Increased visibility has clearly spurred people to come out at younger ages. A study published in 2011 found that the average age of coming out for gay, lesbian, and bisexual people had dropped from twenty-five, in 1991, to sixteen, in 2010. "While life gets better for millions of gays, the number of homeless LGBT teens — many cast out by their religious families — quietly keeps growing," read the lead-in to an article by journalist Alex Morris in the September 2014 issue of *Rolling Stone*. Morris pointed to researchers at San Francisco State University who confirmed that highly religious parents are more likely to reject LGBT children. The number of homeless youth overall has risen in the past several years, with the number of homeless students hitting an all-time high in 2013, at 1.2 million, according to data collected by the National Center for Housing Education, funded by the Department of Education. Several studies have shown that LGBT teens make up 40% or more of homeless teens (an overwhelming number of them black and Latino), even though they are believed to represent less than 10% of all teens. This is not happening just in regions of the country where the evangelical right dominates, either. Carl Siciliano, who heads the Ali Forney Center in New York City, the largest organization providing help for homeless LGBT youth, told Morris, "The summer that marriage equality passed in New York [in 2011], we saw the number of homeless kids looking for shelter go up 40 percent."

How True Are Those Breathless Polls?

So many signs point to the continued entrenchment of homophobia in American society, yet in recent years public-opinion polls and surveys have shown a dramatic shift in support for LGBT rights, including marriage equality. In one widely reported 2013 poll, for example, Pew Research announced that "ten years ago [in 2003], 37% viewed gay men favorably, while 51% viewed them unfavorably; 39% had a favorable impression of lesbian women while 48% had an unfavorable opinion. Today, by a 55% to 32% margin, more have a favorable than unfavorable opinion of gay men. And about twice as many view lesbian women favorably (58%) than unfavorably (29%)." These poll results were breathlessly reported in the media, along with polls showing increasing support for marriage equality. But how much of this shift reflects a true change in beliefs? It may simply suggest that homophobia is assuming a shadowy but no less insidious status, that it is not publicly stated but privately held, and may even be unconscious.

Recent research suggests that, while people say they're more supportive, the change in underlying biases about gays has been "pretty small," according to Rachel Riskind, a social science researcher and assistant professor of psychology at Guilford College in North Carolina. Riskind and her colleagues have done a great deal of research on this question and have also investigated the threat that gender-identity difference poses, particularly to heterosexual men. They used data from the Implicit Association Tests (IATs) of Project Implicit, a joint project created by Harvard University, the University of Washington, and the University of Virginia. Founded by social scientists Anthony Greenwald, Mahzarin Banaji, and Brian Nosek, Project Implicit has amassed data since 1998, including data collected from the project's website. While not random, representative samples, the data sets are massive. More than fourteen million people have taken the tests in categories such as race, sex, gender, and sexual orientation.

In IATs, subjects are shown images and words on a computer screen and asked to quickly make associations, which can be positive or negative. Usually subjects are prompted to match an image with words like *good* or *bad*, but often slightly more complex tests are used. In some cases, participants are provided with information and then answer questions based on it. By measuring the reaction time of subjects while they perform these exercises, IATs assess the presence of attitudes that influence the subjects' answers, biases they may or may not know they hold.

These biases can be classified as explicit or implicit. Explicit attitudes, as the term suggests, are those beliefs and thoughts people express publicly. Implicit attitudes are those which people hold privately, either consciously or unconsciously. "When we talk about implicit attitudes, we're talking about unconscious control or something you're aware of that you don't want to tell people," Riskind explained.

Project Implicit's deep well of data allows scientists to draw conclusions that elude most polls. Over the past few years, the research increasingly shows that, while people have changed their explicit attitudes about race and gender — that is, what they will tell a pollster, or even a friend, when asked if they support equality — privately held beliefs and biases have changed much more slowly, even among younger generations.

The same is holding true for sexual orientation and gender identity. Riskind said that the data sets she and her team are studying in an ongoing research project provide a diverse sample. Thirty percent of respondents were nonwhite, though the subjects were slightly more male and tended to be better educated than the general population. Again, the researchers are using hundreds of thousands of data points to draw sound conclusions. "I think the most striking thing," says Riskind, "is that political identity is one of the strongest predictors of implicit attitudes." In other words, self-identified conservatives tended to show more implicit bias than others. Riskind's research has also shown that heterosexuals, on average, exhibit an implicit bias or "preference" for heterosexuals, as do even some self-identified gay, lesbian, and bisexual people, whose bias exposes what might be internalized homophobia.

Taking the Gay–Straight IAT on the Project Implicit website in April 2014, a subject would learn that 68% of those who'd taken it previously were biased toward straights, showing either a "slight automatic preference to straight people compared to gay people" or a "strong automatic preference for straight people compared to gay people." Riskind and her team are also looking at change over time in their ongoing research.

"Our goal was to say, 'Okay, the public polls say there's been change in explicit attitude. What about implicit attitudes?'" Riskind explained. They found that, as with race and gender, positive changes in explicit attitudes toward sexual orientation and gender identity far outnumber changes in implicit bias. "Implicit attitudes changed, but it's pretty small. It's about half of the size in the change in explicit attitudes. It may be telling us that there are more people who are unwilling to report antigay attitudes."

In her research, Riskind is also pursuing answers to the triggers at the root of homophobia and transphobia. In 2014, Riskind and two colleagues—David J. Lick and Kerri L. Johnson, both professors of psychology at the University of California, Los Angeles—published the results of four studies they conducted, looking at the threat that gender identity posed to straight men. They were particularly interested in how straight men react to men who are gender variant (a category that includes "effeminate" or "stereotypical" gay men) and to gender-nonconforming individuals or those perceived to be transgender, either trans men or trans women. The studies didn't use IAT images of same-sex intimacy, as the implicit-bias study of gays and bisexuals did, but rather presented subjects with photos of faces of various kinds, including faces of gender-nonconforming individuals. "Four studies documented that straight men who feel insecure about their masculinity have heightened recognition of gender-atypical faces. We therefore argue that gender identity concerns play an important role in social vision, arousing perceptual biases that have implications for how men attend to and remember others in their social environments," the researchers concluded.

This research built upon other recent studies that showed men's sense of masculine identity is often threatened by encounters with gender-nonconforming individuals, making them self-conscious of the perception of their own gender. Another series of recent studies provided scientific confirmation that straight men often expressed anxiety about the idea of being falsely identified as gay, and because of that they avoided gay men. This research, published in 2013, affirmed the continued validity of 1990s studies that showed straight men who interacted with gay men were later avoided by other straight men or were perceived by other straight men to be exhibiting behavioral tendencies associated with gay men.

"Specifically, we propose that straight men who feel insecure about their masculinity may remember gender-atypical faces in order to avoid socially contagious interactions and to strengthen their feelings of gender identity," Riskind, Lick, and Johnson concluded. "Straight men unconsciously attend to gendered facial cues, processing gender-atypical others with remarkable efficiency when they have an insecure sense of their own masculinity." The researchers concluded that straight men who feel threatened about their masculinity avoid gender-nonconforming people and men they perceive as gay.

From Threat to Violence

In sum, the vital research that Riskind and others have conducted shows how the deep-seated and often unconscious impulse to identify and exclude those who are different can sometimes supply an undercurrent of threat to interactions between heterosexual and LGBT individuals. And any threat, of course, can materialize in abusive forms. People who aren't primed to engage in physical violence may still take the opportunity to exert dominance if they're allowed to get away with it. Almost all LGBT people have been victims of this kind of aggression at one time or another, experiencing a nasty look or comment or being made to feel uncomfortable and perhaps even endangered.

One Sunday afternoon, in the middle of the very gay neighborhood of Chelsea in Manhattan, my husband, David, and I were sharing a quick good-bye kiss when a man passing by called us "disgusting." I witnessed a similar confrontation a few months earlier when a gender-nonconforming man passed by on a bicycle and a man standing next to me, believing the cyclist had cut him off, called out, "Faggot." The man was a young hipster type who appeared to be heading to the art galleries with his girlfriend — in other words, to all appearances, he was probably not the kind of person who would admit to homophobic feelings.

When I've talked about these incidents on my show, the phones light up, again, with people expressing their own experiences. Sadly, many of the experiences they describe are horrific attacks. I don't mean to imply an equivalence between what happened to me on a street corner in Chelsea and the life-altering violence that far too many people have suffered, but I do feel these incidents exist on a continuum. All too often, when a sense of threat comes to a boil, it explodes into violence, and one of the great tragedies of these heady years of successes is that hate crimes against gay and transgender people still occur with unacceptable frequency. In fact, the reported number of such crimes has been on the rise. It is a cruel irony that, in winning marriage equality and becoming more visible in countless other ways, LGBT people have exposed ourselves more than ever before to a violent strain of bigotry that was always present and has now found its object. This is happening all over the country. For example, 2011, the year New York became the fifth and largest state thus far to achieve marriage equality, also saw the highest number of anti-LGBT murders nationally ever reported since the National Coalition of Anti-Violence Programs (NCAVP) began data collection, in 1998, with transgender people the hardest-hit victims.

We have to be circumspect about drawing broad conclusions from this data, as anti-LGBT violence is difficult to track. Overall reports across all types of antigay violence were actually down in 2011 according to the same report, for instance, but this does not necessarily signify a drop in prevalence. In fact, the authors of the NCAVP's report that year posited a link between the rise in murders and the drop in reporting of overall antigay violence: when smaller organizations are overwhelmed by dealing with serious crimes such as murder, they're less able to do the kind of community outreach necessary to educate people about violence and urge them to report it. "I think that hate violence against these communities has been going on for a very long time and the reports that we're seeing may not even be a reflection on the true pervasiveness of the violence," Chai Jindasurat, one of the authors of the report, told Lila Shapiro of the *Huffington Post* Gay Voices vertical. "I think we're really just getting the tip of the iceberg here."

The FBI, police departments, and private groups often provide different numbers, and the lag times in reporting vary, but most of the figures line up in showing an increase in reporting of hate crimes — whether due to more visibility or higher prevalence — over a period of years. According to the FBI's data, in 2012, Washington, D.C., which has marriage equality and full civil rights for LGBT people, ranked number 1 in hate crimes against that population. Next was Memphis, Tennessee, and then, at number 3, gay-friendly Seattle, in a state with marriage equality.

An accounting of this violence in one city alone quickly turns into a kind of litany, and surely it shows how victory blindness can literally be dangerous. Take my own city, New York. In 2013 violent attacks were reported almost every week. In May of that year, thirty-two-year-old Mark Carson, an African American gay man, was walking down a street in Greenwich Village with a male companion when another man reportedly began to harass them, calling them "faggots," according to eyewitnesses, and asking Carson, "You want to die tonight?" The alleged attacker then drew a gun and shot Carson in the face, killing him. The brutal murder sent a jolt through the LGBT community. In September of the same year, Islan Nettles, a twenty-one-year-old African American transgender woman, was beaten to death after a group of men began hurling antitrans slurs at her while she walked with friends in Harlem. The community was outraged when charges against the one man arrested were dropped, because of what the judge called a lack of evidence that he committed the crime. In the fall of 2014, within a two-week period from late September to mid-October, a transgender woman was viciously beaten unconscious by four men hurling slurs in the doorway of her Brooklyn apartment; a twenty-two-year-old gay Brooklyn man was shot as he ran from three men screaming homophobic slurs; and another gay Brooklyn man was attacked with a hammer in an antigay attack that resulted in his getting staples in his head.

The number of reports of anti-LGBT violence in the city increased by nearly 27% from 2012 to 2013, to a total of 584 cases, according to the New York City Anti-Violence Project, which is a member group of NCAVP. The New York City Police Department, which receives reports of only the most severe kinds of crimes, actually claimed a rise of 70% or higher for the same period; this may reflect the police department's receiving reports of only those more serious crimes, an increase in the severity of those crimes, or some combination of these and other factors — but no matter what, it means these crimes continue to occur at alarming rates. Sharon Stapel, executive director of the New York AVP, called it a "surge" and spoke with me on my show about the issue. She sees the increase in violence as a backlash not only to marriage equality but also to increased visibility. "The violence is still disproportionately impacting people of color and transgender people — nearly 90 percent (yes, 90 percent) of the anti-LGBTQ homicide victims across this country were people of color and 72 percent were transgender women," she has written. "For people of color, transgender women and transgender women of color, the violence isn't just increasing, it's an epidemic. Why, in a time where LGBTQ equality is making such progress, when LGBTQ people are more visible (I mean, Laverne Cox on the cover of *Time* — that's visible!), why is this violence still happening?" she asked. The answer, she says, is the "backlash."

Attacking the Victims

Transgender people of color are not only, as Stapel noted, the group most frequently targeted for violence but they are also, along with LGBT youth, the group that can least expect law enforcement to deliver justice. The story of CeCe McDonald, an African American transgender woman, has shone a light on the often brutal treatment of trans people and LGBT youth by police as well as bashers. McDonald and friends were walking down a Minneapolis street when a group of people outside a bar began taunting them. A woman from the group attacked McDonald and threw a glass at her eyes. The glass shattered and left shards in her face. While blood ran down McDonald's face, the woman assaulted her further. "After she hit me with the glass, she decided to pull me into the street by my hair and show how strong she was," McDonald told me in an interview. "It was really difficult for me to deal with that." She staggered away but was soon pursued by an older white man, Dean Schmitz, who physically threatened her and made transphobic comments. As he approached, she warned him to "leave it go," but he wouldn't. Remembering she had fabric scissors in her bag, she pulled them out and warned him to stay away. But he kept pursuing and she had no choice; she stabbed him in self-defense, unintentionally killing Schmitz.

McDonald was shocked when the police came and didn't seem to grasp that she was the victim. "When I stood in that parking lot, I was sure that the police were coming to help me," she said. "And when they arrived, they were ready to attack me. They were so quick to get out of the car and make me the aggressor." McDonald was sentenced to forty-one months in prison for manslaughter; she served nineteen months before finally being released.

A report by the Center for American Progress and the Center for Gender and Sexuality Law at Columbia Law School noted that "the disproportionate rate of LGBT people and [people living with HIV] in the criminal system can best be understood in the larger context of widespread and continuing discrimination in employment, education, social services, health care, and responses to violence." CeCe McDonald is just one of many victims of the pernicious and still deeply rooted feeling that LGBT people are somehow dangerous predators threatening the social body. The fact that this thinking still persists is a stain on our nation.

It's not over. All of these stories, interviews, comments, reports, data sets, and trends point to that simple fact. There's a disconnect between the way we talk about the strides forward and the reality on the ground. This narrowing of scope to talk only about successes — that's victory blindness. And, just as has often happened in the battles against other forms of bigotry in which groups thought they had "arrived," only to see rights stripped away, sometimes decades later, the enemies of lesbian, gay, bisexual, and transgender Americans will capitalize on it. We've got to pay attention now perhaps more than ever before as equality's opponents gather their forces.

3

BIAS AND BACKLASH

*HOW THE ENEMIES OF EQUALITY ARE REBRANDING,
RECALIBRATING, AND READYING FOR BATTLE*

AS STATEMENTS OF EXPLICIT BIAS against LGBT people become more difficult to voice, it becomes a challenge for the Republican Party, which has courted anti-LGBT conservatives for decades. But we can't let the victory narrative allow us to believe that we've conquered the GOP on this score. The radical right's hard-core, blatant antigay message seems to be disintegrating, but, far from gone, it's morphing into something just as sinister. Through trial and error, leaders among our enemies are rebranding themselves, yet we too often dismiss their efforts as futile by pointing to polls showing support among younger Americans (including younger Republicans) for marriage equality and other LGBT rights. This practice is shortsighted and fed by victory blindness.

The GOP, as I noted, is home to a large antigay religious constituency, which has had enormous influence in the party since Ronald Reagan began courting the evangelical right decades ago. Republican leaders could always count on openly stoking homophobia to bring this large, motivated part of the base out to vote. For Senate candidates like Rick Santorum of Pennsylvania or James Inhofe of Oklahoma, explicit gay bashing was a perennial theme of their campaigns and their years in office as standard-bearers for the Christian right. After Massachusetts became the first state to grant marriage equality with a 2003 ruling from its Supreme Judicial Court that paved the way for the first weddings by gay and lesbian couples beginning in 2004, continued scare tactics about gay marriage helped galvanize the party base to secure George W. Bush's reelection later in that year and to pass preemptive bans on gay marriage in many states.

That evangelical base is still very present and influential in the party, raising money for candidates and turning out to vote even as the winds have changed dramatically on LGBT rights and gay marriage. In March 2012, during the GOP primary races for the 2012 presidential election, a survey found that 50% of GOP primary voters identified as white evangelical or born-again Christian. Skepticism about polling notwithstanding, in every poll that shows the majority of Americans supporting marriage equality, a majority of Republicans polled are opposed. But increasingly over the past few years, conservatives in power have found that openly homophobic words and actions, particularly when they gain traction in the media, can often be toxic in the eyes of independents and more moderate Republicans, as well as younger voters. The GOP has been in this situation before. Whether it was civil rights legislation for African Americans or broad gains for women, Republican leaders have found ways to counter progressive shifts by adjusting their side's discourse away from outright bigotry (though certainly we still hear plenty of that) toward covert appeals to the kind of implicit bias discussed in the preceding chapter. They are beginning to use the same tactics to oppose LGBT equality.

This is by far the greatest danger of victory blindness. Yes, polls showing that a majority of Americans say they favor marriage equality are something to celebrate. Yes, we should be proud that the country has embraced many LGBT figures in popular culture with open arms. But these successes must not prevent us from seeing the backlash building right before our eyes. Or before we know it, conservatives will have quietly, patiently built support to chip away at the rights we've won or to keep us from getting further. This could lock us into our own version of the perpetual battles that American women still fight for basic equality (not just in regard to abortion but about everything from pay equity to the persistence of rape culture) and that African Americans still fight over voting rights, police abuse, and so many other issues. If LGBT people and our allies don't meet this threat head-on, right now, we may find that the limits of what we can achieve fall far short of full equality.

"It's Feeble!"

Republican political strategists would be correct in surmising that homophobia is still a powerful force in American culture. They know that they can still exploit homophobia to win elections. But, as I have stated, they are discovering that frank expressions of that bigotry will often be met with swift censure that prevents them from achieving their goals. This shift is a major advance for LGBT people, to be sure, and has provided some of the most inspiring political and legal scenes in recent years.

For supporters of LGBT rights, it was impossible not to be amazed, impressed, and heartened by the questioning that Richard Posner, judge of the Seventh Circuit Court of Appeals, a Reagan appointee, delivered to Wisconsin assistant attorney general Timothy Samuelson, who defended Wisconsin's gay-marriage ban before the court in August 2014. As Samuelson tried to argue that the "tradition" of defining marriage as the union between a man and a woman justified the ban, Posner jumped in:

POSNER: What concrete factual arguments do you have against
     homosexual marriage?
SAMUELSON: Well, we have, uh, the Burkean argument, that it's
     reasonable and rational to proceed slowly.
POSNER: That's the tradition argument. It's feeble! . . . There was
     a tradition of not allowing blacks and whites, and, actually,
     other interracial couples from marrying. It was a tradition. It
     got swept aside. Why is this tradition better?

SAMUELSON: The tradition is based on experience. And it's the
    tradition of western culture.
POSNER: What experience! It's based on hate, isn't it?
SAMUELSON: No, not at all, your honor.
POSNER: You don't think there's a history of rather savage
    discrimination against homosexuals?

Posner wrote the Seventh Circuit three-judge panel's unanimous
decision upholding decisions by district-court judges striking down
Wisconsin's and Indiana's gay-marriage bans. In one particularly
witty, stinging passage, he wrote, "Heterosexuals get drunk and pregnant, producing unwanted children; their reward is to be allowed to
marry. Homosexual couples do not produce unwanted children; their
reward is to be denied the right to marry. Go figure."

In other arenas bigoted political gambits have imploded in spectacular fashion. In 2011 Stacey Campfield, a Republican in the Tennessee state Senate, championed a piece of legislation that became
known as the "don't say gay" bill. It passed in the state Senate and, if
ratified by the state House of Representatives, would have prevented
any discussion of homosexuality in schools, banning students, teachers, and school officials from even acknowledging that sexuality not
"related to natural human reproduction" (in the strangely coy language of the bill) exists at all.

The bill was born in the most abject bigotry. I invited Campfield,
its architect, for an interview on my radio show in 2012, as "don't
say gay" was making its way through the Tennessee House. His comments veered widely, from dangerous and utterly incorrect proc-
lamations about HIV/AIDS ("My understanding is that it is virtually — not completely, but virtually — impossible to contract AIDS
through heterosexual sex . . . very rarely [transmitted] . . .") to equally
dangerous and staggeringly insensitive comments on the connection
between bullying and LGBT teen suicide. "That bullying thing is the
biggest lark out there," Campfield said. "There are sexually confused

children who could be pushed into a lifestyle that I don't think is appropriate with them and it's not the norm for society, and they don't know how they can get back from that. I think a lot of times these young teens and young children, they find it very hard on themselves and unfortunately some of them commit suicide." In other words, Campfield implied that it was "sexual confusion" and homosexuality itself that were driving LGBT teens to depression and suicide, rather than acknowledging how homophobia — the very thing that Campfield promoted — contributes to those feelings of immense despair. I was grateful when the interview drew national attention to "don't say gay" and decent Tennesseans, embarrassed by Campfield's bigotry, spoke out against him. For example, Martha Boggs, a restaurant owner in Campfield's district in Knoxville, told me in an interview that she showed him the door when he came in one day for brunch. "I was incensed that an elected official could make such irresponsible comments," she said. "I saw him at the front door and there was just something that made me decide to not serve him, just to make a point to him [about] how awful he has been. I told him he wasn't welcome here and I wanted him to leave."

The outrage helped opponents of "don't say gay" defeat the bill in the Tennessee House, where it died without a vote in 2012. Campfield would go on to lose the GOP primary in his district two years later. The bill, though, reared its head again in the spring of 2013, now in an even more extreme form. Written by John Ragan, a Republican in the Tennessee House, the reboot dictated not only that homosexuality couldn't be discussed but also that whenever school officials became aware that a student was gay — for example, if the student confided in a counselor — or so much as suspected it, the school would be required to notify the child's parents. In effect, the bill would have forced kids out of the closet to families who might be conservative and antigay and might put them into harmful conversion-therapy programs or, perhaps, even throw them out on the street. This version, thankfully, failed to pass in the House.

Ragan's part in the story has an inspiring afterword that also shows how any one of us can be an activist, defy complacency, and help unwrite the victory narrative. In the same year that Ragan sponsored his version of "don't say gay," he received a ludicrous Reformer of the Year award from StudentsFirst, a right-wing front group founded by the former chancellor of the Washington, D.C., public schools, Michelle Rhee. The group claims to speak on behalf of students but is all about pushing right-wing policy reform; as the *Los Angeles Times* reported, StudentsFirst "spent nearly $2 million" during the 2012 election "to support 105 candidates across the country," 90 of whom were Republicans. Giving John Ragan an education award was not only farcical, it was also dangerous. He said he would bring back "don't say gay" in future sessions, and StudentsFirst's seal of approval might have given him a veneer of credibility that would have made the bill harder to defeat. Eleven-year-old Marcel Neergaard, a boy from Ragan's town, became empowered to take action. He launched a petition and made a video, speaking out. He also wrote a blog post on *Huffington Post*'s Gay Voices vertical, headlined TAKING A STAND AGAINST BULLYING:

> I am Marcel Neergaard, and I am 11 years old. This year I was homeschooled for sixth grade because of severe bullying. If I had gone back to public school, there is a great possibility that I would have taken my own life. That possibility would have grown if a certain bill introduced in my home state of Tennessee had passed into law. This bill was known as the "don't say gay" bill. Though that bill never became a law, Oak Ridge's own representative, John Ragan, introduced a new version of the Classroom Protection Act. It is the "don't say gay" bill, just more homophobic. While he crafted this horrifying bill, he received an award. I wrote a petition to take a stand against this.
>
> During my first year in middle school, I experienced severe bullying. I was called terrible names that were quite hurtful. At that time, I had just realized that I'm gay, and the bullies used the word

"gay" as an insult. This made me feel like being gay was horrible, but my parents told me otherwise. Their support was tremendous. But as powerful as their love was, it couldn't fight off all the bullying. I don't want anyone else to feel the way I did. No one deserves that much pain, no matter who they are. This was my reason for writing the petition.

Marcel called on StudentsFirst to rescind the award, and with the help of gay activist Scott Wooledge and his powerful and creative social-media campaigns, enough pressure was brought to bear. StudentsFirst withdrew the award, and Marcel and his dad, Mike, came on my show to celebrate and also to empower other young people and their parents across the country. It is only because of brave young people like Marcel coming forward that we can see this kind of action.

The sad truth, though, is that while Tennessee is safe for now, eight other states already have what are known as "no promo homo" laws, which, like the original "don't say gay" bill, restrict to varying degrees what educators can say about homosexuality. Arizona's, for example, mandates that "no district shall include in its course of study instruction which . . . (1) promotes a homosexual life-style . . . (2) portrays homosexuality as a positive alternative life-style . . . (3) suggests that some methods of sex are safe methods of homosexual sex." Antigay conservatives understand that one of the best ways to slow, halt, or even roll back progress toward LGBT equality is to keep gay lives invisible and gay voices silent, and these laws aim to do that in one of the places where it matters most: our public schools. Republicans will not stop trying to pass these bills.

But, as they have discovered, explicit bias — that is, outright bigotry — is no longer a winning strategy. In order to achieve their goals, Republicans are finding a subtler way of appealing to bias toward LGBT people. Increasingly when they talk about gays, they dog-whistle.

The Bias Laboratory

The term "dog whistling" refers to a tactic for talking about race, women's reproductive rights, and other hot-button issues in more covert and coded ways. Republicans began to deploy it in the 1970s, and in more pronounced ways since the 1990s. In his book *Dog Whistle Politics,* Ian Haney López, a senior fellow at the progressive think tank Demos and a law professor at the University of California, Berkeley, reveals how coded signals to underlying racial anxiety are used to convince middle-class white Americans to vote for a political party mainly devoted to serving big business. Appearing in 2012 on the independent TV news program *Democracy Now!* with Amy Goodman, he explained how it works:

> On one level, we hear clearly there's a sense of racial agitation; on another level, plausible deniability — people can insist nothing about race at all. And so, classic examples: Reagan and welfare queens, or Newt Gingrich saying Obama is a "food stamp president." Now, on one level, that's triggering racial sentiment, triggering racial anxiety. On another, of course, Newt Gingrich can turn around and say, "I didn't mention race. I just said food stamps." In fact, he can go further and say, "It's a fact," as if there isn't a sort of a racial undertone there . . . They're using these sort of coded appeals to say to people two things: One, the biggest threat in your life is not concentrated wealth, it's minorities; and two, government coddles minorities, and all these government assistance programs, it's all about giveaways to minorities — oppose them — government is taking your taxes and giving it to undeserving minorities.

In the eyes of many conservatives, LGBT people are yet another "coddled" and "undeserving" minority whose very existence is unsettling and even disgusting. Republican leaders knew they could tap into that sentiment without casting gay people as bearers of disease, perverts, threats to the very notion of the family, or anything else from their familiar repertoire of stereotypes. Instead, they borrowed a page from the same playbook they have used for decades. Now, when they want to talk about gay people, Republicans discuss a threat to "religious liberties" or "religious freedom." And if these terms are the raw ingredients of dog whistling, the Conservative Political Action Conference (CPAC) is the test kitchen where the recipes are developed.

CPAC is an annual convention of conservative activists that draws major GOP politicians, including members of Congress and most of the presidential contenders, as well as activists, analysts, and significant media interest. I've attended for several years, broadcasting my show live from there, interviewing conservative activists and politicians. For me, it's like being a kid in a candy store — a scary candy store — able to speak with the very people who are affecting our lives in such detrimental ways. I try to ask them the hard questions that many in the media won't ask, or expose their bigotry just by talking to them and letting them reveal it frankly. A special treat in 2013 was interviewing the virulently antigay U.S. senator Jim Inhofe of Oklahoma. One of the stranger moments to take place on the Senate floor occurred a few years earlier, when Inhofe, speaking out against homosexuality, held up a photograph of his extended family and said he was "very proud" that "in the recorded history" of the Inhofe family, "we've never had a divorce or any kind of homosexual relationship." At CPAC 2013, the news had just broken that morning that Inhofe's friend GOP senator Rob Portman of Ohio had announced his support of gay marriage after his own son came out to him as gay. I got the chance to break the news to Inhofe in the interview. He seemed to go into shock. "I did not hear that," he said. For several seconds, he didn't say a word. Then: "I'm pretty surprised. I can't really respond to that. It's something I was not aware of until you mentioned it."

In 2014 New Jersey GOP governor Chris Christie spoke at CPAC, as did GOP senator Rand Paul of Kentucky and GOP senator Marco Rubio of Florida, all of whom are opposed to gay marriage and all of whom had been discussed as possible presidential contenders. They were there to test the waters well before the Republican primaries, trying to woo the crowd. Broadcasting my show from the site of the convention, just outside Washington, D.C., in National Harbor, Maryland, I heard plenty of attacks on gay equality coming from the stage during the three days of CPAC. And the various speakers seemed to be trying out different wording.

Former senator Rick Santorum, who was very explicit with me about the harms of homosexuality and gay marriage when I interviewed him at length at the 2008 GOP convention, in Saint Paul, Minnesota, now talked of "reclaiming" marriage and "promoting" marriage — never saying the word *gay*. Ben Carson, the Johns Hopkins neurosurgeon who became a rising right-wing star in the GOP and who damaged his brand when he made a blatant antigay remark comparing gays to pedophiles a year earlier, in 2013, now talked of not offering people "extra rights." I could hear echoes of the "special rights" code that Christian conservatives used to varying degrees for a long time against gays. Ralph Reed was there, too, representing the Faith and Freedom Coalition, the organization he heads. (It's an incarnation of the Christian Coalition, which Reed headed during its heydey in the '90s; the name harmonizes perfectly with a shift from explicit to implicit bias.) Reed blasted "left-wing bullies" for forcing Arizona governor Jan Brewer to veto a "religious liberties" bill and said that Attorney General Eric Holder had engaged in a "brazen act of lawlessness" for counseling state attorneys general not to defend marriage-equality bans. It was at CPAC, during some of the breakout sessions, where I first heard a new term I would hear a great deal later in the year, at the September 2014 Family Research Council's Values Voter Summit: "natural marriage." This was a replacement for the term "traditional marriage," a shift that Adele Stan of *The American Prospect,* who's covered the right for years, attending the Values Voter Summit annually, told me might be a rebranding to reach millennials, who could be put off by the word *traditional,* as young people often are.

I've covered CPAC for years, and this was in fact the first time in several years that there wasn't a panel on how "traditional marriage" was under attack because of the threat of "homosexual activists." In 2012 there was a main-ballroom event moderated by Maggie Gallagher, founder and former president of the National Organization for Marriage (NOM), then the leading group fighting against marriage equality. That panel featured then eighty-seven-year-old Phyllis Schlafly, the Eagle Forum founder and antifeminist leader in the religious right going back to the Reagan years. Most of those on the panel were in fact in their sixties or seventies, and most of the audience was over fifty, while much of CPAC's much younger membership — the majority of attendees — was out in the hallways, not interested in the event.

The following year, in 2013, there was a CPAC panel led by Cleta Mitchell — a prominent antigay board member of the American Conservative Union (ACU), which hosts CPAC and which had banned the conservative gay group GOProud from having a booth in years past — and featuring Brian Brown, then and current president of NOM. Attendance was sparse, while a panel in support of gay marriage — hosted by a libertarian group and featuring gay Republican (now independent) and GOProud founder Jimmy LaSalvia and other conservatives who support gay marriage — was packed.

So, in 2014, it wasn't surprising that there was no panel on the evils of gay marriage, and NOM was relegated to a small table downstairs in the basement of the hotel with the other exhibitors; homophobia had literally been driven underground. Conservative activist and ACU board member Grover Norquist told me that half of CPAC attendees that year, as in the previous year, were under twenty-five. Polling has consistently shown that younger people nationwide publicly support gay marriage, and during the conference several media polls of young Republicans showed them supporting gay rights and even gay marriage, indicating what media pundits and reporters called an increasing generational divide among Republicans on marriage equality. Polling released that week by Pew Research showed young Republicans supporting gay marriage by 61% (in stark contrast to 27% of those over fifty in the GOP who support gay marriage), and a lot of the coverage of the poll and the reported divide in the GOP was tied to stories about

CPAC. In a report from CPAC, using its own similar polling, the *New York Times* ran with the headline YOUNG REPUBLICANS FIND FAULT WITH ELDERS ON LIST OF SOCIAL ISSUES.

Yet much of the media coverage seemed overblown and didn't dig below the surface. I spoke with more than three dozen young people at CPAC, and only a small minority of my interviewees appeared to be actively pro-LGBT and speaking out about it, like Alexander Mc-Cobin of the libertarian student group Students for Liberty, who sat on a panel. A minority seemed to be actively antigay and speaking out about that, like the young men of the American Society for the Defense of Tradition, Family, and Property, a Catholic-identified group that had a presence in the exhibition hall and that gave out fliers depicting the gay group GOProud as a rainbow-colored beaver gnawing at the social-conservative leg of Ronald Reagan's proverbial three-legged stool.

However, it seemed to me that most twenty-somethings at CPAC just don't care about the issue and, quite frankly, don't want to be bothered by it. They certainly didn't want to waste their time sitting in on a panel discussion condemning gay marriage, but they also didn't want to be on the barricades fighting for it. In polling, many of these young people might say they support gay marriage, but it's not something they're passionate about. And, on the basis of my conversations with them, I also don't believe it's going to stop them from supporting an anti-equality, antigay candidate whose fiscal policies or foreign policy they support — in the way that we've seen many Republicans and independents back candidates whose statements or votes on racial issues or on women's rights have been questionable, even abhorrent, but whose other policies they support.

A "Not-So-Subtle Makeover"

The candidacy of David Brat was one prominent example of this phenomenon. Brat, an antiabortion, antigay Tea Party candidate, sent a jolt through Washington when he toppled GOP House majority leader Eric Cantor, congressman from Virginia, in a GOP primary in 2014 in that state's Seventh Congressional District, marking the first time in history that something like that has happened. Brat, who easily won in the general election in 2014, is a hard-core, extreme Christian reconstructionist whose positions on a variety of issues show he ascribes to a political outlook that historian Michael McVicar has called "theocratic libertarianism." Brat and others like him believe the state should be restricted and restrained when it comes to economic issues but completely involved in public policy when it comes to fostering religious beliefs and keeping little separation between church and state. Brat's campaign manager was not some wrinkled stalwart of the Republican establishment but a twenty-three-year-old, Zachary Werrell, who previously worked for libertarian GOP congressman and former presidential candidate Ron Paul's Campaign for Liberty. Werrell is part of a network of young Tea Party Republicans who, in polling, might say they support or have no objection to gay marriage or antidiscrimination laws for gays. Werrell himself is not on record on the issue of gay marriage (though he has scrubbed comments on his social-media accounts that seemed to question abortion rights, after tweets got attention shortly after Brat's win). On social media, he mostly has commented on economic issues, supporting Brat's policies. Young people like him might explicitly disagree with Brat on gay marriage or just not care about it — Brat's campaign website said he will "protect" the "sanctity of marriage," not ever mentioning the word *gay* — but they might still support him for his positions on issues dear to them, such as clamping down on immigration or cutting taxes.

It is true that Barack Obama beat Mitt Romney in 2012 by twenty-four points among all eighteen- to twenty-nine-year-olds. As a group, millennials have been generally leaning with Democrats on a wide variety of issues, supporting many progressive causes. Among white men ages eighteen to twenty-nine, however, Romney beat Obama by thirteen points, and among white women in that age group he beat

Obama by one point. It's fair to say, from what we know of the demographic breakdown of the parties and the way the candidates attracted voters of different racial groups, that the majority of these young white people who voted for Romney are Republican or independent. In polls a large majority of millennial independents say they support same-sex marriage, and even a majority of Republicans in that age group say in recent polls that they agree. Yet most still voted for a candidate who wanted to ban marriage for gays in the U.S. Constitution. Voting trends in recent years show a drop in turnout among all young voters, and particularly among members of minority groups, during midterm elections (which hurts Democrats and progressive causes), while young Republican turnout has been on the rise, meaning that general indifference to LGBT equality among young GOPers can outweigh active support among young people in general. This was predicted in the spring of 2014 by Harvard's Institute of Politics regarding the 2014 midterm elections, analyzing a survey of voters ages eighteen to twenty-nine and noting that "among the most likely voters, the poll . . . finds traditional Republican constituencies showing more enthusiasm than Democratic ones for participating in the upcoming midterms." And that turned out to be exactly right, as exit polls showed voter turnout among the age group dropped significantly, from 19% of the electorate to 13%. Because of that low turnout of young people, looking at voting for members of the House of Representatives specifically, CBS noted, "the Democrats' advantage with young voters was cut in half." In the Republican wave that swept over the Senate, the House, governors' races, and state legislatures in 2014 — and more Republicans were elected to state houses than they had been since the 1920s, which could have implications for some time to come — extreme right-wing and profoundly antigay candidates backed by evangelical leaders were elected. Many of these candidates, like Joni Ernst (elected to the U.S. Senate in Iowa), Tom Cotton (elected to the U.S. Senate in Arkansas), and Cory Gardner (elected to the U.S. Senate in Colorado), had their images softened by Republican strategists (Josh Vorhees at *Slate,* for example, noted Ernst's "not-so-subtle makeover") to bring in young and more moderate voters while still, as exit polls showed, getting strong turnout from evangelical voters in the GOP base who backed them from early on.

In sum, if young Republicans and independents are attracted to a candidate's policies, code words directed toward people who harbor explicit or implicit bias against LGBT people will not alienate those young voters. Only the most blatant bigotry might turn these young people off.

Furthermore, when Mike Huckabee stood before a packed room at CPAC in 2014 and railed about "religious liberty" being under attack and warned of God delivering the "fiery judgment" of "Sodom and Gomorrah" on America, a great many young people were there to join in the standing ovation and raucous applause. As Christian-right leaders try to morph the anti-gay-marriage push into a "religious liberties" and "religious freedom" issue, many of these young people might gravitate toward that message. They may support it out of loyalty, see it as more reasonable, or just rationalize it. For many, implicit homophobic appeals, rather than explicit ones, may work, and certainly the research shows that implicit bias is still quite strong, even though explicit bias has diminished.

Rebranding Bigotry Through Trial and Error

In addition to test-driving antigay dog-whistle rhetoric at gatherings like CPAC, Republicans are trying to write "religious freedom" protections into law in states across the country. We should not be lulled into a false sense of security by the fact that some of these attempts have failed. Like some kind of sci-fi-movie monster, the conservative political machine absorbs everything progressives can throw at it and regenerates itself.

In 2013 a New Mexico lesbian couple were turned away by a wedding photographer, Elaine Huguenin, of Elane Photography. New Mexico, which has had marriage equality since its supreme court handed down a ruling in 2013, has also had, since 2003, a comprehensive law banning discrimination on the basis of sexual orientation and gender identity "in matters of employment, housing, credit, public accommodations, and union membership." The couple sued and won in the New Mexico Supreme Court. (Huguenin eventually asked the U.S. Supreme Court to take the case, but the justices declined to hear it.)

Neighboring Arizona, like twenty-eight other states, has no statewide law protecting LGBT people against discrimination in public accommodations, and passed a ballot measure in 2008 that wrote a same-sex-marriage ban into the state's constitution. So not only were gay and lesbian couples not getting legally married in Arizona at that time, but also, except in a few cities with local protections, no business was or is compelled to serve LGBT people, and any business was free to hang a NO GAYS ALLOWED sign on its doors. Somehow, that wasn't quite enough for conservative Arizona lawmakers, though. They used the New Mexico case to whip up antigay sentiment and fear, and passed a law that would protect business owners' "religious liberties" by granting them broad leeway to discriminate on the basis of their religious beliefs. The law was clearly meant as a countermeasure against LGBT equality, though the lack of statewide protections already gave many business owners all the latitude they needed to discriminate against gays.

The bill backfired big-time. The legislation was not shrewdly worded, and it could have allowed companies to cite "religious beliefs" to discriminate against not only gays but perhaps almost anyone, from single mothers to individuals expressing another religious faith. That glaring problem helped the story gain enormous attention as bloggers and online journalists focused in on it, and it raised awareness of the fact that gays are discriminated against in public accommodations in the first place, something that many Americans hadn't actually believed was legal under federal law. It fell to GOP Arizona governor Jan Brewer to decide whether to sign the bill. In the past, Brewer had backed up Republicans in the legislature almost every time they'd pushed an antigay agenda. Several years earlier, for example, she'd signed a law that reversed previous governor Janet Napolitano's order granting state workers domestic-partner benefits. (The reversal was challenged in the courts, and in 2013 the Supreme Court upheld a lower federal court ruling preventing the reversal from taking effect while the case proceeds.)

But this time, Brewer stalled. Letting the decision drag out, per-haps not sure of what to do, Brewer actually helped to defeat the bill. For days the media built up expectations around the hoped-for veto, and activists had time in the national spotlight to stoke opposition to discrimination. (Even so, as Joe Jervis of the popular gay blog *JoeMy God* shrewdly noted, LGBT groups in Washington, like the Human Rights Campaign, were slow to react.) The delay encouraged major corporations, from Apple to Delta Airlines, to come out against the bill, and even the National Football League weighed in, threatening to pull the 2015 Super Bowl from Arizona. On TV talk shows, commen-tators equated businesses' banning service to gays to refusing to serve a racial or religious minority. Brewer, clearly under pressure from the business community, which itself is a big part of the GOP base, could see how signing the bill could financially impact that state. After a tumultuous week, she vetoed the bill.

LGBT activists, progressives, and media pundits saw it as a huge win, and it was certainly an exciting success. But once the TV crews had decamped and the companies that had pressured Brewer were back to business as usual, many LGBT Arizonans were left exactly where they were when the controversy started. In all but a few cities, it's still legal for businesses to refuse categorically to serve lesbian, gay, bisexual, and transgender customers, for a landlord to turn away LGBT tenants, and for an employer to fire an employee simply for being gay or bisexual. I'm not going to hold my breath waiting for the NFL to protest this unacceptable status quo. Announcing the veto, Brewer said the "religious liberties" law was "unnecessary." She was exactly right. Though certain localities offered protections, the lack of a statewide or federal law banning discrimination already gave bigots everything they need to legally discriminate against LGBT people in much of her state, and still does.

More to the point, we need to recognize Arizona's "religious liberties" bill for what it was: a trial balloon, an early misfire in a much larger battle to drive back the gains LGBT people have made. The GOP-controlled Arizona legislature passed the bill to give some red meat to evangelical Christians in the base during an election year, and it was a major misstep. It cost religious conservatives dearly in the court of public opinion nationwide, and several other states, including Kansas, put similar bills on hold or killed them. But antigay advocates and the politicians who back them vowed to press on, still intent on courting evangelical voters. In fact, only weeks after the debacle, Mississippi Republicans passed legislation that showed how much they'd learned from Arizona's example. The Mississippi bill had been originally worded like the Arizona bill, but the GOP there retooled it to be more vague (but, to many legal observers, no less dangerous), modeled more on the federal Religious Freedom Restoration Act (RFRA). The Mississippi Religious Freedom Restoration Act states that the government "or an action by any person based on state action shall not burden a person's right to exercise religion" without a compelling reason. It doesn't mention gays, but the ACLU and other legal analysts believe it will give the very conservative Mississippi courts justification to allow business owners who oppose homosexuality to refuse services to LGBT people. "Religious right activists clearly envision the Mississippi law as empowering businesses to discriminate against same-sex couples in the name of religion," MSNBC.com reported. Tony Perkins of the antigay Family Research Council, in fact, put out a statement in support of the law's passage, saying that it would allow "a wedding vendor, whose orthodox Christian faith will not allow her to affirm same-sex 'marriage,'" to turn away gay couples. Christian evangelical leaders across the country backed the bill, and they plan to continue this movement in other states.

What many Americans don't yet realize is that religious objections to homosexuality — or to, say, gay weddings — aren't some isolated, special instance that should thus be given an exception because homosexuality has long been condemned in the tenets of several religious faiths. They are in fact connected to a history of discrimination in this country in which religious beliefs have wrongly been used to enforce racial segregation and ban interracial marriage, to subjugate women (according to biblical beliefs, for example), and to deny service to religious minorities. "Religious liberties" bills are a threat not just to LGBT people simply trying to lead their lives but also to all marginalized groups. The federal RFRA, after all, provided the legal basis for the Supreme Court's decision in the infamous *Burwell v. Hobby Lobby Stores, Inc.* case (known colloquially as *Hobby Lobby*), in which the court found that the arts-and-crafts chain store was within its rights to drop coverage of certain forms of birth control from the health-care plans of its female employees. The conservative justices who carried the day reasoned that, because Hobby Lobby was a "closely held" company (meaning a majority of its shares were owned by, at most, five people), owners' religious liberties were threatened by the Affordable Care Act's directive to employers to provide contraceptive coverage. The decision alarmed many civil rights groups, which feared how it would be used; and as Jeffrey Toobin noted in *The New Yorker,* it has already been cited by lower courts in 2014 in ways that raise concern. In one case in Utah, a federal judge ruled that the leader of a fundamentalist Mormon sect that broke away from the Church of Jesus Christ of Latter-Day Saints doesn't have to speak with Department of Labor investigators regarding child-labor practices, because he made a religious vow not to speak of church practices. LGBT groups were so concerned about the *Hobby Lobby* decision that finally most of them were forced to pull their support of ENDA because of its religious exemption, realizing it was a trap, a provision that would be misused by the courts. In other words, ENDA might go the way of the federal RFRA itself. Passed by a large majority of both parties in Congress in 1993 and signed by President Clinton, RFRA was actually intended in part to *prevent* employers from infringing upon the religious freedom of their employees. But conservatives on the Supreme Court, ever inventive, turned it on its head.

The "Victim–Oppressor Dynamic"

In its way, the *Hobby Lobby* decision and certainly the Arizona bill helped draw the chalk lines of the playing field on which conservatives *want* any debate over LGBT equality to take place. As the dust was settling on defeat of the Arizona law, the *Washington Post* ran a front-page story headlined AFTER VETO IN ARIZONA, CONSERVATIVES VOW TO FIGHT FOR RELIGIOUS LIBERTIES. Religious conservatives, the *Post*'s Juliet Eilperin reported, "will continue to press for additional legal protections for private businesses that deny service to gay men and lesbians, saying that a defeat in Arizona this week is only a minor setback and that religious-liberty legislation is the best way to stave off a rapid shift in favor of gay rights." Each of the references to religious liberties in that sentence should at least have those words in quotation marks; to present them at face value is already to buy into the way conservatives have framed the debate. Eilperin also quoted Peter Sprigg, a senior fellow for policy studies at the Family Research Council, who said, "There is a sense of alarm within the pro-family movement and among conservative Christians that there [are] growing threats to religious liberty, and many of those threats do relate to the agenda of the sexual revolutionaries." The article failed to point out that Sprigg himself is an extremist who's called for bringing back sodomy laws and criminalizing homosexuality — in other words, he is not a credible source. I don't mean to single out the *Post* for these lapses, since many outlets are guilty (maybe even unconsciously so) of parroting back the language conservatives use to frame this issue. As we'll explore further in a later chapter, the media across the board often rely on extreme right-wing voices to provide comment on LGBT rights issues, as if bigots represent a reasonable pole of a rational debate. In this case I'm not asking for the *Post* to take sides against religious voters. Precisely the opposite is true: I'm asking the *Post* to accurately report the news by not passively accepting the way conservatives package these topics.

Sprigg's comments resonated with the findings of a chilling report published in 2012 by the Brown University–affiliated scholar Jay Michaelson, a religion expert who has also written extensively on LGBT issues. "The Christian Right campaign to redefine 'religious liberty' has been limiting women's reproductive rights for more than a decade and has recently resulted in significant religious exemptions from antidiscrimination laws, same-sex marriage laws, policies regarding contraception and abortion, and educational policies," Michaelson writes in *Redefining Religious Liberty: The Covert Campaign Against Civil Rights*. "Religious conservatives have succeeded in reframing the debate, inverting the victim–oppressor dynamic, and broadening support for their agenda." When Sprigg refers to "sexual revolutionaries" with an "agenda" threatening the "pro-family movement," he is disingenuously positioning proponents on his side as the victims when in fact they are powerful aggressors. And LGBT people are far from the first group they've fixed in their sights. "In the postwar era, the Christian right defended racial segregation, school prayer, public religious displays, and other religious practices that infringed on the liberties of others by claiming that restrictions on such public acts infringed upon their religious liberty," Michaelson writes. "Then as now, the Christian Right turned anti-discrimination arguments on their heads: instead of African Americans being discriminated against by segregated Christian universities, the universities were being discriminated against by not being allowed to exclude them; instead of public prayers oppressing religious minorities, Christians are being oppressed by not being able to offer them."

As I discussed in chapter 2, this strategy was on full display at the Values Voter Summit in September 2014, the annual convention of conservative activists, where individuals like the Oregon baker Melissa Klein have been presented as victims of the LGBT rights movement.

I sat in on a panel titled "The Future of Marriage." Frank Schubert, mastermind of the Prop 8 campaign and several other antigay ballot campaigns, talked about the strategy the right would employ if anti-equality forces lost on gay marriage at the Supreme Court. (This was just days before Supreme Court in fact surprised both sides, letting court rulings stand in three circuits that had ruled against marriage bans, bringing marriage equality to many more states.) Schubert discussed how antigay activists would model themselves on the anti-abortion movement after *Roe v. Wade* and seek to incrementally chip away at gay rights if the high court ruled in favor of gay marriage; he also said that religious conservatives needed to find a gay version of "partial-birth abortion" in order to appeal to the public.

When I later asked Schubert in an interview what he meant by that, he referred to promoting "conscience clauses" (which would allow religious individuals to opt out of certain duties in their jobs if they believe those duties conflict with their religious beliefs) and passing laws protecting "religious liberties." Other conservatives have discussed laws restricting adoption by gays as one next step. The Child Welfare Provider Inclusion Act of 2014, introduced in July of that year by Senator Mike Enzi (R–WY) and Representative Mike Kelly (R–PA), is, as Zack Ford at Think Progress described it, another "license to discriminate" bill. It would allow religious organizations that receive federal dollars to bar gay and lesbian couples from their adoption and foster-care services. The bill is worded, however, in a way that casts the religious groups as being discriminated against, "inverting the victim–oppressor dynamic," as Jay Michaelson puts it. The bill would "prohibit governmental entities from discriminating or taking an adverse action against a child welfare service provider on the basis that the provider declines to provide a child welfare service that conflicts, or under circumstances that conflict, with the sincerely held religious beliefs or moral convictions of the provider."

This recalibration of the "victim–oppressor dynamic" is exactly what Christian conservatives, with the aid of right-wing bloggers, put into motion after Brendan Eich resigned as CEO of Mozilla. They cast him as a victim of ruthless, organized gay activist groups that were taking away his "religious liberties" — a claim that could not be further from the truth. Too many gay opinion makers fell right into the trap, accepting this reframing, becoming fearful, and running away, fretting about the "optics" rather than challenging the accusation for what it was: a vicious lie and a deception, part of a plot to recast enemies of LGBT equality as victims while they trample hard-won rights. These LGBT thought leaders spoke for all of us who have been overcome with victory blindness and have impulsively reverted to covering our anger and our conviction. And we can't let that happen again.

4

HIDING IN PLAIN SIGHT

THE IMPULSE TO COVER, FROM WASHINGTON TO HOLLYWOOD

WHILE CONSERVATIVES ARE TRYING TO find a new way to talk about gay people, LGBT people and our allies are failing to find a new, more honest way to talk about ourselves. That may sound somewhat preposterous upon first hearing it. Gay, lesbian, bisexual, and transgender people, after all, are visible throughout the media, and the discussion of marriage equality and an array of LGBT rights are front and center in the news. Depictions of LGBT lives, real and fictionalized, are evident across the pop-culture landscape. But when you take a deeper look, even though some more open examples now exist, LGBT people are still too often hidden, obscured, or alluded to without mention in many settings — the old "wink wink, nudge nudge," which still amounts to a dirty little secret. When depicted in more blatant ways in films and on television, LGBT people are sometimes still crude stereotypes or are more often than not sanitized, not a reflection of who LGBT people are. And all of us who support equality are allowing it to happen, perhaps dazzled by being included at all. We're failing to clearly educate, instruct, and demand that the media and mainstream popular culture, including the entertainment industry, portray the complexity of gay, lesbian, bisexual, and transgender lives. And, most important, we're not doing this by example. The most powerful way to turn things around is simply for each and every one of us to stop covering—individually and as a people—and to fiercely resist the imperatives of the covering demand.

On Covering

I've referred to the theory of covering at several points earlier in this book, and I believe this concept is crucial to our understanding of how LGBT people are represented in the public sphere. As Kenji Yoshino writes in his illuminating 2006 book *Covering: The Hidden Assault on Our Civil Rights,* to cover is to "tone down a disfavored identity to fit into the mainstream." The term first acquired this meaning in the work of the highly influential sociologist Erving Goffman, whose 1963 book *Stigma* looked at covering among people who are elderly, obese, or disabled. As Goffman describes it and Yoshino points out, President Franklin Delano Roosevelt, for example, didn't pass as (that is, successfully pretend to be) someone who was not disabled—he couldn't, as he often used a wheelchair or leg braces—but he certainly covered it, diminishing his disability from view and doing everything he could to downplay it.

Acknowledging his debt to Goffman, Yoshino situates covering at the developmental point when marginalized groups—such as women, some racial and religious minorities, and now LGBT people—attain certain basic legal rights but still may be defamed by politicians, mistreated by the criminal-justice system, passed over for advancement at work, misrepresented in popular culture, and beset by other ills associated with discrimination. The response to what Yoshino terms the "covering demand" is an attempt to divert attention from a category of difference. The dominant culture may also "reverse-cover" marginalized subjects, almost as a way to keep them in their place. For example, Yoshino writes of the way, as a Japanese American, white people sometimes say to him, "Speak Japanese so we can hear what it sounds like," or, "No, tell me where you're *really* from."

Applying the concept of covering to gay people, Yoshino, as I noted earlier, distinguishes covering from conversion and passing. The former is about trying to be heterosexual — trying to deny one's homosexuality, torturously, sometimes submitting to "ex-gay" or "conversion therapy" programs. The two most important governing bodies of the mental-health-care establishment — the American Psychiatric Association and the American Psychological Association — as well as many other credible medical organizations have deemed conversion therapy both ineffective and psychologically harmful. The "ex-gay" movement took a huge hit in recent years. Two states, California and New Jersey, as well as the District of Columbia, banned licensed therapists from administering such therapy to gay, lesbian, bisexual, or transgender minors. The largest "ex-gay" group, Exodus International, closed down, and its leader, Alan Chambers, apologized for the harm he'd done — while not renouncing the therapy he himself had gone through. We'll be fighting on this front for a long time. In every state, licensed therapists can legally offer such programs to desperate, confused adults. And many religious organizations still offer various forms of conversion therapy to minors — which is still legal — and adults.

Passing is living in the closet, and as we saw in chapter 2, many more people are passing than we think. As I'll discuss in this chapter, the media are still confused about when to report on public figures who pass, largely because we, by covering, don't push them to figure it out.

We all construct our identities at the intersection of many different categories of belonging. At any given time we may cover certain aspects of ourselves while more fully expressing others. And covering isn't all bad. In many ways, it has helped win rights. When marriage-equality advocates have focused on the desires that many LGBT people share with heterosexuals — to forge relationships, build families, raise children — rather than overtly focusing on our differences, that was a kind of covering (though, as I'll show in a later chapter, it actually was a bit more complicated than that). But while winning rights is a good thing, protecting them is another matter. Deeply embedded implicit bias works against and around those rights, and one thing covering cannot do is challenge this kind of prejudice. That's where covering has reached its limits, and why it's time to stop doing it. Yoshino rightly sees that emphasizing difference rather than downplaying it — assimilating only as much as necessary — is critical now. It's a way of playing offense rather than defense, in pursuit of true equality.

Yoshino is careful to explain, however, that the fact that some or many LGBT people, or members of any group, engage in activities within the dominant culture or lead "average" lives doesn't mean they're covering. Many gay people join the military, for example; or like football or basketball or other popular team sports associated with straight masculinity; or just want to settle down, get married, and raise children in a small town. "We must not assume that individuals behaving in 'mainstream' ways are necessarily covering," Yoshino writes. "My ultimate commitment is to autonomy as a means of achieving authenticity, rather than a fixed conception of what authenticity might be."

But even those who are authentic in behaving in "mainstream ways" — and who among us doesn't engage in "mainstream" activity in one or many aspects of life? — are covering at least some of the time, while others might be covering all of the time. Many, for example, are often covering their individual expressions of sexuality, desire, and love. And we often rationalize this away with the victory narrative, telling ourselves it doesn't matter or isn't important.

The football player Michael Sam, drafted to the NFL in 2014, is a perfect example of someone who decided to stop covering in the midst of intense media attention. And the response showed us why we must keep challenging the dominant culture precisely by not covering. Sam, a man who fits certain aspects of conventional masculinity and plays a stereotypically masculine sport, surely could have just assimilated, even with the world knowing he is gay. But instead, he shocked America's sensibility by kissing his boyfriend at the moment when he was drafted, with ESPN cameras trained on him. He decided not to cover — not to conform to what American viewers wanted and expected — and to simply give his boyfriend the same kind of kiss that any of the straight guys gave their girlfriends or wives when they were drafted.

Because of that, Sam came under attack from many commentators in the sports world and beyond. When asked to comment, Donald Trump said, it "looked pretty out there to me," and, "I've heard many people — I'm not even speak[ing] for myself, but I've heard many people that thought the display after he was chosen was inappropriate . . . But I thought when he — he was really going at it . . . I haven't seen anything like that in a while." What Trump seemed to mean by "pretty out there" was that Sam's kiss crossed a line. Accepting Sam as gay was an act of tolerance. Being expected to see him in even a fleeting moment of intimacy was beyond tolerance.

The day after the draft picks, I was invited on CNN to discuss "the kiss," as the media had come to call it, with Carol Costello, host of *CNN Newsroom*. Costello does a terrific job of grilling antigay crusaders, and I always enjoy chatting with her. But this time I was surprised when she asked me several questions about whether Sam should talk about "the kiss" with the players, and wondered if it would be a problem within the team, stressing that Sam had to see the players regularly in the locker room after that kiss. It made me realize just how clearly this was the new frontier — not covering — and how little people are used to seeing two men or two women kissing, despite all the news coverage of gay marriage.

Slate columnist Mark Joseph Stern wrote a salient short piece whose headline said it all: MICHAEL SAM PROVES IT: GAY PEOPLE NEED TO KISS IN PUBLIC MUCH, MUCH MORE. That got me thinking after my CNN appearance, and that day, in a *Huffington Post* blog post, I launched a project I gave a somewhat grandiose name, "The Great Facebook Kiss-In," inspired by Michael Sam. I changed my Facebook profile picture to a photo of my husband and me smooching (a selfie I took that morning), and I urged others to tweet and post their kissing photos, explaining why this mattered. I told people to kiss a friend if they weren't in a relationship or use another photo — their favorite gay celebrities kissing, say — all with the hashtag "#kissin." It was fun, and I was happy to see the project go viral as it got picked up by other sites. It's the kind of thing we need to do more of, whether out in public or in the media. And that's because merely being out while covering has run its course. Covering tolerates implicit bias and, in turn, allows people to merely tolerate us rather than truly accept us as equals.

Shattering the Glass Closet

The covering demand encourages gay people to be polite "team players," to "not rock the boat." Expanding upon Yoshino's ideas and drawing upon my own work in years past, I would add that at its extreme end, at the hinge point between covering and passing, lies a state of being that is sometimes called the "glass closet." The term refers to public figures who are out in practice but haven't "admitted it." Gay people seeking access to the elite often find that this in/out way of being is part of the membership dues they pay to join the club. The glass closet is malignant, because it is a luxury enjoyed by precisely those people who have the most responsibility not to pass. The rest of us cannot combat the covering demand when the most powerful and influential gay and lesbian people in our community disavow their membership in it so they can enjoy the privileges of in-group access. It's just unfair.

At first it may seem like these people are somehow protecting their right to privacy, but living an open secret is not the same thing as keeping one's sexual orientation private. It requires collusion, the willful blindness of everyone else in the individual's circle. And the most frustrating thing about the glass closet is that it would be shattered in an instant if the media simply stopped respecting it. There is no legal obligation for the media to protect it, an excuse some fall back on. The Supreme Court has given the press wide latitude under the First

Amendment on reporting facts about public figures. But in 2012 New York's highest court went much further, ruling that even falsely saying someone is gay is not "per se defamation." "The decision wiped out decades of rulings," the Associated Press reported. "Without defamation, there is no longer slander, the court ruled unanimously." The court noted that the cases in decades past had been "based on a false premise that it is shameful and disgraceful to be described as lesbian, gay or bisexual." This followed similar rulings in states around the country, including North Carolina.

How can we possibly be near victory if the media still won't report on who is *actually* gay in public life, when it's increasingly not legally considered harmful to even *falsely* say that a public figure is gay? Why won't the media even ask the question when it's relevant or interesting to know about in the same way they inquire about aspects of public figures' heterosexuality? After all, if gays were near complete acceptance, then the media's reporting on gay public figures would be no different from their talking about the fact that a movie star or politician happens to be Jewish or left-handed without asking that person for "permission" to do so. Instead, the media wait for that TV anchor to "admit" that she is a lesbian in a Facebook post or for that actor to "reveal" it during a choreographed interview, though we all already knew because these people were open to large circles of friends, family, and many others, including people in the media, and were often out in the community. Worse than that, there's the more serious issue of the politician who votes antigay while living life as a gay person, engaging in exactly the kind of hypocrisy (and sometimes even corruption) that the media should be reporting — and still he won't discuss it.

When I think back to 2006, when GOP congressman Mark Foley of Florida resigned in a scandal after it came to light he'd sent sexually suggestive e-mails and instant messages to teenage male congressional pages, I can't help but implicate the media in this abuse. By not reporting on Foley's deceitful life for more than fifteen years — during which time he portrayed himself as a heterosexual politician, bringing women to events — the media enabled him. He knew he could get away with his closet, his lie, because no one would report it. Reporters, producers, and editors took part in perpetuating a fiction, one that may well have led to an ugly outcome. True, it's important not to connect Foley's homosexuality to his predatory behavior. But in the zeal to make this point, sometimes we overlook a fundamental issue. Although homosexuality, like heterosexuality, is not inherently dangerous, repressed sexuality — whether it's repressed homosexuality or repressed heterosexuality — can certainly be harmful when the dam bursts. Members of the media later confessed they knew Foley was gay even as he voted for the Defense of Marriage Act. This gave them every reason, not to mention a duty, to report on his hypocrisy and, in the process, avert the harm he would later cause.

By running away from the issue, the media turn a blind eye not just to hypocrisy but also to corruption and abuse. At the 2004 GOP convention, in New York, I interviewed then-twelve-term Republican congressman David Dreier of California. He had an 11% rating on LGBT issues from the Human Rights Campaign. He'd supported DOMA, voted against allowing adoptions by gays in the District of Columbia, and backed the odious Marriage Protection Act, which would have amended the federal judicial code to prevent federal courts from even so much as hearing a challenge to DOMA. For years there had also been rumors about Dreier emanating from the gay community within his Orange County district as well as within Washington. When I asked in the interview not if he was gay but if he was heterosexual, he demurred. "I'm not going to talk about this issue," he said.

A few weeks later, Mike Rogers, who had founded the blog *Blogactive* for the sole purpose of revealing the truth about antigay politicians who were gay and closeted, reported that Dreier lived with his chief of staff, Brad Smith, who was paid an unusually high salary, $156,000 — the highest of any House chief of staff and only $400 less than then White House chief of staff Andrew Card — while even the chiefs of staff of prominent House committees weren't getting that much. *Blogactive* also reported about Dreier's travel records, which Rogers was freely able to obtain at the U.S. Capitol, like any journalist who might take an interest. The documents showed that Dreier and Smith had traveled to more than ten countries in recent years, but they traveled "one day apart, on all the trips," as Rogers later explained when he was interviewed in director Kirby Dick's much-discussed 2009 documentary *Outrage*. "If there was a congressman who traveled with his chief of staff [if she were a woman] continuously around the world, traveling one day before and one day after, that would be in the newspaper," Rogers said. And would it not be reported in major media outlets like the *New York Times* and the *Washington Post* if, say, a Democratic congressman were not only traveling in that manner with his highly paid female chief of staff but living with her as well? You'd better believe it would, particularly if a conservative activist had raised it in a major way on a website. But even though Rogers's story raised questions about the ethics of Dreier's use of taxpayer dollars, none of the media would touch it.

Schocked, Schocked

That was 2004, but the same head-in-the-sand approach continues today.

Take the case of Illinois Republican congressman Aaron Schock. Here is a man who was first elected in 2008 at the age of twenty-eight and is one of the youngest members of Congress, a man who loves to flaunt his body, flashing Instagram photos of himself working out or surfing in Hawaii. In other words, protecting his privacy doesn't seem particularly important to him.

Neither are LGBT rights. Schock voted against "don't ask, don't tell" repeal, was opposed to President Obama's decision not to defend DOMA in federal court, and expressed support for a federal marriage amendment banning gay marriage, only to then hedge, saying he hadn't "really thought too much about it." He also has been rumored for years to be gay and closeted himself, which would certainly render him hypocritical and newsworthy. In a 2009 profile of and interview with him, a *Details* reporter addressed the rumors, which is more than can be said for Washington reporters:

> Schock is hoping his romantic prospects will improve too, once he settles in. He's the only one of his siblings not married with children, and is similarly an outlier among his friends. "I had a group of five or six guys, and we hung out and traveled — ski trips and stuff," he says. "They slowly got picked off — married, married, married." His pals try not to dog him about his love life. "I think he's got enough pressure as it is," says Shea Ledford, a concrete worker who's been Schock's good friend since high school. Indeed, there's been enough speculation about Schock's confirmed-bachelor status that, as far back as 2004, a Chicago newspaper asked him whether he was gay (his response: "No . . . I'm not.").

But the rumors blew up on the web again and again. Most of the discussion was blog chatter, circumstantial evidence, or even stereotyping, such as when a photo of Schock in an outfit he wore to a White House picnic went viral: white jeans, a hot-pink gingham shirt, and a teal belt. (In response to the comments all over the blogs and social media, much of which had pegged him as gay, Schock jokingly tweeted that he'd "burned the belt.") Websites like *Gawker* reported the photo had "made the rounds of gay staffers," while some of the gay press, like Edge in Boston, debated whether an outfit makes a person gay. The rumors blew up again when Schock set off gaydar in certain quarters by posing shirtless on the cover of *Men's Health* in May 2011, as well as being photographed in various poses inside the magazine, promoting health and fitness.

If Aaron Schock had been hypocritically voting the antigay party line while living as a gay man under the radar, that would have been news. In the course of mainstream reporting, if you catch a whiff of political hypocrisy, you follow up on it and collect sources. But the media didn't appear to be interested in finding those sources, not in the ways they are when they have a hunch about other issues. Nor were they interested in simply asking the question.

Frankly, with a horrific record on LGBT rights — a 0 rating from the Human Rights Campaign — Schock should be asked the question again and again, for as long as new rumors keep surfacing. And it certainly should be investigated, and he should be challenged, when an anecdote or story surfaces that is beyond circumstantial evidence or stereotyping. But journalists in D.C. never seem to ask him the question (beyond the routine call to his press office and the predictable "no comment"), though they see him in the halls of Congress and at every swanky cocktail party. Nor do they investigate this issue the way they scour every aspect of Ted Cruz's college years or look into Rand Paul's alleged bong hits.

The rumors only continued. In Tampa, during the 2012 Republican National Convention, *TMZ* descended upon Schock as he walked through the city's gay neighborhood, complete with rainbow flags, stores selling skimpy men's underwear, and what some have said is a local gay bathhouse. (He apparently was coming from a media event.)

I caught up with Schock on the floor of the RNC that weekend at the Illinois delegation, while I was doing interviews for my show with a mic and a recorder in hand. Schock was pleasant and friendly. On why he voted against the repeal of "don't ask, don't tell," Schock said, "I took the advice of military experts that came before Congress. I think that's why you have John McCain and others who have a military background. ["Don't ask, don't tell" supporter] Adam Kinzinger is a close personal friend of mine who's an active-duty member of Congress [in the district] next door to me, and so I think that's why you saw the consistency."

But when I asked about how he responded to those who believe he is gay and who also view his vote against "don't ask, don't tell" repeal as a vote against members of his own group, Schock grew tense and annoyed, and responded, "Those questions are completely ridiculous and inappropriate." He added, when asked if he was confirming that he is not gay, "I've said that before and I don't think it's worthy of further response. I think you can look it up." He then walked off, abruptly ending the interview. I aired the interview and posted it on *Huffington Post,* where it blew up and where Washington media could certainly read it, but nobody followed up.

Almost two years, later, in January 2014, openly gay former CBS journalist Itay Hod caused a firestorm when he wrote on his Facebook page that a friend, whom he described as "a journalist for a reputable network," came home one day to find his roommate and the congressman coming out of the shower together. Hod claimed the journalist knew "in no uncertain terms" who it was.

"Are we still not allowed to out him?" Hod asked. "Let me ask another question . . . doesn't the media have an OBLIGATION to expose his hypocrisy? if he had done something so hypocritical and he wasn't gay, wouldn't we demand journalists do their job? but they can't . . . because we won't let them. you're not allowed to out ANYONE, we tell them."

Hod's status update itself went viral, reported about on scores of blogs, websites, and news sites. He gave an interview to the *New York Times,* which actually ran the story without naming the congressman in question, as if we were in the 1950s. (The *Washington Post,* in a blog post about the controversy by gay editorial-page editor Jonathan Capehart, did discuss Schock by name.) In the *Times,* Hod commented, "I'm not a D.C. reporter. They should be asking those questions; that's their job, and the fact that they're not doing it is because this is still an icky taboo subject."

Is Hod's story hard evidence? Of course not, and certainly no firsthand source is identified by name. But is it interesting information for reporters and pundits to speculate about, discuss, debate, rehash, spin, and make phone calls about, as they do with so many other maybe-true issues about public figures — many of which turn out to be complete nonstories? Yes. Is it something they should ask Aaron Schock about directly as he enters the halls of Congress, heads to the supermarket, or turns up at the next cocktail party? Absolutely.

"No Higher Burden"

Other than Jonathan Capehart — who, to his credit, actually asked for sources to come forward — no journalists, to my knowledge, followed up on Itay Hod's post about Aaron Schock. Instead, there was commentary that criticized Hod or dismissed him. Not only did the *Times* not name Schock, it also put the story in the Styles section, signaling that it was a gossipy piece rather than one that raised an important question about politics and the closet. Brandon Ambrosino, a conservative gay writer, wrote on *Time* magazine's website that wins on gay marriage and the enormous "progress we often forget we've made" now meant it was unimportant or uninteresting to know who is and isn't gay.

This is classic victory-narrative talk, and it seems to have taken hold in the media. Never was this made clearer than when, in 2013, an organization whose name is almost synonymous with the media establishment — the Associated Press — announced that its stylebook, one of the most influential across the industry, would now ban use of the word *homophobia*. The term assumed too much, the AP reasoned, because it determined that those who are opposed to gay rights or have an issue with homosexuality have a phobia, a fear. The word *homophobia* was coined more than forty years ago by psychologist George Weinberg and has a specific meaning in the culture, akin to *sexism* or *racism*. Robbing us of the word that describes the very bigotry we face is the first step toward completely putting that bigotry out of mind while allowing it to thrive. It's the ultimate form of the covering demand: thwarting our ability to label (and thus, to talk about) the particular prejudice we confront.

The media wouldn't collude with the open secrets of glass-closeted public figures and buy into the victory narrative if it didn't serve some purpose for their readers and viewers. The concept of covering helps explain why this happens, too. The covering demand exists in part to protect the sensibilities of a majority whose implicit bias against a minority group, when triggered, produces a feeling of discomfort. Our culture has come around to being able to talk about gay people at all, but gay relationships and, most of all, gay sexuality still make many people queasy. They'd rather not hear about it if they don't have to, thank you very much, and the media honor this unspoken request.

One of the ways the media now police the borders between what can and what cannot be discussed is by claiming (as Ambrosino did) that knowing who is and isn't gay is somehow no longer relevant. The most revealing example of this trend occurred a few months before the Aaron Schock controversy. In October 2013, *Gawker* published a story about some bad behavior the Fox News anchor Shepard Smith allegedly engaged in at a bar — treating a waitress terribly. The piece also mentioned that Smith happened to be there with an unidentified "boyfriend" with whom he often attends the bar, holding hands and being affectionate. In a follow-up, *Gawker* reported that the boyfriend is a Fox staffer who began as a production assistant.

In response, David Carr — the *New York Times* media critic and a journalist who often provides an interesting perspective — wrote a piece critical of *Gawker*, chastising the site because it supposedly "tried to out" Shepard Smith. In order to unpack Carr's response, we need to see it within the context of the history of "outing" — both the word and the phenomenon. *Time* magazine dreamed up the word in 1990. Specifically, it was now-deceased William Henry III, a Pulitzer Prize–winning cultural critic for *Time*, who coined the term to define what he saw as a terrible invasion of privacy against even the most vile and homophobic closeted public figures by gay activists and gay journalists and, most pointedly, by me.

I was an editor at the time at *OutWeek* magazine, and, among other stories, I'd written a cover piece, "The Secret Gay Life of Malcolm Forbes," shortly after the multimillionaire's death, using multiple named and unnamed sources. I considered this simply reporting on a (dead) public figure. There wasn't a special word for discussing details about other aspects of public figures' lives that were relevant to report — from their tax returns and their business dealings to their

latest girlfriends or boyfriends or their divorces — so why invent a
term for reporting that someone is gay or has same-sex relationships?
But Henry had accused me and others of "outing" public figures, and
the term stuck. He chose a violent-sounding verb, and it may have
felt that way to him. Henry himself was rumored to be bisexual and
pursuing closeted affairs with men, a fact his widow confirmed in a
published letter after his death.

What makes the invocation of this trope in Carr's article so revealing is that *Gawker* did not "out" Shepard Smith. His sexuality was
already old news, reported in the film *Outrage,* which aired in heavy
rotation on HBO after a wide theatrical release. In the extensive coverage around the film, writers and reviewers often noted that Smith was
one of its lead stories, and his sexual orientation has been discussed
countless times online both before and since the film appeared. For
several years, Smith has even been included in *Out* magazine's annual
"Power List."

The premise of Carr's piece was that *Gawker*'s supposed outing
didn't "reverberate" (as the headline put it) and wasn't reported much
elsewhere because "the culture has moved on"; and "now that gay
marriage is a fact of life, a person's sexual orientation is not only not
news, it's not very interesting." But Smith's sexual orientation literally wasn't news, in the strictest sense, which helps explain the lack of
pickup. The *Gawker* piece seems like "outing" only if it's an invasion
of privacy to even mention that a well-known gay man was in the
presence of a boyfriend. When was the last time a news outlet was
castigated for noting that a media celebrity of Smith's stature was out
in public with his girlfriend?

"Many argue that there is an implicit contract between the public and celebrities: that if we deem someone famous, and they reap
the benefits of that, they forfeit their right to privacy," Carr wrote.
"But being gay carries no higher burden. Not talking about something that people do not seem to care about is not really a secret. It's
just a choice." It's that phrase, "no higher burden," that makes this so
frustrating. Was Smith's behavior in a bar information that any of us

needed to know? Of course not. *Gawker* is a website that runs a lot of gossip and traffics in all kinds of revelations about famous individuals, sometimes outlandish and sensational. But in doing what it does on a daily basis, if *Gawker* didn't report that a male public figure was out in public with a "boyfriend" when an incident occurred — when it would normally report that he was with a "girlfriend" if he were straight — *Gawker* would actually be giving gays special treatment rather than treating gays equally. This process helps enforce the closet and keep gays invisible. Full equality means equality in gossip, too.

The larger question here is: Why did this particular story inspire a respected media critic to scold *Gawker* and then to criticize the site regarding only this one story, when there are so many other sensational and arguably much more private or invasive issues *Gawker* has reported on about heterosexual public figures and their relationships? It's certainly not about David Carr himself, who's never shown any hostility toward gays. It's rather about that queasiness in general that many in the media still feel about reporting on who exactly is gay, believing they or others are doing something terribly wrong. If we'd reached true equality, as Carr seems to be suggesting by referencing victory-narrative ideas, then a male celebrity having a boyfriend would simply be another detail to report on.

The Treachery of On-Screen Covering

The same squeamishness about addressing gay-related subjects is a fact of life in the entertainment industry. In its 2014 Studio Responsibility Index, an annual study of LGBT representations in the previous year's major Hollywood films, GLAAD reported that, of 102 studio films, only 17 had gay, lesbian, bisexual, or transgender characters of any kind. Most of these were tangential minor roles or, worse yet, as GLAAD put it, "outright defamatory representations." The LGBT characters "received only minutes — or even seconds — of screen time, and were often offensive portrayals." And those fleeting depictions were also remarkably racially homogeneous: "Of the 25 different characters counted (many of whom were onscreen for no more than a few seconds), 19 were white (76%) while only 3 were Black/African American (12%), 2 were Asian/Pacific Islander (8%), and 1 was Latino (4%)."

Although smaller, independent films have focused on gay plotlines since the '70s and '80s, when *Brokeback Mountain* became an unexpected box-office hit in 2007, and after 2008's Oscar-winning *Milk*, many thought that, surely, Hollywood had broken a final barrier. But building gay, lesbian, bisexual, or transgender characters into a film's central plotline — especially when that involves depicting physical intimacy — is something the industry is still reluctant to do. In 2013 director Steven Soderbergh couldn't get his biopic about Liberace, *Behind the Candelabra,* made by any major studio, even with huge stars like Michael Douglas, playing Liberace, and Matt Damon, playing Liberace's partner Scott Thorson, and a relatively small budget of $5 million.

Soderbergh said he was "stunned," telling *The Wrap* that every major studio turned him down. "They said it was too gay. Everybody. This was after *Brokeback Mountain* . . . it made no sense to us," he said. But where *Brokeback Mountain* represented sex between its two cowboy characters as tender and nonthreatening, *Behind the Candelabra* was proudly garish and up-front in its depictions of gay intimacy — some of it in groups, lots of it in hot tubs. Even though, as characters, Liberace and Thorson were living in the glass closet, the film itself refused to "cover" them. Its main character was gender-nonconforming, to be sure. By portraying the older Liberace, the flamboyant queen, meeting and seducing the much younger Thorson, *Behind the Candelabra* activated the kind of threat — the fear — that Rachel Riskind's work has uncovered in straight-male response to gender-nonconforming faces.

"Studios were going: 'We don't know how to sell it,'" Soderbergh said. "They were scared." HBO picked up the film, which won several Emmys, perhaps breaking through that fear — and challenging it

—but only HBO was willing to take that chance. HBO is notable for its successes with LGBT-themed work, including the series *Looking* (which is one of few shows to deal even remotely honestly with gay men's lives today, and which was renewed after its first season) and the groundbreaking 2014 film of Larry Kramer's *The Normal Heart,* produced and directed by Ryan Murphy, which reached far beyond a gay viewership and set records for HBO. But these are the rare break-outs that garner massive media attention or win awards. The overall landscape is bleak.

In television, too, we tend to focus on the shows that buck the trend of invisibility or undisguised defamation. Landmark moments—like Laverne Cox's performance in Netflix's *Orange Is the New Black,* or the Amazon-produced series *Transparent*—are the exceptions that prove the rule. GLAAD's 2013 index noted that LGBT representations are less "scarce and regressive" in television than in film, but the group still found the paucity "surprising." It's great that we have *RuPaul's Drag Race* serving up fabulous entertainment on the niche gay network Logo. And Ryan Murphy's *Glee* has been among the few standouts aimed at a wide audience and has done an enormous amount to affirm LGBT young people, depicting openly gay teens expressing physical intimacy and tackling homophobia and bullying. But by and large, LGBT characters on television, when they are represented at all, tend to be offered up in covered forms, with their difference diminished to a note so soft you can barely hear it, especially on network shows. It's a response to what is often called the "ick factor," the fear of turning off an audience by challenging its implicit bias. ("Is TV too gay?" one news story on a Fox affiliate asked a few years ago, referring specifically to *Glee.*) Just as people who find the thought of LGBT relationships uncomfortable may still tell a pollster they support gay rights and equality, they also might not mind the character of the funny gay friend or neighbor who comes in and out on a sitcom or drama. They wouldn't want to see these characters fired from their jobs or prevented from marrying, but they'd also prefer such characters remain sexless and, thus, harmless. A study published in the

American Sociological Review in November 2014, in fact, concluded that though a large majority of respondents said they supported full civil rights for gays and lesbians, they would rather not see same-sex public displays of affection. "Of the heterosexuals interviewed, 95 percent said they approved of a scenario in which a straight couple kissed each other on the cheek in public, but only 55 percent approved of a gay couple doing the same," *Al Jazeera America* reported of the study, which surveyed one thousand Americans. "When asked if it were a lesbian couple, 72 percent of straight people approved." And these results represent those who actually would admit to implicit bias. Rachel Riskind's research, described in chapter 2, would suggest that a much lower percentage truly would be comfortable with same-sex intimacy. Also reflecting Riskind's research, this study found that heterosexual men appear to be more threatened than women, with a larger percentage of that population disapproving of public displays of affection among same-sex couples.

Salon writer Daniel D'Addario has pointed out that ABC's *Scandal* features "a semi-realistic depiction of a married gay couple," though their "homosexuality was less important than their love of power." And he criticizes *Modern Family* for its depiction of a gay married couple that treats the characters as "vehicles to show how tolerant straight people are." (*BuzzFeed* writer Louis Peitzman memorably described *Modern Family*'s Mitch and Cam, who rarely show intimacy of any kind, as "two gay men who don't even seem to like each other.") This is covering. Having a couple on TV who are dads who don't have sex isn't enough, not in 2014, if we're to challenge assumptions and break through implicit bias. "By and large, gay characters are sexless," Peitzman wrote following a comparative study of portrayals of kissing and sex among characters in opposite-sex and same-sex couples on TV shows. "And when they're not, their trysts are still more insinuation than anything explicit. It comes down to depictional equality: If the straight couples on a show are making out, the gay couples ought to be able to make out too."

Gay and transgender characters continue to be deployed as reliable laugh lines on television sitcoms too. (Jokes at the expense of gays are endemic on late-night shows and in stand-up comedy as well, with hardly any repercussions.) CBS's hit *Mike and Molly* has been notorious, using the terms *shemale* and *tranny* to refer to transgender women, and came under criticism from gay groups in early 2013. The ugly jokes continued. Blogger Sue Kerr laced into the network later that year in a blog essay on *Huffington Post,* noting how in the first fifteen minutes of a randomly selected episode she counted jab after jab at lesbians, gay men, and transgender women — ten in total.

Transgender people are perhaps the least well served by television representations, as in so many areas. GLAAD studied ten years of transgender depictions in 2013, looking at every major broadcast network and seven cable networks. Most of the depictions were abysmal. Transgender people were slotted into a victim role at least 40% of the time, and were killers or villains at least 21% of the time. Antitrans language and slurs were present in 61% of portrayals. The reality — including the brutal hate crimes and the disproportionate criminalization of transgender people of color — is barely reflected in popular culture.

HIV, meanwhile, is a reality in the lives of both transgender women and gay men, communities in which infection rates hold steady at roughly the same rate per year as they were in the '90s. Yet HIV and AIDS are treated like yesterday's drama in films and on television. *Dallas Buyers Club* (2013) was an important film about the early years of the AIDS epidemic — based on a true story of a straight man with AIDS who organized a club to bring unapproved drugs into the country — and garnered great attention and Academy Awards for its stars, Matthew McConaughey and Jared Leto, who played a transgender woman. But while gay and bisexual men and transgender women are the groups most affected by HIV today, accounting for 63% of infections in 2010, HIV is essentially invisible in the lives of gay characters living in films and television shows set in the present day. Right now, gay and bisexual men and transgender women who are HIV positive manage a lifelong illness as well as the stigma attached to it — not to mention, for some, the harsh reality of criminalization laws — and HIV-negative gay men of every generation grapple with and debate prevention methods. Hardly any of this exists in films and television. "I think it's one of the reasons we have the infection rates we do," AIDS activist Peter Staley told me, pointing to the complacency that invisibility in both the media and popular culture helps fuel. "I think it is interrelated to all these victories and this depiction of who we are as a community and how [gay life is] more mainstream now [with] families and kids and marriage and fighting in the military. HIV is in such conflict with all those story lines. In a sense it threatens all those story lines."

In other words, dealing with the realities of HIV doesn't gel with the victory narrative. Speaking about it and portraying it means frankly dealing with sex, which simply isn't possible in covered portrayals of gay lives.

Hollywood's "Gatekeepers" Still Rule

With so much animus against LGBT characters and so much fear among studio executives about their marketability, it's no surprise that the closet is still the law in Hollywood. A few years ago, Todd Holland, an openly gay television director who's won three Emmys, said he counsels actors who are gay and male to stay in the closet. After his words caused a stir, he wrote a piece in which he clarified, saying that if you're in "that fractional .002 percent of the young male actor population, and you really have the goods to become a true leading man . . . I can't tell you to come out." He pointed to the "gate-keepers" who "abound at every level," from agents to casting directors and others in the industry, who tell actors to stay closeted.

In a 2012 survey of a set of Screen Actors Guild–American Federation of Television and Radio Artists members conducted by UCLA's Williams Institute and which received some media attention in 2014, more than half of LGBT actors who responded believed directors and producers are biased against LGBT performers in hiring, and more than half also reported hearing anti-LGBT comments on set. Only 36% of lesbian and gay respondents were out to their agents. And only 13% of lesbian and gay actors and 2% of bisexual actors were open to industry executives.

This is true even though in recent years, directors, casting agents, producers, and even studio executives, from Disney to DreamWorks, have come out of the closet themselves. The very people running the television and film industry include openly gay, lesbian, and bisexual people. Yet these creators, too, often complain that they can't get LGBT-themed projects made and that invisibility, covering, and the closet prevail. It's an industry in which a young Welsh actor named Luke Evans actually went back into the closet. When he was an actor on the London stage, Evans quite matter-of-factly told *The Advocate* in 2002 that he was a "gay man," but when years later it came time to embark on a Hollywood action-hero career, he was suddenly romantically linked to a woman, briefly, and his agent told *The Backlot* in 2011 that he would "not comment" on Evans's sexual orientation and that Evans had "learned not to engage the press in his personal life." In October 2014, Evans came out again, delicately, in an interview with *Women's Wear Daily*.

Evans is one of a small, brave group of people in the entertainment industry who are coming out more than ever before, even if, for many of them, it means accepting a more limited career. A handful of younger actresses, including Anna Paquin and Megan Fox, have publicly self-identified as bisexual. Ellen DeGeneres and Rosie O'Donnell are perhaps daytime TV's most famous lesbians. And there are Cynthia Nixon, who is married to a woman, and Portia de Rossi, who is married to DeGeneres. Openly gay Neil Patrick Harris starred on a TV sitcom and on Broadway, as has Jesse Tyler Ferguson of *Modern Family*. Matt Bomer, a star of *White Collar* and Murphy's *The Normal Heart,* came out without fuss and became a heartthrob of gay men. Comedian Wanda Sykes is one of a small number of African American LGBT celebrities to have come out. Some young actors, like Zachary Quinto and Jonathan Groff, are pursuing their careers as out gay men, carving out a place for themselves in the entertainment business. And of course there's Laverne Cox, who has broken barriers as a transgender actress playing a transgender woman.

There's hope among younger people who are refusing to play along with passing or covering. Ellen Page, nominated for an Academy Award for her role in the 2007 film *Juno*, came out as a lesbian in 2014, during a speech in which she decried the pressures of "an industry that places crushing standards on all of us." "You have ideas planted in your head — thoughts you never had before — that tell you how you have to act, how you have to dress, and who you have to be," she said. "And I've been trying to push back to be authentic and follow my heart, but it can be hard."

Page told a story that underscored the pressure within the industry to follow strict norms on both sexual orientation and gender identity. She said she'd happened to see an article on a website that mocked her for wearing baggy clothes, calling her a "petite beauty" who insisted on "dressing like a massive man." "There are pervasive stereotypes about masculinity and femininity that define how we're all supposed to act, dress, and speak, and they serve no one," she said. "Anyone who defies these so-called 'norms' becomes worthy of comment and scrutiny, and the LGBT community knows this all too well." Page's speech is a sharp challenge to victory-narrative thinking, reminding us that even in the entertainment industry, a piece of our culture often pegged as a left-wing bastion, public figures still experience a crushing pressure to pass as straight.

Coming out is one part of the story; covering is another. Maybe we'll see more of a push to stop covering in depictions, at least on television. In the fall of 2014, ABC debuted *How to Get Away with Murder*, starring Viola Davis; it's the newest show from prolific producer Shonda Rhimes (of *Grey's Anatomy* and *Scandal*), and the show features a gay main character who, like many heterosexuals in TV dramas, enjoys lots of physical intimacy and passionate sex (of course, with other men), such as we've never seen before on any network program. Peter Norwalk, who is a co-executive producer on *Scandal,* created the new show. He told *Variety* that this character was important for him as a gay man, and he told *E! Online* that he knew he wanted to "push the envelope" on the gay sex "to right the wrong of all of the straight sex that you see on TV." "I didn't see that growing up," he said, and then alluded to what may be an antidote to the discomfited reactions that greeted Michael Sam's kiss. "I feel like the more people get used to two men kissing, the less weird it will be for people. I just feel like it's a lack of vision that you don't see it on TV."

Uncovering

Certainly we need laws passed and judicial decisions handed down that will protect LGBT people against discrimination, whether we're talking about marriage equality or the federal protections in employment, housing, and public accommodations. Getting those rights is essential. But, as Kenji Yoshino notes in his discussing of covering, winning rights is only one part of the battle. To keep them, we have to change the culture, and that means resisting the demand that we cover and conform. In the closing pages of his book *Covering,* Yoshino writes that this can't be done by lawyers but needs to be done by all of us, gay and straight. Not only LGBT people but also all those straight allies who want to make progress need to change how we talk about LGBT lives and about equality. Yoshino argues that we need to popularize the term *covering* in the way the term *closet* has become popularized and that we need to take all of these discussions to the public square, including to our nation's schools.

That, in fact, is where real change will take place — future filmmakers and TV producers and actors and politicians and editors and reporters are in grade school right now, after all — but change is also about stopping homophobia before it begins and ending bullying in our schools and gay bashing on our streets. We need to create no-closet, no-covering environments from the moment a child steps into kindergarten. And that is what California is now embarking upon, leading the way for the rest of the country.

For years California's public primary and secondary schools have been mandated to teach the history and contributions of Native Americans, African Americans, Mexican Americans, Asian Americans, women, and other groups. Then, through a law that was passed in 2011, California became the first state to mandate the teaching of gay, lesbian, bisexual, and transgender history in K–12 education. The law, the Fair, Accurate, Inclusive, and Respectful Education Act, also requires schools to teach about the contributions of people with disabilities.

Schools were given a great deal of time to get up to speed with the expanded curriculum, and, because of California's budget crisis, new and revised textbooks would not be published until at least 2015. Still, supporters of the bill saw it as something that would truly reshape how young people are taught about LGBT life and history. The groundbreaking bill was introduced by state senator Mark Leno, who is openly gay. He came on my radio program both when he introduced the bill and, later, when it was passed. "Imagine — wouldn't it be an amazingly different experience for a child to have some information that LGBT people, not unlike Jews and people of color, were all marked and tagged, even like those who had mental disabilities, by the Nazis, that they were considered under this Nazi regime all to be inferior and they were sent away to camps?" he said. "That this is a page in history," he explained. Leno painted a picture of a world in which American schools help to humanize LGBT people as well as vividly show the discrimination they've faced. "We then move from the '30s, the '40s, into the '50s, [teaching] that there was something called the Mattachine Society [an early gay organization]," he continued. "That brave people stepped from out of the shadows, where they risked their livelihoods, their family connections, their entire lives, to state proudly that they were who they were as LGBT people."

The argument for passing this bill, which now needs to be made in statehouses across the country (an admittedly tough, long-term battle that, in several states, will mean repealing "no promo homo" laws first while battling further passage of such laws in other states), isn't just that it gives kids the facts or teaches them about LGBT people in the same way we teach the histories of other groups; it also embraces the specificity of LGBT experiences in a way that defies the impulse to cover. And it's a tool — a weapon — in the battle against bullying and gay bashing.

A study conducted in several California districts where this kind of curriculum had been in place already shows that this tool is working. The Preventing School Harassment Survey found that in schools where the majority of youth report having learned about LGBT people in the curriculum, only 11% of students report being bullied, which was half the number of students who reported being bullied in schools that do not teach this history.

How could such a curriculum not change things? To see gay, lesbian, bisexual, and transgender people as real human beings, with a history, a culture, a shared struggle for civil rights, and a quest to be treated with dignity can only help to cut down on bias and violence. Kids may be taught misinformation or bigotry at their churches or in their homes, but at school, perhaps before those ideas can solidify, something else is challenging them with facts.

There will, of course, be enormous pushback to pursuing this effort across the country, a fact which itself defies the victory narrative as well. In California, too, there was the predictable uproar from the Christian right. Even conservatives who were less hard-line spoke out against the curriculum as well, an example of the resistance that we'll surely face nationwide. Tucker Carlson called in to *Fox and Friends,* the Fox News morning show, claiming this law promoted "propaganda" and amounted to "blackmail." He claimed that history is meant to "teach what happened. Not what you wanted to happen." And he said it was blackmail because "you're basically saying if you don't do this, kids could die." That is a massive distortion of the law.

The law is in fact about, finally, teaching what has happened, countering the lies and twisted stories that kids pick up elsewhere.

In 2013 in Los Angeles, some schools were already working the lessons into the teaching plan. As the *Los Angeles Times* reported, the L.A. Gay and Lesbian Center and the Los Angeles Unified School District joined forces to create Project SPIN (Suicide Prevention Intervention Now), and they brought in Jamie Scot, from the ONE National Gay and Lesbian Archives at the University of Southern California, as a consultant to help create the county schools' history curriculum and lesson plans. "We don't want to interrupt what [teachers are] already doing," Scot said, explaining that the ONE institute will be training teachers on how to implement the curriculum. "We want them to be able to fold it in so it's seamless, so it's not like 'Today, here's gay history day.'"

"There's a lot to study, a lot to learn, a lot to discuss," Mark Leno told me. "For children, in an age-appropriate fashion, to have an opportunity to say, 'Why did we discriminate? Why do we discriminate? Why did we do this to black people then? Why did we do this to women then? Why did we do this to LGBT people?' Better understand themselves, better understand the broad diversity of the human experience. And isn't that what an education is supposed to be about?"

5

WORTHY OF DEFENDING

CHALLENGING BULLYING AND CREATING EMPOWERMENT

THE NAME-CALLING WAS ALMOST CONSTANT. *Faggot, fag, queer.* Alex, sixteen at the time, felt inundated. But one day, as he pulled into a drive-in restaurant in rural southern Illinois, he just wasn't in the mood to hear it again.

"This guy from school cornered me, as I sat in my car, and was calling me *fag* and other names in front of a crowd from school to make himself look like a big shot," he recounted. It was autumn of 2011, and the media were focused on a number of horrible stories of LGBT youth being bullied and sometimes taking their own lives. I asked my radio listeners to call and write in about their experiences fighting back against bullies. Alex was one who responded. His and others' stories illustrate that it's vital we offer young people more ways to empower themselves so that they can stand up and be proud; if we're going to challenge and transform our society for the long term, rather than buying the false promise of the victory narrative, we have to help young people foster self-confidence, now and for the future.

Alex said the years of verbal abuse had taken their toll, and teachers and administrators didn't do anything about it. He'd finally had it. "Just about everyone from school was there that day," he recalled. "I got out of my car and up in his face and said I was gay — for the first time ever to anyone! And I asked him what he was going to do about it. He backed down. But when I walked away he hit me from behind."

So, Alex said, he hit back. While other students from his high school looked on, he won a fistfight against a bully. "I never had another problem in school again."

Alex's story is jarring, to be sure. But there's a lesson in it for LGBT youth and adults, and really for anyone who is being or has been bullied or harassed. No, I'm certainly not talking about taking enjoyment in fighting back. Alex, in fact, went on to say he didn't feel good about beating someone up, nor was he promoting violence. But the important point is this: Alex fought back.

Too often, LGBT individuals internalize the homophobia that society has forced upon them. As gay, lesbian, bisexual, and transgender people, from early childhood onward most of us receive messages from popular culture, and, sadly, often from our churches and families, that we are feeble, frail, lowly, despicable. We're told we are weak, we are cowardly, we cannot stand up for ourselves. For gay men, so much of this is tied to being called less than a man, a "sissy" and a "girl," and the current of misogyny in our culture that gives those accusations their sting obviously affects the lives of women, too, including lesbians and trans women. We internalize that homophobia at a young age, and as teenagers the rules are set: The bullies are tough, strong, and macho. We are weak and defenseless. Some of us become the bullies, to prove we're not queer, while others run away or seek refuge even when there isn't any. The experience drives many people to desperation, including depression and suicide.

While we've seen great change in pressuring school administrations and local governments to take the issue seriously, and while expansion of gay–straight alliances in schools has had a big impact, even with local and state antibullying laws in place, the problem of anti-LGBT bullying stubbornly persists. According to the most recent National School Climate survey, published in October 2014 by the Gay, Lesbian, Straight Education Network (GLSEN), the groundbreaking alliance that has been enormously affirming for LGBT kids in schools across the country, 74% of LGBT students surveyed were harassed within the previous year because of their sexual orientation, and 55% because of their gender expression. "Progress is being made in our nation's schools," Eliza Byard, GLSEN's executive director, said in a statement. "But when more than half of LGBT youth continue to report unsafe or even dangerous school climates, we all have a responsibility to act."

"You have to feel you're worth defending." That's how Kevin Jennings, President Obama's former antibullying czar (director of the Office of Safe and Drug-Free Schools in the Department of Education) and a founder of GLSEN, put it when he called my show that autumn after hearing others talking about how they fought back. Jennings's statement reminds us that the issue isn't about putting the onus on the victims. When bullying occurs, the people targeted are never at fault if they don't or can't fight back. Rather, he raises a different question: How can you defend yourself, truly — not just physically but also emotionally — if you believe society's message that you don't deserve to be defended? Self-defense is thus not just about learning martial arts or fighting techniques or avoidance tactics; it's about building self-confidence and becoming empowered.

Jennings himself took a self-defense course called Model Mugging, describing in a later interview how it made "a huge difference in my personal life over the last twenty years." He explained that it gave him the ability not just to stand up to attackers but also to carry himself differently every day, sending a message that he's not to be messed with. In no way does that mean he lets the schools or the justice system off the hook. He's spent much of his life changing the system and holding people accountable for bullying. But he firmly believes we must empower young people in the here and now.

"The coping technique we were taught as children is if you keep your head down, that nobody will hurt you," he said. But it's a false promise, and a bad strategy, one that seems tailor-made for victory blindness. The point is to keep your head up, and it can only help to have the confidence that comes from feeling you could take on the bashers and bullies if you needed to. Self-defense training has long been a cornerstone of the women's movement and continues to help women achieve a sense of empowerment, but it has never held a similar place in the LGBT-rights program. It's time for that to change. Studies confirm that when people learn how to fight back, they feel better, more confident, and more emotionally and physically healthy. It is one of the most practical and powerful tools LGBT people have for combating the internalized homophobia and sexism that say we are weak, and stopping the self-doubt that eats away at us. And it's up to adults, including educators and school administrators, to send that message to young people, especially children who may be gay, lesbian, bisexual, or transgender.

The Brutal Stories We Can't Ignore

A wildly disproportionate number of teens who take their own lives are LGBT. The statistics are sobering. Several studies have confirmed that LGBT teens make up almost 40% of all suicides in that age group. The Suicide Prevention Resource Center, in a 2008 meta-analysis of studies published over one year, estimated that between 30% and 40% of LGBT youth have attempted suicide. According to a report from the U.S. Centers for Disease Control and Prevention published in 2011, gay, lesbian, and bisexual youth were four times as likely to attempt suicide as heterosexual peers. Of course, each case is complex, and many elements may be in play when a young person decides to end his or her life. Also, just the fact that someone is gay doesn't mean he or she will attempt or think about suicide. But so many of us who are LGBT know the feelings of isolation and depression — the kinds of states that can sometimes lead to suicide — and bullying has often been a contributing factor.

The stories in the media have been ghastly and enraging, and they've continued. If the unabated persistence of these stories is not a wholesale indictment of the victory narrative, what is? Some received a lot of attention, like that of Tyler Clementi, the Rutgers University student who jumped off the George Washington Bridge to his death

when he believed a roommate had spied on him having sex with another man and then had discussed it on Twitter. The cyberbullying
was compounded by his mother's reaction when, before leaving for
Rutgers just weeks earlier, he'd told her he was gay; she "completely
rejected me," he wrote in a letter. Clementi's older brother James is
also gay, and he came out to Tyler shortly before Tyler left for college.
But getting that kind of support was perhaps too little, too late.

"I definitely felt like there was a lot of bravado [on Tyler's part]
that was covering up maybe more fear and more anxiety," James Clementi told me in an interview on my show, about his coming out to
his brother. (Neither brother had come out to their parents at that
point.) "But I guess as a brother I didn't want to parent him or try
to lecture him. I wanted to give him space and some freedom. But I
did tell him there's always going to be situations that come up where
you're going to need a friend and need a brother to talk to and let
him know I would be that person. But I don't know how much that
message sunk in."

Other stories that garnered less attention over the past several
years were no less heartbreaking. Sirdeaner Walker, the mother of an
eleven-year old African American boy, Karl Joseph Walker, told me
of terrible bullying her son endured in his school in Springfield, Massachusetts, especially in the days leading up to his hanging himself in
his room. "He played football, basketball, soccer," she said in an interview on the show. "He was a Boy Scout. He was involved in different
programs. Earlier on in the school year, he started having problems.
When he started having problems, he told me that there were some
kids at school who were bothering him, picking on him, just bullying him. He told me at that time that they were calling him gay. 'You
think you're gay. You act like a girl.' Something along those lines. I
was outraged, because I knew this was really hurting him."

And there was Jamie Rodemeyer, a fourteen-year-old boy from
Williamsville, New York, who took his life even after his parents
thought he'd gotten past the worst time. "[The bullying] started in
about fifth grade," Jamie's father, Tim Rodemeyer, told me when he

came on my program. Jamie's parents were accepting when he told them that he "might be gay" (Jamie's words, as relayed to me by his father), though they told him there was no need to "rush into anything" and that he should take his time figuring himself out. (Jamie had told a friend he was bisexual.) "Jamie was a very sensitive boy," Tim Rodemeyer said. "He gravitated to hanging out with the girls in school, because he 'got' the girls. He understood them. They're sensitive. He didn't like when the boys would make fun of girls and how immature boys could be in grade school."

His parents thought things had gotten better when he entered middle school, but almost immediately he was cyberbullied. "They were telling him to kill himself, and 'you're not worth living,' and things like that," Tim Rodemeyer said. And it was nine days after beginning at the school that he took his life. Jamie was someone who had tried to build a bulwark in himself against despair. He had once made an "It Gets Better" video, expressing hope for so many others who were struggling with being gay, lesbian, bisexual, or transgender. His father told me that Jamie had even talked a young person who described herself as transgender out of taking her own life. And yet the continued bullying, intensified by the societal homophobia he, like all of us, grew up with, was perhaps too much for him to bear.

Sometimes the media report the stories of children who've taken their lives or been beaten senseless by bullies, but most times they don't. The reports come from all across the country, from rural areas and small towns to big cities where many think gays are completely accepted. These stories — combined with the fact that anti-LGBT assaults persist and may even be more frequent — are the clearest evidence we have that the victory narrative is an utter fiction.

The It Gets Better Project was one enormously successful response to the increased reports of bullying in schools and suicides among LGBT youth. It was founded in 2010 by Dan Savage and his husband, Terry Miller, two gay dads who'd had enough and wanted to give kids hope and support. They made the first "It Gets Better" video, telling young people that life truly would get better once they got past the hatred they were experiencing in school, and they told others to make videos, too. The project grew into a worldwide phenomenon, encompassing thousands and thousands of videos. Major public figures, celebrities, and even President Obama made videos. "It Gets Better" testimonials on the project's website and on YouTube empowered young people to think about the future and plan for a day when they could live their lives on their own terms. It was uplifting and forward thinking, using online channels to reach gay, lesbian, bisexual, and transgender children and teens who otherwise couldn't or wouldn't communicate with supportive adults and other young people.

Giving kids hope for the future is vital. But what if teachers and administrators won't help them? If kids are lucky enough to have parents who are understanding, who might be open to other possibilities when schools won't step in, what other options might those parents make available to themselves and their kids in the present? What can we do to stop the madness and to make kids feel strong and empowered, and what initiatives might young people take on their own, even without supportive parents? Those were the questions I asked on the show and thought about myself, looking to my own past.

When I was a kid, planning for the future was always part of my strategy for dealing with the bullying I experienced. I looked forward to being an adult, getting through school, playing a kind of "It Gets Better" speech in my head. But in the moment, my own instinct was also to fight back. Years later I realized that that was the basis of all of my eventual activism and writing.

How Self-Defense Equals Self-Preservation

In my first book, *Queer in America*, I wrote about knowing I was gay from as early as five years old. I had crushes on boys in first grade (and on Davy Jones from the Monkees), and I preferred to play with the girls. I knew that most of the boys thought something was wrong with me. I was bullied throughout my childhood, and most intensely beginning in fourth grade, when other boys started calling me a "faggot." Once, I even ran away; in reality, I just disappeared for a couple of hours into the bushes at my school, St. John Villa Academy in Staten Island. Shortly after I surfaced, I confided in a male teacher about homophobic bullying I experienced. He had a tear in his eye as I told him about being taunted and shoved and kicked around; in retrospect I realize he was gay. He told me it would be better when I was an adult. He told me he'd try to do whatever he could to stop the bullying. He even lectured the entire class, shaming people for what they'd done. Some kids came up to me and apologized. But a few days later, the bullying started up again, as if nothing had happened to challenge it.

I cried myself to sleep many nights. The outgoing, vivacious me — the true me — was replaced by a fearful, reserved child who tried not to call attention to himself. I remember standing on the edge of the Staten Island Ferry many times as it sped across the harbor, thinking about jumping in the water and ending it all.

But I never gave in to that, and managed to build self-confidence. My father had taught me how to fight — not only how to defend myself against threats and against physical attacks but also how to feel confident — starting as far back as I can remember. Even growing up in a much less accepting time and in a Catholic Italian family, where I knew I could never talk about the possibility I might be gay, I began to realize that fighting back against bullies was something I had to do in order to survive emotionally. The idea was simple: If I used the skills my father taught me about how to fight, then if I got bullied, if thugs at school picked on me, if they shoved me and hit me, I'd know how to pack a wallop that would send them running home to Mom. And they'd never bother me again. More importantly, my whole demeanor could send the message that they'd better not mess with me, long before I ever needed to defend myself.

My father is the son of Italian immigrants and grew up in working-class Brooklyn neighborhoods in the 1940s and '50s. His intention in teaching me self-defense was to empower me to ward off those who might bully me for being Italian. In his day, Italian Americans were called "greasy dagos" and faced discrimination. That was a real issue then; in my day, not so much. But the training was still invaluable for me. I began to apply it all to being queer.

After this realization, when bullies laid a hand on me, I felt self-confident in a way that said loudly and clearly, Mess with me at your own peril. Still, I had to throw a few punches when bullies were stupid enough not to get the message. I didn't enjoy hurting anyone. I often even felt sympathy for the bullies. But I also felt empowered and in control. I felt that I could change the course of the treatment against me, which the school, teachers, and my parents just couldn't do. I certainly don't mean to imply that by standing up to a bully, you magically, automatically become accepting of yourself as gay. I surely didn't. In fact, later on in high school, still grappling with internalized homophobia, I briefly even *became* a bully in order to prove I wasn't gay, though I am glad I recognized what I was really doing in time to stop it. Still, I think back to those earliest instances of fighting back and to how empowering those experiences of standing up for myself were. And that spirit carried through into adulthood. When the man I referred to in chapter 2 called my husband and me "disgusting" after seeing us share a quick kiss on the street, we stood up to him, knowing that in that moment, together, we could do so, shaming him by pointing to him and calling him a "homophobe." He quickly scurried out of the neighborhood, and I'd like to think he may refrain from repeating that behavior, knowing that more of us, when we can, are standing up to harrassers like him.

So, on the show in the past years, thinking back on my own childhood, I wanted to know what others did — older people as well as younger people today — to see if they, too, had fought back and felt empowered. I heard from people of all ages: lesbian and transgender teens who were in the midst of struggling with being bullied, right up to a seventy-year-old gay man who "bashed back," as another man put it. I got a call from a woman named Connie, a lesbian from Michigan, who is a martial-arts instructor and has devoted her life to teaching young gay people to fight back. "I tell my kids, if you're being assaulted, you have the right to kick their ass," she said.

She told the story of a gender-nonconforming boy who was being picked on. His mother didn't know what to do, and teachers and administrators only paid her lip service. "You had to see him when he came to me," she said. "Crying, crouching, very weak emotionally, very scared. I trained him. He used his self-defense. He is now one of my best students. If a parent brings someone to me, I'm going to make that child confident to fight back."

Matt, another listener, wrote me after hearing that story on the air. He explained that he is gay as well as intersex. Intersex people are born with both male and female reproductive or sexual anatomy, or sexual anatomy that doesn't quite fit the definition of either gender. (Often intersex infants are assigned a gender at birth or shortly thereafter by doctors who decide to remove physical aspects of one gender. Intersex activists have fought against this practice for years, saying it can cause psychological harm, especially when a doctor chooses to assign someone a gender other than the dominant gender identity the individual has as he or she grows up.) "Part of being intersex was always being the shortest and skinniest boy in school," Matt wrote. "I had to be given testosterone shots to mature at all and that doesn't work as well as mother nature, so at 15 I still looked like I was 11. Part of my persecution was because I'm gay, part because I was behind everyone else in development.

"When I was 13, I was assaulted every morning at my locker by a jerk who called me a *faggot* and slammed my locker so hard that if it had hit me it would have hurt me. We shared a homeroom and science class together where he would literally scream me down if I raised my hand to answer a question asked by the teacher, or tried to answer a question the teacher asked me. Finally, this same teacher told me, 'The next time [he] slams your locker like that I want you to drop whatever's in your hands, say nothing—just turn as fast as you can and punch him with all your might right in the nose.' 'No not like that, like this.' (He showed me.) So, I did it, and it worked and never again did [the bully] try it on me."

It's true that, at a physical or even emotional level, not every person can actually repel an attacker, nor is every situation going to lend itself to fighting back. To act in a threatening manner toward other people even if they've threatened us is not something we often feel we want to do. Some of those who called me and wrote to me described having mixed feelings. "I have to admit that I really believe violence is not the answer," Matt wrote. "Yes, it did stop the bully, but I truly wish that there would have been some other way. It was against my nature back then, and even to this day, to fight, and I must be pushed to the breaking point before I retaliate in kind."

Matt's story raises an important point in this discussion. At its base, self-defense training is worthwhile for the feelings of self-confidence and empowerment it can instill. But when a child is forced to put that training into practice in a school, a worst-case scenario results. It is, first and foremost, the responsibility of educators and parents to create safe environments for kids. The teacher in Matt's story probably had little or no recourse to stop the bullying by going to the school's administration himself, which is why the burden of self-defense fell to Matt at all. So many teachers in schools across the country, in the past and today, hit a brick wall when they try to get schools to institute policies — or enforce existing ones — that end bullying. This has been the basis of lawsuits going back to a landmark case won by Jamie Nasbosny, an Ashland, Wisconsin, high school student who was brutally bullied and whose lawsuit resulted in a federal ruling that said schools have an obligation to protect LGBT students from being bullied.

Certainly the stories of these listeners, sometimes acting impulsively and not trained in self-defense, may not be textbook examples of how to fight back. It would be much more effective if they learned tried and true techniques to defend themselves. With teachers and administrators often unwilling or unable to help, it is only right that young people be taught how to protect themselves. In the best of circumstances, kids will reap the emotional and physical benefits of this training but never have to actually use it. But we know that we don't live in the best of circumstances. LGBT people are under assault, sometimes from very young ages, and we have not focused enough on teaching them self-defense.

Turning Back to the Women's Movement

Ideas around self-defense, which many lesbian feminists and trans women promoted from the '80s into the present, are thoroughly rooted in a self-empowerment perspective that did help women to take control of their lives during the early years of the feminist movement. Books like Linda Tschirhart Sanford and Ann Fetter's 1979 *In Defense of Ourselves* helped inspire many women not to succumb to societal pressure that they be passive and feel uncomfortable for standing up physically to a victimizer. They were among feminists throughout the '70s who advocated that women could empower themselves, have more self-confidence, and effectively defend themselves against attackers.

Brooklyn Women's Martial Arts was one of many groups that began during that time as a response to violence on the streets against women. Lesbian feminists were very much a part of this movement, and many saw self-defense and self-empowerment as weaving together their status as women and their status as a minority group under attack. Today Brooklyn Women's Martial Arts has grown into the Center for Anti-Violence Education (CAE), leading the country in self-defense training for women and gay, lesbian, bisexual, and transgender people. "The common thread throughout our 38-year history is our dedication to actively creating a more just and equitable world through individual empowerment and community building—and our ability to meet the evolving needs of our communities," the group states on its website. CAE is committed to training women and transgender youth — including preteens, free of charge — and it does off-site training for gay boys and men, including preteens.

"Each class builds community and respect through talking circles, movement games, and other activities encouraging and empowering teens to take risks, grow, and feel pride in their minds, bodies, and spirits," the group states. CAE was the first group to begin offering self-defense classes to transgender people, in the 1980s, and to people targeted because they have HIV or AIDS. Its curriculum focuses on prevention of violence — ways to keep bullies and bashers from making that first attack. Basic self-defense techniques include "strikes, blocks and kicks; ways to get out of different grabs and holds, verbal exercises, roleplays & discussions about dealing with attackers who are strangers, acquaintances or intimates." Similar self-defense training has occurred across the country.

Annie Ellman is a self-identified queer antiracist feminist who was one of the founders of Brooklyn Women's Martial Arts, in 1974. "It was a time where sexual violence, different kinds of women's oppression in general, was coming to the forefront, getting media attention," she said about the early '70s. "We rented spaces. And we taught women basically karate, to define ourselves, to give us more power, build our self-esteem, to help us heal from violence. At that time I didn't know that so much of what we were doing would be countering the shame, the humiliation associated with violence. Really, at that time it was about giving women the power."

Building Collective Self-Esteem to Fight Back

For Ellman it was about community building in addition to raising individual self-esteem. "We gave people a range of ways to protect themselves, starting with awareness," she said, describing CAE's techniques as centered on avoiding confrontation. "We showed students how to block their heads and gave them ways to practice verbal responses. If people were harassed on the street, you could choose to respond or powerfully ignore the taunts. The main thing was that people choose their responses."

Ellman and many others I've asked are not sure why the LGBT movement hasn't adopted, in a more integrated and outspoken way, the same kind of self-defense and self-empowerment model as the early women's movement. "It's a really interesting question," she said. "I think it's kind of not seeing value in what is perceived as self-defense. I for years have wanted to change the name [of 'self-defense']. Many feminists have called it the empowerment model of self-defense. People's image of self-defense is that you're just engaged in the physical aspect. I think in general, there is still such bias against understanding what self-defense can offer you. It's so much about strengthening us to keep on going and healing from wounds of societal violence."

Ellman talks about the way people, including young boys and girls who are experiencing bullying at school, learn self-confidence and reshape how they feel about themselves through training. "When people do take self-defense, there is a way they feel like they're giving birth to themselves," she explained. "I have noticed it's been hard to get people to attend LGBT self-defense classes. There's a lot of shame around issues of violence. People don't want to admit their feelings of powerlessness and are worried about being able to do the physical techniques." But she believes that shame is based on stereotypes and misinformation. "Some of the men remember how it felt when they were young and not able to function in macho gym classes," she said. "In our last class there was a gay man around fifty who could not believe how important learning self-defense was to him and how proficient he felt."

The question of why self-defense has never been a frontline defense against bullying and bashers in the larger LGBT movement, even with its roots in the lesbian-feminist movement, is a perplexing one. It hasn't even come up much as part of discussion, either in the gay press and among gay activists or in the larger media, amid the frenzy of reporting on bullying and suicide among LGBT people in recent years. Sure, there are many self-defense courses offered at LGBT centers and among private schools around the country, in Los Angeles, San Francisco, Seattle, and elsewhere. But self-defense doesn't seem connected to the movement itself, not in the way it was connected to the feminist movement, nor is it automatically turned to, as it should be, in addition to changing schools' policies, raising awareness, and passing antibullying laws.

Kevin Jennings, who had experienced bullying as a kid and was determined to empower himself, completed the Model Mugging course he described earlier as an adult. The course's "full-contact self-defense program," as he described it, takes a much more aggressive stance than, say, CAE does. It's clear that there isn't one program that might be right for everyone.

"I carry myself completely differently, because I've had to fight off attackers in a structured setting," he told me. He also has taken on potential bashers on the streets. "A guy started harassing [me and my husband], and I got up in his face. I have recommended to every gay man, 'Go take the Model Mugging program.'"

Jennings agrees that self-defense is one part of the solution to dealing with bullying in schools, while not letting schools themselves off the hook. "What I would say to parents is two things," he said. "Enroll [your kids] in self-defense, for confidence. The second thing is: Don't let that be a substitute for holding your school accountable for protecting children. You need to do both."

Research suggests that young people who stand up to their bullies are happier and more productive later in life. Studies show that fighting back not only prevents them from being bloodied and beaten now but actually instills young people with the tools of self-confidence later in life.

In one recent study, researchers at UCLA concluded that children who stand up to their bullies earn the respect of other students and teachers and are more likely to develop strong emotional and social skills. Melissa Witkow, the leader of the UCLA study and now a professor at Willamette University in Oregon, said, "The children who are not disliked by anybody are the most well-adjusted, not surprisingly. However, among kids who are disliked by a peer, our research suggests it may be [helpful] for some young adolescents to return that peer's dislike than to either not be aware or to continue liking that peer."

That means not standing there and taking it, being subservient to and trying to gain the acceptance of the bully. It means fighting back. Witkow told the *New York Times*, "You have several options, as I see it, when you become aware of someone else's antipathy. You could be extra nice, and that might be good. But it could also be awkward or disappointing, and a waste of time. You could choose to ignore the person. Or you can engage." Her study, she said, showed that "when someone dislikes you, it may be adaptive to dislike them back."

The late Ruth Peters, the clinical psychologist specializing in adolescent development and a best-selling author who died in 2010, noted that "a significant part of the bully–victim dynamic is based upon the personality and behavioral style of the child who is being picked upon," and observed that "part of this dynamic may be based in the victim's avoidance of 'fighting back' and the bully's interpretation of this as a weakness.

"Discuss with your child what physical actions he can take — if tripped, shoved, or pushed, should he push back a bit to show that he's not going to passively take the abuse?" Peters once wrote, advising parents on how to help their bullied son to cope. "Would knowledge of and expertise in self-defense give him the confidence to better stand his ground and to not retreat so quickly? I'm not suggesting that you teach your child to deal with teasing and harassment by automatically using aggression. It's more a matter of giving the perception that he will not run away, back down, or tolerate the bully's abuse. Standing firm, distracting with humor, or calling upon the aid of friends are tactics that are often sufficient to stop a skirmish and to persuade the bully to take his attentions elsewhere."

Self-Empowerment Online

When we focus only on transforming institutions and they don't change fast enough, young people can infer a message of hopelessness and despair. Many parents today accept their LGBT children — indeed, in many of the high-profile cases of bullying, assault, and suicide recently, the parents were accepting — so not only must we demand accountability from administrators and politicians but also accepting parents owe it to their kids to enroll them in self-defense and other self-empowerment programs. Often the techniques being taught focus on defusing potentially dangerous situations. Lashing out with a punch might not be as strategic, and highly developed skills that organizations like the Center for Anti-violence Education teach are meant to minimize escalation. But self-defense does mean standing up to bullies and saying, "I'm confident. I'm in control. And I'm not going to take it."

There are those, however, who say fighting back doesn't work and isn't a strategy to employ. But these opponents appear to reject fighting back because it doesn't work every time, rather than seeing it as one of many tools in our toolkit. "This type of 'superior force' advice shows a lack of appreciation for the complexities of the bully–victim dynamics of today's world, where bullying often takes place in new arenas, such as on the Internet," says Carrie Goldman, author of *Bullied: What Every Parent, Teacher, and Kid Needs to Know About Ending the Cycle of Fear.* "Sure, if a victim fights back and flattens his bully, the bully tends to back off. But what if the bullies are hiding behind computer screens? What if the target is physically incapable of taking down the bully, which is more often the case?"

This is a great point, but in the rush to show how bullying has transformed, we forget the aspects that stay constant. Yes, cyberbullying is a different animal, and it needs to be addressed in complex ways unto itself. But studies show that teens still report greater stress from bullying in school than from bullying online, something Danah Boyd, who has spent years studying the online lives of teens, points out in her book *It's Complicated: The Social Lives of Networked Teens*.

Boyd, a principal researcher at Microsoft Research and a research assistant professor at New York University, came on my show in 2014 and discussed her conclusions after looking at reports of cyberbullying in the media and then reading the literature on bullying. "I found something really surprising to me," she said. "Bullying has not actually risen in the last thirty years, which is really confusing when you think about the rise of it on the Internet, and then I looked at these national surveys and found that young people continuously report that bullying is far worse at school, with greater emotional duress and more significant consequences." In other words, what's happening online may not represent an escalation of bullying, as the popular belief would have it, so much as reflect the bullying and bias we've always seen. "What I found is that the culture of meanness and cruelty, the culture of racism, it appears online as well," Boyd explained. "So the technology allows us to see the world we live in, good, bad, and ugly, and forces us to contend with it."

Of course, the Internet does have the potential to amplify bullying to a larger audience. But what is also larger is the potential support group that a young person can organize to combat bullying. And since bullying becomes documented on the Internet, and thus more visible, it gives us opportunities to challenge it. We can't discount the horrendous instances of cyberbullying and its terrible consequences that we've seen reported in the media. But Boyd also described how the Internet and social media allow both for parents to witness the bullying and do something about it, and for young people to band together, defend one another, and take on bullies in their social circles.

Such instances probably result in the more mundane stories we're less likely to see reported. Boyd observed that parents often think the Internet "is just an extension [of what's going on in school], and that's why the Internet is problematic." But when she spoke with teens, she got a different picture. "They were, like, 'No, actually, I can get a lot more support online from my friends than I can in school, where we're in these separable environments, where it's really structured, and so the Internet is actually a great value for me,'" she explained.

Young gay, lesbian, bisexual, and transgender people, along with allies, can organize and fight back, sometimes connecting with people who live far beyond their geographical locale but who are experiencing the same kind of bullying. These connections can keep them grounded early on in life and can ward off seduction by the victory narrative, allowing them to grow up strong and ready for the battles and bias that as adults they will face. For them the experience can generate self-empowerment similar to the comradeship that Annie Ellman and Kevin Jennings see in group self-defense classes. Connecting with others can help us each walk proud on our own, in the here and now.

6

NOT UP FOR DEBATE

ABANDONING THE MEDIA'S "BOTH SIDES" DELUSION

LEARNING TO DEFEND OURSELVES IS one thing LGBT people can do, in the here and now, to deal with the reality of homophobia that's concealed by the victory narrative. We also need to pay attention to the way homophobia still persists in public discussion every day.

One of the things the victory narrative assumes is the existence of a gay-friendly media. LGBT civil rights successes make front-page headlines, where once gay people and their stories were barely mentioned in the news at all. There are openly gay reporters at newspapers and online news sites, and openly gay anchors and talk-show hosts all over television news. Robin Roberts is out. So are Sam Champion and Rachel Maddow and Anderson Cooper. Newspapers' editorial boards advocate for marriage equality. *Time* charted the "transgender tipping point," with Laverne Cox on the cover.

Look more closely, though, and you'll find that television networks — beyond Fox News and its longtime hostile coverage — and Washington reporters and columnists still give purveyors of antigay, antitrans hate a platform on which to recite lies that have been dispelled ten times over. Victory blindness often has us accepting this practice under the assumption that we should be "magnanimous" in our supposed victory, when in fact such bigotry should simply no longer be acceptable. By excusing it, we allow ourselves to be treated as less legitimate than any other group. Neither CNN nor any of the broadcast networks would invite a member of a white-supremacist group like the Council of Conservative Citizens as a commentator, but they still accept homophobia from their own commentators. One of the media's responsibilities is to keep up with the boundaries of what is and is not acceptable speech in our civil society. Yet as those boundaries have shifted, the media have not shifted with them.

Giving Legitimacy to Hate

The Family Research Council (FRC), founded in 1983, is a powerful and viciously antigay right-wing group. Its founder, James Dobson, who is also responsible for the conservative advocacy organization Focus on the Family, is considered perhaps the most influential anti-gay Christian-right leader in America. In commentary he wrote for CNN.com, he once compared gay marriage to slavery (lamenting the number of years it took to end the British slave trade and comparing that to how long it might take to overturn gay marriage), and has said that legalizing gay marriage would lead to "group marriage," "marriage between daddies and little girls," and "marriage between a man and his donkey." Tony Perkins, FRC's current president, has said that gays "are intolerant. They are hateful. They are vile. They are spiteful." He also claimed that gay young people "have a higher propensity to depression or suicide because of that internal conflict; homosexuals may recognize intuitively that their same-sex attractions are abnormal." An FRC official, Peter Sprigg, in 2010 said on MSNBC that "homosexual behavior" should be outlawed once again, and the group has distributed a pamphlet that depicts gay men and lesbians as physically and mentally ill pedophiles who can be cured. It was also revealed that the FRC contributed $25,000 to stop a congressional resolution to condemn what was known as the "kill the gays" bill in Uganda, which would have made homosexuality punishable by death in that country. The FRC said that it worried the resolution could make it appear that homosexuality is acceptable.

In 2010 the Southern Poverty Law Center (SPLC), which has monitored hate-group and extremist activity for more than forty years, added the FRC to its list of hate groups. A group doesn't need to be violent to earn this designation. The SPLC decided that the label applied in this case by using the same logic it uses to determine racist and other extremist groups: the FRC promotes defamation and promulgates known falsehoods. Many of the groups the SPLC lists as hate groups on its website are not violent, and some even claim to oppose violence. Included on the hate-group list are the Nation of Islam and other black-separatist groups, as well as neo-Confederate groups that espouse "white pride." The FRC earned its place on the SPLC's list.

In August 2012, a deranged gunman identified as twenty-eight-year-old Floyd Lee Corkins went to the FRC's Washington headquarters and began firing shots, allegedly saying, "I don't like your politics." A heroic security guard struggled with the gunman and was shot, but was able to stop Corkins from shooting others. (The guard recovered.) Corkins had recently volunteered at a gay center and was carrying a backpack full of Chick-fil-A sandwiches, perhaps referring to recent inflammatory antigay statements made by the fast-food chain's owner, Dan Cathay. It was a horrific crime perpetrated by an unhinged individual. In the days that followed, though, Dana Milbank, a *Washington Post* reporter and columnist, published a piece that argued the FRC's hate-group label was unjustified, and that the label actually incited the shooting. Milbank received a fair amount of criticism for the piece from progressive bloggers and LGBT commentators (but, curiously, virtually no criticism from his colleagues in the mainstream media). I invited him onto my show to try to find out why such a smart and respected journalist would defend a hate group. After all, Corkins's actions, while obviously condemnable, are one isolated incident. Compare that with the unbroken history of hate crimes committed against LGBT people because of the homophobia that lies, deceptions, and outright defamation propagated by groups like the FRC help stoke. I wanted to understand Milbank's thinking.

"[The Family Research Council] is a Washington think-tank, not a group that puts on sheets," Milbank said, alluding to the Ku Klux Klan's white robes. "This is a group that was founded by James Dobson," he continued, explaining that Dobson was "widely respected around town." I found Milbank's comments — and those of his editor, who tweeted his support after the column was criticized, calling the criticism "idiotic" — immensely revealing. Many in the media would say they support LGBT rights and abhor anyone who promotes hatred. But, often enjoying a cozy relationship with antigay figures who've been around for a long time, they go to great pains to distinguish them from others who promote hate. Milbank and his editor aren't to blame for this phenomenon, of course, but this story points to the existence of a much wider problem that affects our entire public discourse around LGBT issues. The idea that there is some difference between people who propagate lies against gay and transgender people and those who do so against other groups — people who "wear sheets" — betrays a double standard on LGBT defamation even in this supposedly more enlightened time.

Tony Perkins and James Dobson are by no means the only ones given this legitimacy and mainstream visibility. In 2014 ABC News announced that it was hiring far-right radio host Laura Ingraham to be a new commentator on the very mainstream *This Week with George Stephanopoulos*. Ingraham, who often shields herself by reminding opponents that she has a gay brother, nonetheless has defended people who condemn gay rights, like Perkins and the FRC. When the Guinness Brewery pulled its support of the annual St. Patrick's Day Parade in New York that year, protesting the parade organizers' longtime, annual decision to bar an Irish LGBT-pride group from marching, Ingraham attacked Guinness, commenting, "Welcome to the new totalitarianism." (A gay group from NBC/Universal, the parade's main sponsor, would finally be allowed to march, it was announced in 2014.) In 2013, she ridiculed transgender people, attacking what she called the "gender-bending phenomenon" while discussing a story about a gender-variant ten-year-old, Ryan, who identifies as female. Ingraham actually charged that parents are "pushing kids" into being transgender, because Ryan's parents decided, after much soul-searching and research, to accept Ryan's self-identification. In August 2014, on Fox News, Ingraham called hormone treatment for transgender youth "child abuse." Does ABC actually see this kind of ugly distortion and misinformation as legitimate? Would the network legitimize someone who makes blatantly stinging comments about a racial or religious group by making that person a commentator? Certainly, television-news coverage and much other coverage still makes racist and bigoted assumptions in what producers and editors decide to cover and not cover; nor should it be discounted that Ingraham herself has made remarks that promoted racist views, such as when she mocked an immigration protester in 2013 for speaking with an accent, or when she lambasted Michigan's governor in 2014 for making it easier for immigrants to move to Detroit. But the antigay comments are much more blatant — a higher level of vocal hate appears to be tolerated of all pundits when it's directed at gays.

A League of One

Positioning herself as speaking from "the Catholic perspective," Ingraham slammed the Supreme Court's decision striking down DOMA in June 2013, saying it would make people who are "religiously inclined" into "persona non grata at the moment." This resonated with public statements by other self-avowed Catholic pundits and commentators who are opposed to gay rights that have popped up on all the major networks and have been quoted in newspapers for years, such as Bill Donohue of the Catholic League. Donohue's "league" appears to be a one-person operation, yet he is brought on talk shows continually to speak for "the" Catholic point of view and the church's stand on gay rights. Appearing on Piers Morgan's show on CNN in 2012, he said, "I want the law to discriminate against all alternative lifestyles, against gays and unions. I want to promote and to put in a privileged position that institution of marriage between a man and a woman, which has been shown over and over to be the gold standard."

The list of Donohue's antigay comments in the name of American Catholics is sprawling, and I've debated him on my own show several times — bringing him on the show to take him on for his comments, not, like many among the media, presenting him as the "other side" or the voice of Catholics. The biggest problem with his presence in the media isn't that he's antigay but that it's implied that he's speaking for the majority of American Catholics. That couldn't be further from the truth. Though we have to be skeptical of poll results on this issue (for all the reasons discussed in chapter 2), it is significant that, in every major poll for several years now, a clear majority of Catholics support gay marriage. A Quinnipiac poll in 2013 found that, among all Catholics, 60% support gay marriage versus 31% opposed; that would mean the proportion of gay-marriage supporters among Catholics is higher than the rate in the general population, which the same poll found to be 56%–36% in favor. That poll also found that even a majority of Catholics who "attend church weekly" support gay marriage (53%–40%). So Catholics, if the polls accurately reflect public opinion (as the media certainly tell us they do), are actually leading the way on this issue.

If that's the case, why is Bill Donohue paraded on television as a Catholic leader when he would appear to be in the minority of Catholics and when his group seems to be a one-man show? Why is he on TV representing the church when even the pope has pulled back on antigay rhetoric and has criticized church leaders for becoming "obsessed" with the issue? Why isn't there a Catholic leader from a progressive Catholic group — and there are several pro-choice and pro-gay Catholic groups — on television all the time rightly representing the majority-Catholic view when gay marriage comes up?

This phenomenon goes beyond the Catholic community to encompass other groups, as GLAAD noted in an analysis of television-news commentators issued after President Obama announced his support for marriage equality in May 2012: "Overall, the religious spokespeople used in both written articles and television segments do not reflect the American people's views on marriage equality. Although white spokespeople are shown as being split evenly in terms of support for marriage equality, African American and Latino spokespeople are presented as being highly unsupportive, when they are, in fact, more supportive than the white population. Media outlets spoke overwhelmingly to straight male Christian clergy . . . These voices came disproportionately from the Baptist tradition."

In a study analyzing a three-year sample of news reports, published by the University of Missouri Center of Religion and the Professions in 2012, the researchers concluded, "Media outlets persistently quoted sources from Evangelical Christian organizations to speak about LGBT issues, and the messages those sources conveyed were significantly more negative than positive."

> By persistently reducing a diverse range of religious voices, intra-denominational progress, and public policy debate on LGBT issues to a "religion versus gay" frame, the news media is largely omitting a pro-LGBT religious perspective and ignoring individuals who identify as both LGBT and religious, particularly those who identify as Christian. As a result of this binary framing, it is likely that media consumers have distorted views of the relationship between LGBT people and religion.

It's hard to guess why that range is not called upon. Why, for example, is Donohue used to represent all Catholics when he obviously does not? It could be that media executives are bowing to religious conservatives' charges of a liberal and pro-gay bias in the media. Laura Ingraham has been noted as one of the biggest purveyors of this myth, and it obviously worked out well for her, winning her a spot on ABC. Or perhaps they like the sensationalism and theatrics that result, which help gin up ratings. Whatever the reason, this practice is misguided, irresponsible, and distorted, and it dehumanizes an entire group of people.

Christians aren't the only group whose views are being misrepresented by the commentators selected by the media. In a curious twist, the media similarly often overrepresent conservative or contrarian gay voices, too, making it appear as if these individuals speak for most LGBT people. There's a long history of this practice, but one prominent recent example was the hiring of a young, inexperienced writer, Brandon Ambrosino, for a coveted fellowship at the newly launched progressive-leaning site *Vox.com* in March 2014. After graduating from the late antigay crusader Jerry Falwell's evangelical-based Liberty University in 2007 and pursuing a career as a professional tap and jazz dancer, six years later Ambrosino started a virtual cottage industry writing articles online for publications from *Time.com* to *The Atlantic* that criticized gay activists and certainly weren't representative of the thinking of LGBT Americans on issues such as taking on defamation in popular culture or coming out. Because his often-undeveloped, weak arguments could not go uncriticized, his pieces got attention and brought a lot of traffic to those media sites. This may have been the rationale behind *Vox*'s decision to hire him, which rightly came under fire from many LGBT critics. (*Vox* editor in chief Ezra Klein denied that charge but did admit on his Facebook page that he "could've, and should've, handled this hire a lot better.") As with Donohue standing in for all Catholics, the media's hunger to attract as many eyeballs as possible seems to be at the root of this penchant for sensational contrarians, providing heat rather than light.

In from the Fringe

The same sensationalism and recklessness are in play when megaphones are given to voices far outside the mainstream. When channels with broad audiences welcome in people with extreme views, it gives these commentators a credibility that they soak up, only to return to the right-wing outlets they came from, their profiles elevated. CNN in particular has a habit of hiring extreme right-wing commentators whose ideas don't come close to representing any of the smart and interesting thinking going on in conservative circles right now, but who say controversial things likely to spike the ratings for the often-ratings-challenged network. And rarely do they invite someone from the progressive side to challenge these people, as they're often paired in debate with a moderate or an "objective reporter."

Dana Loesch, who was a Tea Party organizer in St. Louis, was hired by CNN in February 2011 as a commentator during the 2012 election cycle to offer the Tea Party perspective. Her caustic comments sparked outrage. For example, she applauded U.S. Marines who urinated on the bodies of Taliban soldiers (and said she'd have done the same). By 2013 CNN stopped bringing her on, apparently the result of comments like that. But during her time on the network, wearing that badge of CNN credibility, Loesch on her radio show defended a fourteen-year-old radio host who said President Obama was "making kids gay." And she went on a screaming rampage against a woman who called up and identified herself as a conservative Christian who said she stopped eating at Chick-fil-A because she opposed the comments of the restaurant chain's owner. "You only prescribe to certain aspects of Christianity," Loesch screeched. "Have you read the Gospels? I'm well full and clear to talk about it. So you think God is hateful? You are literally calling Christ hateful. That's not my opinion. That's what's in the Gospels. I don't want false Christians. You embarrass the faith. Get away from me, you evil . . ."

Loesch also railed against allowing transgender women to use women's rooms, because it's a "safety issue," and compared the struggles of transgender students to her dream of wanting to be a flower when she was a child. She castigated Dan Savage for trying to "take out homosexual rage on children." She called marriage "a covenant between a man, woman, and God before God on His terms. It is a religious civil liberty, not a right granted by government."

By using CNN to raise her profile, Loesch made herself a media commodity. By the time CNN got around to deciding not to book her anymore, it was too late. Even with Loesch's homophobic, transphobic baggage, ABC's *The View* eventually brought her on as a guest host in February 2014, perhaps similarly tantalized by the ratings spike that her ugly views could generate. "ABC's *The View* reportedly plans to mainstream conservative talk radio host Dana Loesch by featuring her as a guest co-host on the February 3 program," the watchdog group Media Matters for America reported. "The decision to give Loesch a national platform on a highly-rated television show is troubling considering Loesch has gained notoriety for her inflammatory rhetoric."

CNN also built up extreme-right *RedState.com* blogger Eric Erikson, whose blog has consistently published attacks on LGBT rights, giving him a platform on a legitimate network and making him a star. CNN had him on contract for three years until 2013, a period in which he, too, made controversial attacks that had critics calling for him to be fired but that also raised his profile from the far-right blogosphere to mainstream TV. Erikson has said gay people "must repent" and "not act on their sexuality" and claimed that "comparing gay rights activists to the Nazis is fitting." In 2014, taking up the distorted "religious liberties" meme that antigay leaders are now using to turn themselves into victims, he wrote on *Townhall.com*, "Enormous energy is being expended by the left in America to make Christianity and Christians unacceptable . . . As gay rights activists use the tactics of [segregation-era Alabama official] Bull Connor to push for what they declare civil rights, they are targeting churches, religiously affiliated groups and Christian businesses for harassment and lawsuits." Would CNN or ABC give such a platform to an out-and-out racist who said blacks are like the Nazis or said Jews "must repent"?

Now Erikson spits his venom from Fox News, which has been biased against or ignorant of LGBT rights since its inception. There he joins Keith Albow, perhaps the most transphobic commentator in all of the media, who has said, among other things, that he considers Chaz Bono's transition "a psychotic delusion — a fixed and false belief," adding that there is "nothing substantially different from a woman believing she is a man than there is about a woman believing she is a CIA agent being followed by the KGB (when in reality, she is, say, a salesperson at J. Crew)."

In another instance, discussing a California bill in 2013 to allow transgender students to choose the bathroom and sports team that fit their gender identity, CNN brought on "pro-family" Christian evangelical leader Randy Thomasson, whose group, Save California, the Southern Poverty Law Center also lists as a hate group. Among other defamatory remarks, Thomasson called the LGBT rights movement a "tsunami of perversity." There was no reason to bring on a religious or self-described pro-family person to debate this issue. Thomasson isn't a psychologist or psychiatrist. It's one thing to bring on someone who disagrees but who is a trusted expert. But if media actually tried to meet that benchmark, they would quickly discover the simple truth that there are no reputable psychiatrists, psychologists, sex therapists, or other mental-health professionals or medical authorities who believe homosexuality and transgenderism are unnatural or harmful to individuals or destructive to institutions. The American Medical Association, American Psychological Association, and American Psychiatric Association support gay and trans people. But rather than report the story in an accurate way that won't cause any fireworks, the networks put on a circus by bringing in a nonexpert who promotes bigotry.

The Widening Media Landscape

Getting the media to cover LGBT issues more responsibly will require consistent pressure. Equality Matters reports that since it has begun petitioning CNN and MSNBC to stop using Tony Perkins, and having people write and complain to the network, the leader of the Family Research Council has shown up less and less often. That has happened only because Americans across the country, LGBTs and allies of equality alike, have engaged in online campaigns pointing out the bigotry. The widely dispersed and more democratic media landscape that the Internet makes possible has also allowed a flourishing online world of LGBT and progressive blogs, commentators, and reporters that isn't afraid to take on defamation by the major outlets. In the past, with only print publications, it was impossible for a gay newspaper to get the message about anti-LGBT defamation out to a wide audience. But criticism of a media outlet by the gay press, independent blogs, and media watchdogs today can escalate and embarrass these major outlets for promoting homophobia and transphobia.

To reject the presence of extreme and defamatory views in American media is not to call for "censorship," as some on the right hypocritically claim (while they try to stop progressive and LGBT voices from being legitimized). No one wants the government to step in and prevent voices from being heard. Rather, we are asking media corporations to be responsible, to treat all groups equally, and to stop legitimizing defamation as rational debate, particularly when genuine debates on many of these issues have long since ended. Sure, they are in the business of making money, but it shouldn't be at the expense of demonizing LGBT people and instead could actually be in the service of exposing homophobia.

That is in fact what many LGBT activists and bloggers have been able to do in taking on bigotry, from as far back as the vibrant AIDS demonstrations of twenty-five years ago and up to the stories that go viral today on the Internet. The media's penchant for sensation can also make them a force for good. Every chance we have to direct clicks and eyeballs to stories of LGBT discrimination and ugly incidents of rejection and bigotry is an opportunity to challenge the victory narrative, cut through victory blindness, and lay the groundwork for the hard, necessary fights ahead.

7

WINNING TRUE EQUALITY

HOW THE GRASS ROOTS ARE VITAL TO FULL CIVIL RIGHTS

I BEGAN CHAPTER 2 OF this book by describing the bigoted, demeaning treatment that Olivier Odom and her wife, Jennifer Tipton, received from a guard at the Tennessee amusement park Dollywood. Winning an apology and changing the status quo in that instance took more than just filing a complaint. In fact, the women and the Campaign for Southern Equality, which helped them, didn't initially get the kind of response they wanted. It was the energy of the LGBT community nationally that made an impact. The women took their story to local media, and that story then went viral and exploded in the national media. This put Dollywood in the hot seat and pressured Dolly Parton herself to respond. As with so many of the stories of discrimination I've discussed in this book, there was a resolution only after there was collective action and shaming brought to bear by perhaps thousands of people. Time and again we've seen the power of joining together, of taking a stand as a people, whether on the streets or, increasingly, online. The victory narrative seduces us, however, to pull back just when we're beginning to win, in fear of taking further risks. The covering demand draws too many of us in, as our enemies put us on the defensive when we must remain vigilant and constantly on the offensive in attaining civil rights. That means being vocal, organizing at the grass roots, and collectively demanding action.

That's how we've won every right for LGBT people. This has cer-

tainly been true since the beginning of the Stonewall era, but especially so since the emergence of AIDS drew a sharp line and instilled
in us an attitude of "never again." Like other marginalized groups,
we'd experienced suffering and mass death, and we knew that we
would never be the same. There's a direct line from ACT UP and
AIDS activism — the vibrant street demonstrations of the late '80s and
early '90s — to everything the LGBT rights movement has achieved
today with marriage equality and beyond. AIDS painfully woke up
the LGBT community to the reality that we were hated and despised,
thought of as second-class citizens whose lives were not worth saving.
We would never be silent again. The mantra of ACT UP, "Silence =
Death," has been in the DNA of every other aspect of the movement
from then on. We weren't going to rest.

We have learned that making noise via collective action is the only
way we can get what we truly need: a full civil rights bill, something
much bigger than ENDA, that encompasses employment, housing,
public accommodations, education, and all banking and lending,
without a religious exemption any broader than the one in the Civil
Rights Act of 1964. We must not settle for anything less.

A Much Bigger Lift

Collective action from the grass roots, to put pressure on our politicians and LGBT leaders in Washington, is also one way through
which we can get HIV-criminalization laws repealed. The Repeal
Existing Policies That Encourage and Allow Legal (REPEAL) HIV
Discrimination Act, introduced in 2013 by Democratic senator Chris
Coons of Delaware in the Senate and California Democratic representative Barbara Lee and Republican representative Ileana Ros-
Lehtinen in the House, would require a federal review of these harsh
laws across the country; it has languished, and a previous version of
it, introduced by Lee, died in three subcommittees in the Republican-
controlled House. In the Democratic-controlled Senate, after Coons

introduced the bill in 2013, there was no action on it, and it failed to get a Republican cosponsor.

At a time when several reports have shown that the CDC's HIV-prevention campaigns targeted toward gay and bisexual men and that those targeting transgender women are dramatically underfunded (those groups together represent almost two thirds of new infections but benefit from far less than half of prevention funds), it's going to take a lot of pressure if we want the CDC to finally take comprehensive action to slow HIV infections with real, fully funded prevention campaigns.

Though the repeal of "don't ask, don't tell" cleared the way for gays and lesbians to serve openly in the military, the same is still not true for transgender people. We will not have achieved the full promise of the end of "don't' ask, don't tell" until that changes. The obstacle isn't a law but an outdated, insulting Pentagon regulation that disqualifies anyone from service with "current or history of psychosexual conditions, including but not limited to transsexualism [and] transvestism." (The term *transsexualism* stopped being used in the American Psychiatric Association's *Diagnostic and Statistical Manual* in 1994. The word *transvestism* is also now discouraged.) In 2014 a commission led by former surgeon general Jocelyn Elders concluded there was "no compelling medical rationale" for the ban. The policy could be ended with the stroke of a pen at any time. Secretary of Defense Chuck Hagel said in 2014 that he was "open" to reviewing it. Even with a review under way, history tells us sustained pressure would still be needed.

Ending the ban would bring the U.S. military up to speed with many of our allies that have allowed open service by transgender people for years, including Canada and the United Kingdom. Instead, the military is currently ejecting valuable people at a time when they're most needed. I interviewed Landon Wilson in 2014; Wilson served as a dominance warfare specialist in the U.S. Navy, stationed in Afghanistan. Then his life was turned upside down one day in December 2013, when it was discovered that he was a transgender man after a routine paperwork check uncovered that he'd enlisted when he was biologically female, before transitioning. The story of this valued sailor, whom the military had spent a half million dollars training for an important and specialized intelligence job, is just one of many that prove this harmful and outmoded ban must end.

We also need a nationwide antibullying law like the Safe Schools Improvement Act — also stalled in Congress — to help stop the bullying we see among teens and young children that has resulted in numerous reports of suicide. With bullying occurring so widely and for so many reasons, this issue is vital to all children, no matter their sexual orientation or gender identity, and the fact that antigay currents in the GOP prevent many lawmakers from seeing that fact is mind-boggling. An antibullying law would be a pivotal act of education reform and would make our schools safer for all Americans. Opponents need to be shamed into doing this for the sake of all American kids, including their own.

These are just a few examples. Winning these federal protections, policy changes, and much more would certainly be a bigger lift than taking on an amusement park over a T-shirt. But it is a difference of degree, not a difference of kind. If we're serious about winning equality, collective action is the only force strong enough. We cannot rely on Beltway lobbying to take the lead.

To pass legislation and a big federal civil rights bill that includes no broad religious exemption will mean bringing relentless pressure, both online and on the ground. It will mean protesting, practicing civil disobedience, carrying out online campaigns and, perhaps, planning right now for another march on Washington. It will mean pressuring Democratic candidates in upcoming elections who will want the LGBT vote but must earn it by promising to support a full and comprehensive civil rights bill and all of these other measures, and nothing less. Instead, with a Hillary Clinton 2016 presidential campaign almost assured, we already see LGBT groups lining up behind her or fawning, such as when Fred Sainz of the Human Rights Campaign (HRC) told the *New York Times* in August 2014, "We get her like we get our moms. We've seen the travails she's been through and the fact that she's not just a survivor but a conqueror." We should not be comparing Hillary Clinton to our mothers, and we certainly don't owe her filial obedience. She is a politician who now must make major promises if she wants our support in any political race.

Incrementalism's Failure

With so much to be done, with the closet still tyrannizing so many Americans and discrimination in public accommodations and employment so rampant, it's shocking that, aside from a hate-crimes law, we don't have any significant federal legislation of any kind to protect us. And, as Sainz's words suggest, that's partly because advocates in Washington haven't really demanded it; instead they have played nice and put faith in politicians who profess to be our friends. Most problematically, the strategy that Washington LGBT advocates have pursued could best be described as incrementalism. The logic of incrementalism is that by asking for a little bit at a time and winning a little bit at a time, you can eventually achieve the full complement of your goals. But in fact that's not how Washington works, certainly not in the current environment. You need to demand something big, something your opponents see as even outlandish, and then fight it out. You walk away with what you can get, which may be even more than you thought was possible. Incrementalism is, in many ways, a legislative version of covering: not shaking things up too much, playing by the rules, being on the defensive rather than the offensive.

It wasn't until July 2014, for example, that HRC, the largest gay group, would even say publicly that the LGBT movement should "put its weight behind" a broad and comprehensive civil rights bill. Not until December 2014 did the group release a report calling for such a bill. But even given that intention, HRC will still have to be pushed hard, because its default has always been to settle for less, placating politicians rather than making demands. Well into 2014, HRC was still pushing that narrow employment bill the Employment Non-Discrimination Act, with its dangerous, broad religious exemption that would allow continued discrimination by the very institutions that do most of the discriminating. Only after the Supreme Court's *Hobby Lobby* decision was HRC finally forced to listen to what other groups and the grass roots of the movement had been saying for years.

The incremental approach of HRC and Beltway lobbyists, when it comes to legislation, is self-defeating. It's flawed because it's going to take just as long to get a little bit done — ENDA was introduced more than twenty years ago and has gone nowhere   as it would to get much more done. So why not ask for as much as we can? After all, making wild demands is how Republicans have often gotten away with their most brazen legislative achievements. Why can't the same strategy work for us?

When we don't ask for much, we also send a message that we're not really serious. Incrementalism — legislative covering — and fear of going big and fighting it out have actually created roadblocks, sending us on the run with our enemies going on the offensive. In contrast, the movement for marriage equality, which has been greatly successful, broke from the standard approach, providing a multifocused, uncompromising, grassroots-generated model for action and results. It demanded something big — something seen as outlandish and unrealistic — and made it a reality.

"ENDA is not as new, as sexy, and frankly, I think the branding around ENDA is just terribly bad," said Michael Crawford, director of online programs at Freedom to Marry, comparing marriage equality's messaging to the employment bill's. He was speaking on a panel I moderated in San Jose in 2013 at the annual progressive activist conference Netroots Nation, a live broadcast on my radio program. Crawford, speaking for himself as an activist and not as a representative of Freedom to Marry, pointed out that marriage-equality activists tapped into the public's imagination. And he said the same needs to be done in regard to federal legislation — we need to tap into the public's imagination.

It was a discussion that took me back to Kenji Yoshino, who in his book sees marriage equality as a complicated and interesting issue that is sometimes about covering — fitting in — and other times is not, especially when it challenges how people think about gay and lesbian relationships. The way Crawford talked about marriage equality, it wasn't about covering. Pleading for "rights" can often be a covering strategy, especially when we posit that we're exactly the same as heterosexuals and ask the dominant culture not to notice our differences (such as when, in discussion of employment protections, we say we do the "same job" as a heterosexual counterpart when, perhaps, we should say we bring something new and interesting to the table). Crawford was instead talking about appealing to the general public on the level of the things that connect us all rather than hiding who we are, even as gay people are different and unique in how we love.

Crawford noted that it wasn't until recently that we saw marriage as a winning issue rather than a losing one. "When you look at marriage, you see a strategic shift in messaging," he explained. "We stopped talking about it as 'rights.' When straight people want to get married, it's about love and commitment. How can we make that transition around ENDA? I think a much more interesting way to look at it is if we reconceived how we push for nondiscrimination at the federal level. A broader bill that was bigger, bolder, had the chance to captivate the public's imagination. Rebranding, talking about it in ways that resonate with the general public and put pressure on elected officials."

Beyond the messaging, another important aspect of the marriage-equality movement that gives us some guidance moving forward is that it was driven not by the Beltway but by average Americans who wanted equality and who worked with visionary legal advocates. Many activists in Washington in the early '90s saw marriage as utopian — and outlandish — certainly not part of their incremental plan. Their first priority was passing the tepid and narrow ENDA (first introduced in 1994), and they believed same-sex marriage would just create backlash and divert their attention. Marriage equality was driven by couples in Hawaii who sued in 1993, getting a preliminary positive ruling with the help of their lawyer Dan Foley at the local ACLU; Evan Wolfson, then of Lambda Legal, became a co-counsel on the case and pioneered the marriage-equality movement, going on to create the group Freedom to Marry. I went to Hawaii at the time and reported on the movement there for *Out* magazine, and I certainly remember the fear back in Washington among activists who fretted.

It did in fact cause a backlash. That's what happens when you're not covering — it shakes people up. In Hawaii a ballot measure was launched that allowed the legislature to define marriage as a union between a man and a woman, blunting any action the courts would take — and gay groups in Washington hadn't done the work to beat it back, not from early on. At the federal level, conservatives responded with the Defense of Marriage Act, which they then saw as a great fund-raising tool and fear-mongering weapon. Again LGBT groups responded with panic rather than planning far ahead. But the point is that we needed to have this fight. And while many can argue about what could or should have been done and how we could have gotten our allies to support us more, the fact remains that it is the fight itself, standing up against the hate because we dare to demand equality, that changes the culture and brings people to the cause.

Marriage Equality and the Force of the Grass Roots

In fact, the recent trajectories of the marriage-equality movement and the repeal of "don't ask, don't tell" provide all the proof we need that timid, incremental approaches are no way to chart a path forward. This chapter doesn't at all purport to be a complete history of achievements on marriage equality and "don't ask, don't tell"; there are many books and articles, some of them excellent, that do tell those stories in much fuller detail, and there will surely be more. But simply in sketching out the course of events, particularly in regard to pressuring Washington politicians and the White House, we can see how making big demands and building support from the grass roots up were the secret to our greatest wins.

In the years after the battle in Hawaii and the vote on the Defense of Marriage Act, couples in Massachusetts took the lead. Their guide was the pioneering attorney Mary Bonauto at Gay and Lesbian Advocates and Defenders, who fought right up to the Massachusetts Supreme Judicial Court. That state became the first to achieve marriage equality, in 2003. (Bonauto later went on to successfully challenge DOMA in federal court.) In the following years antigay ballot measures were passed in states across the country, and the backlash against marriage equality was used by George W. Bush and the GOP in elections year after year, including in 2008, when Prop 8 was passed in California.

In response, the American Foundation for Equal Rights — cofounded by filmmaker Rob Reiner and his wife, Michele, producer Bruce Cohen, screenwriter Dustin Lance Black, and Chad Griffin, who now is president of the Human Rights Campaign — was formed to take Prop 8 to federal court. It was bold of Griffin and others in Hollywood to create a group and bring in superattorneys Ted Olson and David Boies. This sent a message that we wouldn't just sit back. It put us on the offensive, even as other LGBT groups at first opposed the idea, worried about a possible setback. The Prop 8 trial was important in changing public opinion. Getting a federal ruling striking down a marriage ban in California was an important achievement.

Jo Becker's book *Forcing the Spring,* which covered the Prop 8 case but presented itself as a history of the entire marriage movement, rightly came under scrutiny for ignoring the early history and groundbreakers like Evan Wolfson and Mary Bonauto, as well as gay and lesbian writers and pundits like Andrew Sullivan, E. J. Graff, Gabriel Rotello, and others who'd been making the case for marriage equality since the late '80s and early '90s. As many critics (including me) pointed out when the book was published, it overplayed the Prop 8 case, which in the end didn't do what its architects set out to do: end same-sex-marriage bans across the country. The monumental, pivotal case, which got short shrift in the book, was *United States v. Windsor,* in which Edie Windsor, represented by attorney Roberta Kaplan, won at the Supreme Court, and DOMA was struck down. Dozens of federal judges then used that decision to crush marriage bans in the states.

What fewer commentators have mentioned is that *Forcing the Spring* also ignored the importance of the grass roots and the Net roots, a widely dispersed but powerful collection of progressive activists. It overlooked the sheer will of LGBT people across the country who pressured a president and a political party to honor the big promises they had made.

As we'll see again with "don't ask, don't tell" repeal, HRC was acquiescing to the Obama White House, falling in line after making one initial slap at the administration when it chose antigay evangelical pastor Rick Warren to give the invocation at the presidential inauguration in January 2008. HRC often made excuses for inaction on the part of President Obama and the Democrats, likely fearing that it would lose access if it continued with any criticism. "People wrongly assume that having Democratic majorities in Congress means that your legislative goals will be met. That's not the case," said HRC vice president Fred Sainz to the Associated Press in June 2010, apologizing for our allies' inaction in taking on DOMA and passing antidiscrimination legislation, even as Democrats had control of the House and the Senate with a big majority (and, for a very brief period, even had a supermajority in the Senate, able to break a filibuster).

Not only was President Obama not inclined to take quick action on LGBT rights — and getting excused for it by Beltway gay groups — but his Justice Department was actually defending DOMA in court, just as George W. Bush had done. It took the grass roots and the Net roots to make him stop. OBAMA DEFENDS DOMA IN FEDERAL COURT. SAYS BANNING GAY MARRIAGE IS GOOD FOR THE FEDERAL BUDGET. INVOKES INCEST AND MARRYING CHILDREN read the headline on the outspoken gay and progressive news-and-commentary site *AMERICAblog* regarding a Justice Department brief filed in 2009, one of several that the administration filed into 2011. The story exploded across the Internet, onto all the major gay and progressive blogs, and into the mainstream media. It now wasn't just activists but ordinary LGBT Americans and their allies who put the pressure on. The Beltway groups, including HRC, followed suit, breaking for the moment from offering apologies, seeing the anger in the community, and realizing others were leading the protest. *AMERICAblog*'s John Aravosis and Joe Sudbay would, in fact, continue a relentless campaign on their site for more than two years, targeting the administration for pandering to our enemies rather than championing our cause.

David Mixner said the brief "could have been written by Pat Robertson." Soon bloggers inspired some LGBT donors to boycott Democratic National Committee fund-raisers. Aravosis attacked what he called the "Democratic effort to milk money from our community at the same time Democrats are equating us with incest and not lifting a finger on any of our legislation priorities in Congress or the White House." The White House claimed it had to defend DOMA. Spokesperson Tracy Schmaler said the Department of Justice had an obligation "to defend federal statutes when they are challenged in court" and couldn't "pick and choose" which statutes to defend.

But former Clinton-administration officials, among others, pointed out that if an administration doesn't believe a law is constitutional, it doesn't have to defend that law in court, instead allowing Congress to do so. Both President George W. Bush and President Clinton had, in fact, used that tactic. The online campaign heated up over the next year and a half, joined by protests as well, demanding the president stop defending DOMA each time a brief had to be filed in various cases. *AMERICAblog* forcefully took on what Joe Sudbay later called "apologists (mostly obsequious job seekers and lobbyists) from the LGBT community" who claimed the president simply had to defend DOMA.

In January 2011, the Obama administration defended DOMA in court in yet another case, incurring more wrath from grassroots activists and an avalanche of negative press. But just one month later, the administration made an about-face. The Justice Department announced that it believed DOMA to be unconstitutional and that it would not be defending it in court. By that point as well, Joe Sudbay had asked President Obama about his position on marriage during an interview in the White House conducted by Sudbay and several other bloggers — Obama's first sit-down with the Net roots — and he'd elicited the now-famous line that Obama was "evolving" on gay marriage. "Attitudes evolve, including mine," Obama said. "And I think that it is an issue that I wrestle with." That happened in October 2010, and Obama would go on to mention his "evolving" several times in the following months.

After Obama signaled that the winds might be shifting, grassroots activists, leading thousands of LGBT Americans and allies across the country, didn't let up. At the June 2011 White House LGBT Pride reception, Dan Savage wore a pin with the words EVOLVE ALREADY!, a phrase that AMERICAblog had made the new mantra of the pressure campaign. Savage told the Associated Press, "I think the gay community has to keep the pressure on." Even HRC had, by this point, urged the president to support marriage equality, putting out a statement shortly after the DOMA brief in January.

As the 2012 elections neared, many of us made the point that Obama needed to energize his base, especially young voters who supported marriage equality, if he wanted to win a second term. Activists argued that what was good for us was good for Obama in the election. He needed to create a sharp difference between himself and Mitt Romney, who claimed to oppose antigay discrimination but didn't support gay marriage. (In other words, Romney was positioning himself similarly to Obama at the time.)

A month later, in May, Joe Biden made his infamous slip-up or trial balloon — however you perceive it — and came out for marriage equality. Within days the president announced his support in an interview on ABC, and it did help to change public opinion. He led the way, and there's no question it helped in four states where gay marriage was on the ballot: Minnesota, Maryland, Washington, and Maine. Next, the White House filed a brief with the Supreme Court, urging it to strike down DOMA. Surely there were many insiders in the gay groups, as well as gay people close to the White House and the president, who both shaped Obama's thoughts and helped manage pressure from the outside. Tobias Barrington Wolff, the University of Pennsylvania School of Law professor who served as an adviser on LGBT issues during Obama's 2008 campaign and an informal adviser to the president since then, comes to mind. But none of it would have happened, and their counsel wouldn't have been as urgently needed, without the grass roots, the Net roots, the bloggers, and the protests that allowed thousands of Americans to pressure the president to do the right thing for LGBT Americans (as well as for his reelection campaign) and for the country as a whole.

"Continue to Pressure Me"

The same was true in the battle for "don't ask, don't tell" repeal. We can't discount the role that insiders played, but the determining factor was the grass roots. Without pressure from outside, this achievement would not have happened.

In 2009, while the Democrats controlled the House and had a supermajority in the Senate, the Matthew Shepard and James Byrd Jr. Hate Crimes Prevention Act was passed. But that long-overdue bill had languished for years. It was low-hanging fruit, the bare minimum expected. It was great that gay and transgender people would finally be protected under hate-crimes statutes; but why wasn't President Obama tackling laws written expressly to target and harm us?

During the 2008 presidential campaign, Obama had described himself as a "fierce advocate" of LGBT rights. When the new administration failed to move quickly to live up to that commitment, Richard Socarides, an openly gay former Clinton aide, wrote a *Washington Post* op-ed in May 2009, deriding Obama and asking, "Where's our 'fierce advocate'?" In a *New York Times* article, David Mixner asked, "How much longer do we give [Obama] the benefit of the doubt?"

HRC, again likely fearing loss of access, allowed Obama to stall repeal, often apologizing to the gay community for his actions or offering tepid press releases expressing opposition. After a meeting in May 2009 at the White House, HRC's then leader, Joe Solmonese, lauded the president on his efforts on repealing "don't ask, don't tell," even as activists across the country were speaking out loudly and angrily about the president's continued refusal to move forward with an equal-rights agenda. "They have a vision," Solmonese told the *New York Times*. "They have a plan."

But there was no plan of any kind. Shortly after that interview, Solmonese came on my show and further defended the White House, even as grassroots activists organized protests and David Mixner and San Francisco activist Cleve Jones called for a march on Washington, the National Equality March, for the fall of that year. The passage of Proposition 8 had only further energized activists in California and across the country, and people weren't going to accept the foot-dragging or the apologies from HRC. The National Equality March was led by organizers Robin McGehee and Kip Williams, doing much of their work online and on a shoestring budget. Almost two hundred thousand people, by some estimates, came to Washington that October 2009 — just a few months after the call to march — to demand that the president follow through on his promises.

"Let us be clear to America, we are looking at a system of gay apartheid," Mixner said from the stage. "One set of laws for LGBT citizens and another set of laws for the rest of America. We elected you, Mr. President, not to be led by Congress but to lead Congress . . . And then you will have the moral authority, and we will be behind your back demanding that Congress repeal 'Don't Ask, Don't Tell.'"

The White House, realizing that upwards of two hundred thousand people were coming to town, had scheduled Obama to speak at HRC's annual gala in Washington for the eve of the march, where the president said ending the ban was a priority — though he gave no idea of when that would happen. And he laid the bait, urging those attending to "continue to pressure me."

With the pressure on, a few months later, in his State of the Union address in 2010, the president said, "This year, I will work with Congress and our military to finally repeal the law that denies gay Americans the right to serve the country they love because of who they are." Defense Secretary Robert Gates and Joint Chiefs Chairman Michael Mullen soon voiced their support for repeal.

But time was running out. Democrats were still in control of both branches of Congress, but many observers — gauging the political climate and seeing the rise of the Tea Party — knew that control wouldn't last. And in February 2010, Gates announced that the Pentagon would undertake a nine-month study of the issue, though there had been study after exhaustive study done in years past showing that gays served with distinction and that there would be no problems with open service. It seemed like the military was stalling, and the president wasn't challenging this tactic out of fear of upsetting conservatives. (Not until Obama's second term would the administration painfully come to realize the futility of pandering to people who would never meet them halfway.)

This trepidation notwithstanding, it was expected that repeal would be included in the president's Department of Defense authorization bill that spring. But Kerry Eleveld at *The Advocate* reported in April 2010 that "multiple sources say some administration officials counseled the president against acting on the military's gay ban in 2010" and that at a February 1 meeting gay advocates were told "it would not be going into the president's Defense authorization budget proposal."

If not for the emergence of the protest group GetEQUAL, the stalling would only have continued, by both Democrats in Congress and the president. The direct-action group grew out of an idea proposed by the National Equality March organizers and got off the ground with the help of former Clinton aide Paul Yandura and funding from Progressive Insurance heir Jonathan Lewis. GetEQUAL sprang into action in the spring of 2010. The actions of Robin McGehee, Lieutenant Dan Choi, Autumn Sandeen, and other GetEQUAL activists who were arrested for chaining themselves to the White House fence, among other protests, sent a message to the administration and Congress that they would only continue to be embarrassed for this gross negligence. Choi had even gotten a public promise from Senate majority leader Harry Reid when he challenged him from the audience as Reid was being interviewed onstage at the progressive Netroots Nation conference.

The Net roots kept up the pressure, as did the Washington-based Servicemembers Legal Defense Network, which was eventually shut out of a key meeting at the White House even as HRC was still included and quietly went along. Think tanks like Palm Center, then at the University of California, Santa Barbara (and specifically the critical research on sexual minorities in the military from the center's Nathaniel Frank and Aaron Belkin), provided much-needed ammunition to activists. Democrats lost control of the House of Representatives as the Tea Party surged in the 2010 midterm elections. The eventual vote on "don't ask, don't tell" took place that December, after Republicans surprised Democrats by pulling support for a massive federal spending bill, suddenly creating room for "don't ask, don't tell" on the agenda. Repeal passed during the lame-duck session, literally in the last hours of the Democrats' full control of both houses of Congress. Right up until the week before the final vote on a stand-alone bill repealing the policy, Michigan Democratic senator Carl Levin, chair of the Senate Armed Services Committee, complained that the White House still wasn't pushing hard enough to influence the senators whose votes were crucial. The repeal drive took on a life of its own in those final hours, however, and the White House could only embrace it and accept the win, which it surely needed.

None of this showed there was a "plan," as Joe Solmonese had said. Had Republicans not pulled support for the spending bill, those last hours of the Congress would have been focused on it and not on "don't ask, don't tell," and that law would likely still be in existence today. Persistent, vocal activism was one of the main reasons "don't ask, don't tell" got to be slated for a vote once the spending bill was off the table. It was the grassroots action that began way back with the

National Equality March that had continued to pressure the White House and Reid until they ultimately responded. The GetEQUAL activists, the National Equality March organizers, and the key bloggers and other activists were invited to the historic repeal-signing ceremony that December; it was the White House's way of acknowledging the role the grass roots played.

It's Not Inevitable

"Don't ask, don't tell" repeal and marriage equality's success are the key examples in the recent past of how we can win by thinking big and organizing collective action that includes everyday LGBT Americans and allies across the country. As a movement, we actually once thought big about a comprehensive civil rights bill, too. In 1974 New York congresswoman Bella Abzug and New York congressman Ed Koch (the closeted gay man who would go on to become New York City's mayor, and then, with aspirations to the governorship, shamefully ignored the burgeoning AIDS epidemic) sponsored a gay civil rights bill. They modeled their bill after the Civil Rights Act of 1964 and worked with the oldest still-existing Washington gay group, the National LGBTQ Task Force, then known as the National Gay Task Force. Following in the footsteps of the civil rights movement, the Equality Act of 1974 was a sweeping bill that would have prohibited discrimination on the basis of sex, marital status, or sexual orientation (defining sexual orientation as "choice of sexual partner according to gender") in employment, housing, and public accommodations.

The late '70s, however, saw the rise of the new right — a backlash to the '60s reform era — and antigay crusades, most notably the successful Anita Bryant–led "Save Our Children" campaign against an anti-discrimination ordinance in Miami-Dade County. By the '80s there came the AIDS epidemic and the backlash to that as well, with the Reagan administration bowing to religious extremists.

Perhaps more notably, however, there was also a shift in the balance of power in the gay leaders in Washington, from the more grassroots-focused National Gay Task Force (now the National LGBTQ Task Force) to the Human Rights Campaign Fund (now the Human Rights Campaign) and its insider, access-driven lobbying approach. The latter group was funded in large part through black-tie dinners and big donors and a decidedly less radical crowd. And that's where the incrementalist strategy was born.

Soon enough the narrow version of ENDA would be introduced, the idea being that asking for only a little was an achievable goal. But it never passed, even as it came close. Our enemies weren't about to give us even an inch. Why were LGBT advocates in Washington still pushing ENDA in 2013? Why didn't we just scrap it long ago and go for broke?

In July 2013, in an interview on my show, I asked Senator Tammy Baldwin of Wisconsin why we hadn't introduced a full and complete civil rights bill. Baldwin was the only openly gay or lesbian person in the U.S. Senate, and she has fought hard for LGBT rights throughout her career as a great advocate, so her response was disappointing.

"With regard to what has been called before an omnibus approach to LGBT equality and sort of dealing with multiple facets in one bill, I'd actually — I find myself keeping on referring to my service in the House of Representatives," she said, referring to her time as a member of the House representing Madison, Wisconsin.

> One of the challenges is that a bill like that would be referred to four or five or more committees. And if you think it's hard to get a bill through one committee, let me tell you how hard it would be to get a bill through four or five or more committees in the House . . . Actually threading that needle and actually getting a bill through all those committees would probably be quite a challenge and I think we want to see progress faster than that. In fact we want to see it yesterday. But we prefer to see it tomorrow than many years off.

Baldwin was absolutely right that we want to see progress yesterday. But when powerful figures in our community, like Baldwin,
default to incremental approaches, it's time to shift our thinking. If
the twenty years we've spent trying to pass one bill — ENDA, with its
broad, conciliatory religious exemption — are any guide, focusing on
what seems achievable to us now is no shortcut. It will take us years
of relentless pressure to accomplish anything, no matter what. So why
not use those years to educate members of Congress and the public
and do all the work to get support for a big bill? Why not just wait it
out, introducing the bill and lobbying and educating people as the
Republican Party nears implosion (pulled apart by the Tea Party and
the religious right), and have it ready to go when Democrats come
back into power? Why not demand that every Democratic candidate
make a promise to get on board?

And, if Democrats are so supportive of gay rights — with almost
every Democratic senator racing to come out for marriage equality
before the Supreme Court's decision on DOMA in 2013 — then let's
make them work for us. Let's keep them busy in committees defending our full civil rights in return for our full support and let them use
it as a wedge issue against the GOP. The last thing leading Republicans want to do, after all, is have an open conversation about LGBT
equality. They know the bigotry that appeals to the party base is toxic
to the mainstream, yet they can't run away from their fiercest supporters. Let's force them to talk about an issue they wish they just
didn't have to discuss. Why instead allow Republicans the time to
regroup and come up with new strategies to push homophobia below
the radar and use implicit bias, when we should be on the offensive?
It's victory blindness that prevents us from moving forward, thinking
full equality is coming to us when it won't unless we make it happen.
Encouragingly, by December 2014 some longtime Democratic allies,
like Senator Jeff Merkley of Oregon, were getting that message, noting that a comprehensive bill is where we need to go no matter how
long it takes, jumping off from HRC's long-overdue report. He said
he planned to introduce a full civil rights bill in the spring of 2015,

though he acknowledged that the question of when it might ever get passed is a "hazy, crystal ball question."

The truth is, we'll be fighting for quite a while, and we'll be fighting on many fronts, but we can win. Legal advocates are turning to the courts: it's possible the Equal Employment Opportunity Commission will rule that the prohibition against employment discrimination on the basis of sex found in Title VII of the Civil Rights Act applies to gay, lesbian, and bisexual people in the same way it ruled that transgender people were covered under that statute. The battle has to be multi-pronged. In 2014 the Gill Foundation — founded by the gay high-tech multimillionaire philanthropist Tim Gill, whose group changed the political landscape in Colorado by backing pro-gay candidates and taking down antigay candidates and who's donated an estimated $300 million to the cause of LGBT rights — announced it was putting $25 million toward fighting for gay rights in the South. Until there are federal laws banning discrimination, it could take many years before many southern states, where homophobia is still entrenched in the political environment, pass such laws — unless activists there, who must lead the fight, get the help they need.

"This is a point in time where we've accomplished a number of things in easy states and where you hear some people saying gay rights is inevitable," Gill told *Politico* in 2014, discussing states like Texas where politicians continue to push antigay bills. "It's clearly not." HRC also announced in 2014 that it was opening field offices in Alabama, Arkansas, and Missouri and put $8.5 million toward its Project One America effort in the South.

Getting full equality under the law for every LGBT American may take a long time, but in the meantime, just as thousands of people did in rallying around Jennifer Tipton and Olivier Odom in taking on Dollywood, we can work collectively and change the culture and challenge homophobia, which can only help our efforts in the courts and the legislatures.

We can fight back in the creative ways we already have been using. When the two men in Pittsburgh, Texas, were told in May 2014 by

Big Earl's Bait House, "We don't serve fags here," people took to the Internet to write reviews on Yelp describing Big Earl's as the gayest place around. "Lovely place to bring your same-sex partner to and show how much you love him/her as much as their food! The more flamboyant, the better!" read one review. Another read, "On the positive side, it says, 'Bait House' but the place was more like a Bath House with all the horny Texas cowboys flirting and slapping each other's behinds. Very gay-friendly atmosphere!" (Yelp eventually removed these reviews, but only after they garnered a lot of online and media attention.) And a group of people from Dallas planned to make a trip to Pittsburgh to hold a queer eat-in.

Then there was Pamela Raintree, a Shreveport, Louisiana, transgender woman who appeared at a city council meeting in January 2014 to challenge city councilman Ron Webb, who'd proposed a repeal of an LGBT antidiscrimination ordinance that had passed three months earlier. Raintree addressed the council, stood in front of Webb, and lifted a stone high in the air. "Leviticus 20:13 states, 'If a man lie also with mankind as he lieth with a woman, they shall surely put him to death,'" Raintree said. "I brought the first stone, Mr. Webb, in case your Bible talk isn't just a smoke screen for personal prejudices."

Raintree told me in an interview on my show, "I saw him cast his eyes down when I slammed that rock down, and you could see on his face, 'Oh, this one's over.' He didn't make any public comment about it, so I'll never know. He whispered in the clerk's ear what he wanted to do. He didn't have a leg left to stand on." Shortly thereafter, Webb dropped his proposal, and Raintree's story went viral. Her stone has been donated to the local ACLU, which collects historical artifacts.

Raintree is a hero, as were all the people who challenged Big Earl's on Yelp and then headed there to eat, as is anyone who stands up and confronts bigotry. We can be heroes by speaking out, using traditional protests — marching and putting our bodies on the line — as well as online organizing and creative actions like Raintree's. Each instance of just being our fullest selves, resisting the victory narrative and not covering, moves the needle.

8

FIELDS OF COMBAT

MAJOR-LEAGUE BIAS AND THE END OF BIGOTRY

MANY HAVE CALLED THE WORLD of male professional team sports —
long seen as a bastion of straight-male masculinity — among the final
frontiers in confronting homophobia and bias against LGBT people
in American culture. Whatever you think of professional sports, its
powerful influence is impossible to escape. If LGBT people are to be
fully equal and respected in America, every institution as American
as apple pie must be transformed, and that certainly means the world
of male professional team sports. Only with equality on that playing
field will we be equal in the playing field of American society. And
if creating a legal framework for LGBT civil rights is a big lift, the
world of male professional team sports is, in many ways, the heavi-
est lift we have to make in changing American culture, requiring us
to wield enormous pressure and make demands, and not passively
follow the victory narrative. Not only is it important to create a space
where players can be openly gay, something we're only beginning to
see; it's also crucial that professional sports not tolerate homophobia
and transphobia and that its stars not telegraph to young people, who
look up to them as heroes, that queer bashing and discrimination are
acceptable. For the short term, this means making sure there is zero
tolerance for bigotry in sports; for the long term, it means raising
boys in our society without the homophobia and misogyny that are
still embedded within the culture of male team sports.

The Fallacy of the Insider-Only Strategy

Openly LGBT athletes in the wider world of sports, beyond the major leagues of male team sports, have struggled, but many have broken barriers in coming out and competing. It's true that transgender female athletes, in particular, face discrimination regarding whether they have an advantage over other female athletes. That charge runs counter to the rules of the International Olympic Committee, the National Collegiate Athletic Association, and other licensing boards, which have deemed that changes in hormones after transitioning diminish any advantage. Renée Richards fought to compete in tennis in the U.S. Open as far back as the 1970s, and Fallon Fox in recent years battled to compete in women's mixed martial arts. But openly gay, lesbian, and bisexual athletes outside the major leagues have experienced more acceptance and more breakthroughs for a longer period of time, evident from the careers of many individuals, from openly lesbian tennis legend Martina Navratilova to the young, openly gay current diving champion, Tom Daley. Sheryl Swoopes came out as gay in the Women's National Basketball Association in 2005. (A few years later she became engaged to a man, but she also made a point of not identifying herself as straight.) When WNBA player Brittney Griner came out as a lesbian matter-of-factly during an interview in 2013, there was, as *The Atlantic* noted, "a collective shrug." Griner's fellow player Ellen Delle Donne, on the WNBA team the Chicago Sky, was asked the question about having to share the locker room with other women that the media always seem to recite when an athlete comes out as gay or lesbian. Donne responded, "In our sport, we're fine with it . . . Hopefully the men can one day adopt that same attitude that we have." Compare that to the barrage of media attention and slew of homophobic tweets that followed Jason Collins's coming out in the NBA in that same year.

When it comes to changing attitudes among "the men," the conventional wisdom is that outside pressure on male professional team sports isn't effective and can even be counterproductive — and that only working on the inside, educating the coaches, owners, and players, is effective at creating change. I've been told this by many activists at LGBT groups and by gay journalists who cover the sports world. The thinking goes that the people who run professional sports — largely straight men — are playing to an audience of largely straight men, and they really don't care that much about gay people (and women), even if a great many fans are LGBT (and women). These observers are right that the leadership of male professional team sports is dominated by straight men. In 2011 I interviewed Rick Welts, the president of the Phoenix Suns, who that year became the first openly gay NBA executive when he came out. (Welts is now president of the Golden State Warriors.) He said he hoped others would follow, but he's still the only one. Major-league sports is far different from, say, the entertainment industry, where many openly gay as well as closeted gay people are in the upper echelons, running movie studios and television networks, playing to an audience that includes the vast majority of LGBT people, in addition to many other people.

But observers and critics are just plain wrong when they claim that professional sports doesn't respond to outside pressure. Every single institution responds to outside pressure to curb homophobia, provided enough pressure is ultimately brought to bear, particularly in a capitalist society, where money talks. Some Christian denominations have changed in America and now welcome gay, lesbian, bisexual, and transgender people, even blessing unions and supporting LGBT clergy. Even the Vatican, the archetype of conservative institutions, has been forced to respond to outside pressure in a changing culture within the West. I would argue that, partially because many of us may be indifferent or afraid, and partially because we've been busy taking on politicians and other culture makers, there's been very little pressure from the outside to date on male professional team sports regarding homophobia. And working only on the inside, as some groups are now doing, just isn't enough to make this vital change. Educating players, organizations, and fans is good work, and important work, but holding up those activities as a replacement for outside criticism and grassroots activism is counterproductive. Our history — and this book — has shown this to be true, time and again. Working only on the inside is gentle, a covering strategy, and for that reason it's very limited.

Yes, we can point to Jason Collins's example, as well as the first openly gay football player drafted, Michael Sam, and the strong support they both received from their respective league presidents. It's true that Collins, in announcing his retirement in November 2014, leaves Sam, as of this writing, as the only openly gay player in the big four major sports leagues. (The L.A. Galaxy's Robbie Rogers came out in Major League Soccer, which is slowly gaining in popularity.) And Sam's late-round draft pick only to be cut from the St. Louis Rams, and then eventually cut from even the Dallas Cowboys' practice squad, was suspect to some prominent sports analysts and could inhibit other players from coming out. But though Sam had these difficulties, and both he and Collins saw an avalanche of homophobia from some fans, a few players, and even some sports commentators when they initially came out, they received enormous positive support among many others both inside and outside professional sports, including the president and first lady. Their coming out was heralded in much of the media as a new day in their respective sports leagues.

Champions of Bigotry

Yet how is it that in 2014, the same year Michael Sam was drafted, the New York Giants could see fit to hire someone with clearly homophobic views to be the team's "director of player development"? Coach Tom Coughlin described the new job like this: "It is the working relationship with the players to aid them in their continuing education, their development as young men . . . It is there to help instruct them, make them aware of the issues and the problems that exist out in the community and the world to try to keep them focused on their job and not fall into trouble." The person the Giants chose to fill this role was former player David Tyree, a man who worked tirelessly to stop gay marriage, is connected to extreme Christian ideology, and has advocated for "pray-away-the-gay" therapy to "cure" gays of homosexuality. The hiring clearly suggested that the goal of creating an environment in which any player on the Giants team who might be thinking about coming out as gay or bisexual could feel comfortable — or an environment in which a player harboring or acting upon deep homophobia might have his views challenged — meant nothing to the team.

Tyree not only held beliefs opposed to homosexuality, he also spoke out loudly about them and joined the antigay National Organization for Marriage (NOM) as a spokesman in 2011. Tyree became a Super Bowl hero when the Giants faced the New England Patriots in 2008; he made a late-game catch that allowed the Giants moments later to score a touchdown and beat the previously undefeated Patriots. Tyree saw his catch as an act of God, what he called a "gift." But he told the *New York Daily News* in 2011 that he would trade the win at the Super Bowl to stop gay marriage. "Honestly, I would," he responded to a reporter who asked. "Being the fact that I firmly believe that God created and ordained marriage between a man and a woman, I believe that that's something that should be fought for at all costs," he added.

Tyree also said that the "gift" of the catch may have been God's way of helping him to prevent gays and lesbians from having equality. "Perhaps God orchestrated that play to give me a platform for what I'm doing here today: To urge political leaders all over our nation to reject same-sex marriage," he said.

That interview occurred during the same June week in which marriage equality was being debated in Albany and ultimately was passed and signed into law in New York State by Democratic governor Andrew Cuomo. But before it passed, there was intense lobbying from religious conservatives to stop it, and Tyree stood front and center in the effort, working for the National Organization for Marriage. Tyree made a video for NOM that week in which he said, "If this does pass, it will be the beginning of our country sliding toward — it's a strong word but — anarchy . . . That will be the moment our society loses its grip with what is right." He also took to Twitter during that time to vouch for the effectiveness of conversion therapy, saying he had "met former homosexuals. That's the #truth."

It would be unthinkable that a sports team or any private company would hire as an executive a person who had gone public with such open-faced disparaging comments about Jews, Latinos, or African Americans, no matter what religious beliefs he couched them in. To its credit, the Human Rights Campaign launched the first public criticism of Tyree's hire in 2014 and created headlines throughout the sports media, sending out a strongly worded press release and forcing the Giants to respond. This was actually quite out of character. Unlike their acknowledgment of defamation in most other areas, major LGBT groups have often remained relatively quiet in the face of homophobia in sports, buying into the idea that sports is different and that fighting homophobia there requires working from within; some people at GLAAD have told me as much. They often leave that work to other, newly formed groups that focus specifically on creating alliances for LGBT people in the world of sports, and they work with the leagues and teams in partnerships and rarely publicly criticize them. When San Francisco 49er Chris Culliver said in 2013, "We don't got no gay people on the team. You know, they gotta get up out of here if they do," for example, and calls for the team leadership to impose a harsh penalty on Culliver were extensively covered on TV news, groups like GLAAD stayed out of the spotlight. GLAAD, in fact, appeared satisfied with Culliver's issuing a boilerplate apology and going into "sensitivity training," when a fine, a suspension, or both would have been more appropriate.

Whatever the reason for HRC's speaking out about Tyree, it was both unusual (GLAAD remained relatively silent again) and good. The Giants seemed taken aback. Responding to criticism, the Giants' general manager, Jerry Reese, said, "Sometimes you say some things that maybe you don't want to say or shouldn't have said and can get blown out of proportion to some degree. But I'm not here to talk about social issues or somebody's personal opinion about their beliefs." But if Tyree had said "some things that maybe [he didn't] want to say," then he needed to clarify that much earlier. It no longer is acceptable to say that the "belief" that gays can convert to heterosexuality is a belief that should be respected.

The NFL at the time was coasting on lofty words of support for gay players and against intolerance, having put out a positive statement about Michael Sam's draft, welcoming an openly gay player to the NFL. Days before the Tyree hire, another homophobic outburst had come from former NFL coach Tony Dungy, who said he wouldn't have drafted Sam, not because he's not a good player but simply because he's gay and would be some sort of distraction. That was flat-out bigotry, and Dungy's clarification — that he gave an "honest answer" and did believe "the media attention that comes with it will be a distraction" — did little to change his original comments. The St. Louis Rams coach responded that Sam was "not a distraction" of any kind, but there was silence from NFL officials. In November 2014, in a revealing and insulting display of hypocrisy, Dungy, who said he wouldn't have drafted Michael Sam because he's a "distraction," said that he would welcome back with open arms Ray Rice — the Baltimore Ravens running back who had punched out his then fiancée in an elevator earlier in the year and was the center of a massive furor, eventually suspended indefinitely by the NFL — if he "learned from his mistake," as if Rice's presence would not be a "distraction" of any kind.

Major-League Covering

HRC's criticism of Tyree was short-lived; after one more press release on the matter, it dropped the issue. The controversy died quickly, largely because the Giants were given cover by the You Can Play Project, one of the insider groups partnered with the NFL, whose direc-

tor criticized HRC in the media for speaking out. You Can Play was
cofounded in 2012 by its current president, Patrick Burke, a straight
ally of gay rights (his deceased brother was a gay athlete) who cofounded the group to help try to make sports more gay-affirming.
Burke works for the National Hockey League and obviously has many
connections and friendships within the world of professional sports.
After he criticized HRC, openly gay former NFL player and You Can
Play's executive director Wade Davis further helped the Giants get
past the controversy. Davis does some important work with the teams
and coaches, including with the Giants, attending events and educating about homophobia. This time, Davis wrote a blog post saying he'd
met Tyree in the past and had spoken with him after the hire, and that
Tyree had given him a statement. "He approached me [at an event in
the past], introduced himself, offered his hand and said, 'I want you
to know I really respect what you do,'" Davis wrote. "After having the
opportunity to speak with David, I realized he is on a journey when it
comes to understanding the LGBT community. He is evolving." And
then Davis reiterated the statement Tyree gave him to give to the public: "My interactions with Wade over the past few months are much
more representative of my current beliefs toward the gay community
than some tweets from several years ago. Christianity teaches us love,
compassion, and respect for our fellow man, and it is in that light that
I will continue to work with Wade and others to better serve the gay
community. I would absolutely support any player on the Giants who
identified as gay, in any way I could. And I will continue to stay in
touch with Wade to ensure I am aware of the right ways to do that."

But the blog post left important questions unanswered; giving a
statement to an advocate working with the teams wasn't satisfactory.
Tyree refused to give journalists interviews that might allow him to
be quoted directly and to engage in a dialogue. In a column headlined
DAVID TYREE HIRE A BAD MOVE FOR GIANTS, the widely read
ESPN sportswriter Dan Graziano noted, "While I don't think wrongheaded views should necessarily prevent a person from seeking and
holding a job in his chosen field, I'm surprised that the Giants would

make such a tone-deaf move in the current NFL and social climate . . . and Tyree declined to comment about the criticism when contacted by ESPN New York.com."

Cyd Zeigler, a gay, longtime sports journalist at the site *Outsports* (which he cofounded), made a video in which he stated that he, like Davis, had spoken with Tyree and that Tyree doesn't support conversion therapy and "doesn't even know what conversion therapy is." There was no evidence of the back-and-forth discussion journalists engage in with a subject — and no quotes of any kind, in fact. Again, Tyree had refused to speak for himself. Zeigler also criticized those who aren't working as insiders in sports, as if criticism from the outside were useless or counterproductive.

The claim that Tyree knows nothing about conversion therapy was also difficult to fathom. Just two weeks before, on Twitter, Tyree lamented that there are not enough men for "single Christian women," because too many men are "effeminate." He also had retweeted a tweet from a religious-based therapist who promotes "ex-gay" therapy, Meg Meeker: "We must be bold enough to throw aside political maneuvering and do what's right for our kids." Meeker, on her Facebook page, promoted her radio show: "What would you do if your son or daughter came home from college to tell you that they're gay? How would you respond? On today's broadcast, Dr. Christopher Yuan and his mom Angela will share how God not only brought Christopher out of a life of homosexuality and into a relationship with himself, but healed Angela's broken heart." (David Tyree's Twitter feed was completely deleted soon after HRC's press release criticizing him was issued.)

Within days of Tyree's hire, a watchdog of the religious right, Rachel Tabachnick at Political Research Associates, unearthed Tyree's business and religious connections to "apostle" Kimberly Daniels, whom he called his "spiritual mother" and with whom he coauthored a book in 2008 about his career and his religious beliefs, *More Than Just the Catch*. She's at the forefront of an extreme Christian movement, the New Apostolic Reformation, which believes in a complete religious takeover of government. Following what is known as "Seven Mountains" theology, the group professes that Christians must control — and place individuals at the top of — the "seven pillars of society," from government and media to the worlds of business and entertainment, including sports. Daniels is an avowed "demon buster" and wrote a book in 2009 that included a "prayer against the homosexual agenda" and a "confession to come out of homosexuality/lesbianism."

Winning with Outside Pressure

I don't mean to single out You Can Play, the Giants, the NFL, or David Tyree. There are other groups that work on the inside with other teams and leagues and that also might not be likely to offer criticism. And in other leagues as well, like the NBA, we've seen antigay outbursts from players, with only minor penalties incurred.

In 2012 Amar'e Stoudemire of the New York Knicks lashed out at a critic on Twitter, calling him a "fag!" He received a mere $50,000 fine, a pittance for an NBA player whom the Knicks had signed to a five-year, $100 million contract, and wasn't suspended; it's likely his punishment would have been much more severe if he'd slurred any other group. Matt Barnes of the Los Angeles Clippers, arrested in 2013 on an outstanding warrant, called the arresting officer a "fucking faggot"; the NBA didn't penalize him at all. A gay caterer in 2014 alleged that several members of the Houston Rockets taunted him with antigay slurs while he was setting up in the locker room at the Barclays Center in Brooklyn. "Get this faggot out of here!" the lawsuit alleges was said. "He's trying to catch a sneaky peeky!" The caterer alleges in the suit that the incident was witnessed by a member of the Brooklyn Nets staff, who urged him to "just leave." He said he received a formal apology from the Nets senior vice president of human resources. (As of this writing the Nets have yet to publicly respond.) In 2013 Roy Hibbert of the Indiana Pacers blurted out "no homo" while laughing, speaking at a press conference, and received a mild, $75,000 fine. Sports columnist Dave Zirin of *The Nation* got it right when he criticized the NBA, whose commissioner, David Stern, had also spoken against homophobia in the past: "The NBA had an opportunity to say and do something about anti-gay bigotry and draw a line in the sand. They could have announced all kinds of systemic reforms aimed at dealing with this head-on . . ."

Some leagues and teams have been better, particularly recently. Major League Baseball in 2014 partnered with the group Athlete Ally and hired openly gay former player Billy Bean as its first "ambassador of inclusion," announcing it was taking a stand against "homophobia and transphobia in sports." The Chicago White Sox, in the summer of 2014, announced it would begin sponsoring LGBT Pride Night: Out with the Sox, in partnership with Equality Illinois. In December 2014, an MLB umpire, Dale Scott, came out as gay, and was supported by the league.

I raise the example of David Tyree and the Giants, however, to make the point that, just as in all other areas where we've made change, both insiders working with the team and, perhaps most importantly, outsiders putting on intense pressure are necessary. It's vital that the teams send a message, right now, to young people that homophobia is not accepted. And that means giving more than a slap on the wrist for homophobic comments and actions, and it means not hiring virulently antigay individuals in prominent positions.

When Ray Rice brutally pummeled his then fiancée, Janay Palmer, and the NFL initially gave him a mere three-game suspension in July 2014, it took just that kind of outside pressure to get the league to suspend him indefinitely a month later. It was only after uproar from activists on the outside, after a new video of Rice attacking his fiancée in an elevator went viral on *TMZ*, that NFL commissioner Roger Goodell responded with the harsher penalty. An online community of more than eight hundred thousand women, UltraViolet, flew a banner over MetLife Stadium in New Jersey during an Arizona Cardinals–New York Giants game, calling for Goodell to resign. A black women's coalition, the Black Women's Roundtable, which includes leaders of various women's groups, demanded a meeting with Goodell, bringing a petition with thousands of names and focusing on procedures for anti-domestic-violence training that were necessary. Goodell promised action and more meetings as the media spotlight was directed on him. NFL sponsors such as McDonald's, Campbell's Soup, and FedEx were pressured to speak out and criticize the NFL, worried about their brands. U.S. senators, including Kirsten Gillibrand of New York and Richard Blumenthal of Connecticut, lambasted the league. Discussions erupted in Congress and among city and state government leaders about ending massive tax breaks that the NFL receives. The league has nonprofit status, yet Goodell made more than $44 million in the previous year. (In November 2014, an arbitrator reinstated Rice, granting his appeal based solely on the NFL's shifting position on a penalty due to public pressure, underscoring why the NFL must mandate a harsher penalty for domestic abuse from the outset.)

Domestic violence is far more urgent and severe than verbal slurs. But we can also see how the campaign to get the Washington Redskins to change its racist name — a slur against Native Americans — has involved outside activism, protests, and pressure on companies and politicians to speak out against the team's owner and demand action. Hundreds of people protested in November 2013 in Minneapolis, for example, where the city council passed a resolution calling on the team to change its name. So did the Washington, D.C., City Council, and fifty U.S. senators signed a letter demanding the team change the name. Many sports analysts believe it's only a matter of time until the team's owner relents. We saw the same pressure from the outside on the NBA and the Los Angeles Clippers in 2014 when that team's owner, Donald Sterling, was revealed to have made horribly racist comments and was forced to sell the team. Sterling's remarks even inspired California legislators to pass a bill prohibiting team owners from exempting league fines on their taxes, a bill Governor Jerry Brown promptly signed.

Liberating Everyone

When we don't demand similar actions in regard to homophobic slurs and behavior, we're engaging in the very covering that had gay pundits and opinion leaders fretting over Brendan Eich's resignation when we should expect a workplace that does not condone homophobia. We're buying into the victory narrative, thinking that complete acceptance will come on its own, succumbing to victory blindness rather than speaking out forcefully and loudly. When it comes to antigay actions and slurs in the major leagues, we've seen hardly any outside pressure — certainly not from major gay groups, let alone politicians urging action at those groups' behest — while advocates still believe in the strategy of working only on the inside.

The closest we've come is when seventeen state lawmakers in Minnesota sent a strongly worded letter to the Minnesota Vikings owner demanding much more serious response after special-teams coordinator Mike Priefer had said, "We should round up all the gays, send them to an island, then nuke them until it glows." Written by openly gay state senator Scott Dibble in August 2014 and copied to Governor Mark Dayton, the letter demanded the Vikings give Priefer a harsher penalty and raised the issue of the tax breaks that the Vikings get from the state. Priefer was given a three-game suspension — reduced to two games if he completed sensitivity training, which he did — although many expected that after making such extreme statements he'd be fired.

Priefer had made the comments to a group of players in the locker room, including Chris Kluwe, the Vikings punter who became a champion of marriage equality and who was later cut from the team. Kluwe alleged that his advocacy was the reason for his being cut and threatened a lawsuit; he told me on my show that Priefer made derogatory comments about gays in front of him several times. The Vikings undertook an investigation. Priefer at first denied making the remarks several times, but then admitted to it after witnesses corroborated what Kluwe said. (Kluwe settled with the Vikings for undisclosed donations to five LGBT organizations over a five-year period and for an agreement that the Vikings would host a symposium on LGBT issues and athletes in the spring of 2015.)

Senator Dibble came on my show to discuss the letter to the Vikings' owner, which threatened to withdraw continued tax breaks the Vikings expected, noting that its new stadium had been paid for by taxpayers as well. "Mike Priefer said something that was pretty horrendous," he explained. "And he lied about it repeatedly . . . No one has really ever contemplated what exactly he said. And it's been dismissed in various reports including by leadership of the Vikings, as, 'Well, you know, people say these things. He said it in jest. He's a good man, etc., etc.' It wasn't just homophobic, it was genocidal. It was violent. It was really horrific. And when you contemplate it for just a second, if he had said let's destroy all African American people, let's destroy all Jewish people in this country, let's put them on an island and nuke it until it glows — that's what he said — he wouldn't have his job today."

What Senator Scott Dibble did was enormously important, getting politicians to pressure a team and publicly shaming the team owners and the league. It probably helped in getting the team to settle with Kluwe and to donate money to LGBT groups; but without much more support and a sustained campaign, it clearly wasn't enough to have the Vikings invoke a harsher penalty, as the issue died down. Until there is sustained pressure from the outside, that will continue to happen.

Ultimately, however, harsher penalties and getting the leaders in the leagues, the team owners, and the players to take these issues seriously are a Band-Aid approach, even if they are necessary now to stem the message of hate being sent to young people. The real change for the future has to begin in our schools, within the sports programs themselves — where homophobia and misogyny are still condoned. While activists have been able to make change in many places, it's still too routine for high school and college coaches in male team sports to demean the players during training by calling them "girls" or "ladies" if they don't perform well, or even going further, calling them "pussies" and "pansies." And what are these terms really all about? The idea that women are less than men, and that being less than a real man — whether that means being like a woman or being like a homo — is the worst thing you can possibly be.

That has to stop in all sports programs, and education needs to begin. And it needs to happen in our classrooms, too, which brings us back to California's pioneering law that will mandate the teaching of LGBT history and the contributions to American history of prominent people who were gay, lesbian, bisexual, or transgender — something we must make happen in all fifty states. Only when heterosexual young people are taught at the earliest ages about gay and lesbian and bisexual and transgender people will they understand and connect with LGBT people as fellow humans and not as people to be mocked. And only when everyone, gay and straight, whatever his or her gender, is taught about sexual orientation and gender identity and understands the complexities will we see masculinity redefined for men in a way that is not about promoting misogyny and homophobia and transphobia.

As I said at the beginning of this chapter, this will be quite a heavy lift. But look at how far LGBT Americans have come in such a short period of time. We went from invisibility, derision, and shame, through a time of loss and death of unimaginable proportions and society's indifference, to, now, marriage equality across the land and so many LGBT people standing tall and proud. We now also have the collective force of so many allies — parents, friends, educators, coworkers, and other supporters of full equality. There's no reason why we can't go much, much further. It's about breaking a cycle that continues into adulthood and then is passed down to the next generation. It's about liberating everyone, including straight men, who also often feel they must conform to a rigid idea of masculinity, and it's about upholding values that don't confine women to constricting gender norms. And for gay, lesbian, bisexual, and transgender people, it means getting beyond mere tolerance and winning true equality.

CHARTING A PATH FORWARD

IT'S TIME FOR ALL OF US—gay, lesbian, bisexual, and transgender people; heterosexual family, friends, and coworkers; and all progressives and anyone of any political party or persuasion who claims to believe in equality—to stop accepting mere "tolerance" or half-hearted measures. If we don't, we will never see full equality. In fact, it's time for us to be *intolerant*—intolerant of all forms of homophobia, transphobia, and bigotry against LGBT people. People often use the phrase "let's agree to disagree" when they respect but do not share the different positions of their friends or colleagues. But it's time that all of us who support LGBT equality no longer agree to disagree on full civil rights for LGBT people. Anything less than full acceptance and full civil rights must be defined as an expression of bias, whether implicit or explicit. And it has to be called out—even if that means challenging our friends, coworkers, and others we know and respect —if we're to get beyond tolerance.

There are steps we can all take in our lives right now and every day to move forward, each individual working with others to create a powerful force that can't be held back. Here are seven actions that every gay, lesbian, bisexual, and transgender person and all allies of full equality should think about deeply, encourage in others, or take themselves:

Break from victory blindness, and scrap the victory narrative. It's empowering and necessary to talk about our wins and celebrate them when they occur. But as the gay philanthropist Tim Gill noted, the achievement of gay rights isn't inevitable. You have to make it happen. Equality supporters have won some battles, even major ones, but that doesn't mean we'll win the long war against bigotry, nor does it give us any assurance of when that might happen. We need only look to other movements to see how gains have been rolled back in ways that would have seemed unimaginable forty years ago, from voting rights for minorities to access to contraception for women. We can't let our wins convince us we're offending people or pushing too hard — or not being "magnanimous" — when we demand full equality now and refuse to accept mere tolerance. Be aware that we'll likely have to defend hard-fought wins, push for further gains, beat back our enemies, and battle bias and violence for generations to come. Empowered with that realization — that knowledge — march forward and fight the backlash that is surely under way.

Stop covering, and reject the covering demand. For those of us who have come out and declared our sexual orientation or gender identity, the struggle doesn't simply end when we've told those around us the truth about ourselves. Every day we have to strive not to cover — not to play down who we are — and to resist the covering demand. And that goes for our allies, too, who must understand how and why the covering demand exists in order to stop enabling its enforcement. It also means giving both Hollywood and the media clear guidelines on why covering is wrong. Demand that they stop colluding with the powerful to preserve the glass closet, which makes us invisible and still treats being queer as if it's a dirty little secret. Call for a rejection of slurs and bigotry by pop-culture figures and sports stars, and in Hollywood portrayals, and call for real penalties for such actions. We can vote with our wallets and our viewing habits — and use social media, websites, and blogs in all the ways they've been harnessed in recent years — to demand true, realistic portrayals on television, in films, and in popular culture that more accurately reflect the complex lives of LGBT people. That means including our struggle for equality and for physical and emotional well-being, as well as the threat of violence against us. It means not making concessions to the sensibilities of those who might be uncomfortable with homosexuality and transgender people. If being ourselves makes some people uncomfortable, so be it. Challenging them may be the only way to (for lack of a better word) desensitize them to who we truly are.

Teach self-defense and self-empowerment. Let's use every tool available — certainly for LGBT youth, but also for adults — to empower people to stand strong. We need to build the self-esteem and fortitude to stand up to bullies and bashers, and that means learning how to defend ourselves emotionally as well as physically. And everyone who supports equality needs to encourage self-empowerment, including parents. Not only will this help us all, young and old, in the here and now, but also it will build the kind of self-confidence and fortitude it takes to defeat gay bashers in the legislatures, in the media, and throughout society.

Revolutionize education. We need to galvanize people in a way that makes them invested in changing our schools and making sure that LGBT history and culture are taught in an age-appropriate way as part of the curriculum from kindergarten through twelfth grade. The onus here also has to be on all parents who support equality, to make their own kids aware that LGBT people exist and are among both their classmates and their classmates' parents. Parents themselves need to be aware that teaching this vital history is about creating a safe, hostility-free environment for all, including their children. This is the core long-term strategy to stop bullying, bias, and bigotry well into the future and to make sure all children mature into adults who feel accepted for who they are and who don't discriminate against others. Our nation's schools have a responsibility to cut through the lies and distortions that people may learn in their homes, at their churches, and on the streets. Let's take California's lead and commit to passing laws in all fifty states that require teaching the contributions of LGBT Americans in history in all public schools — and get the existing "no promo homo" laws in several states repealed. That would truly revolutionize education nationally by doing something both simple and profound: teaching the truth.

Tell the media the debate is over. Under the pretense of offering "balanced" coverage, the media continually rehash debates that have been settled for years, and invite religious leaders to represent the "other side" rather than calling on legitimate experts (particularly in medicine and mental health). When it comes to LGBT civil rights, as with other marginalized groups, our fundamental personhood is not an issue that has two sides. Again, it's about no longer agreeing to disagree; that debate has come to an end. What I'm proposing isn't censorship; it's a matter of the media's responsibility for their choices about which voices to showcase or not. Every individual has a constitutional right to free speech — but no one has a right to appear on a television talk show. When the media legitimize people who promote hate against LGBT people, we can easily use social media to express our outrage and tell the reporters, editors, and producers responsible that they've made a mistake. We've seen people, sometimes just one person, begin a critique that goes viral and forces the media to apologize or make amends for defamation. Each of us has the power to take on TV, print, and online news media and demand a new standard for how discussions about gay and transgender issues are dealt with in the public sphere.

Settle for nothing less than full civil rights. Incrementalism is dead. Piecemeal approaches and exemptions have not served us well, and, moving forward, we simply cannot accept them. Let's not rest until we pass all the laws needed, from repealing HIV-criminalization laws and aggressively promoting HIV prevention to fighting bullying in schools and ending all discrimination in the military. Demand full civil rights in employment, in housing, in public accommodations, in banking, in education, and throughout every institution, either with a comprehensive bill — an LGBT Equality Act — or even with LGBT people being added to the Civil Rights Act. Prepare for a fight. Pressure, call, and e-mail LGBT leaders — who too often can revert back to incremental thinking, even after they swear it off — as well as Democratic and Republican politicians, and let your voice be heard. Use your money to back campaigns, and withhold money from those who don't support equality; push presidential candidates who want our votes and money to pledge support for a full civil rights bill, and accept nothing less. If you can, organize protests. Confront politicians in the streets, at their events. Get involved in campaigning for those who work for equality. Plan for marching on Washington again. And, again, use the power of social media and blogs to create pressure, whether on an antigay politician or a homophobic business, letting your voice be heard. And don't delay — the time is now.

Develop a new attitude that is uncompromising and empowering. Defend yourself, resist the covering demand, settle for nothing less than full civil rights and true equality, and no longer agree to disagree — all of that and more adds up to a whole new attitude. There will be an impulse now to accept less than what we deserve, especially with conservative and Republican voices increasingly proposing that we cut deals and make compromises on equality. With your bold new attitude, draw a line in the sand. Tell yourself that mere acceptance and mere tolerance are not enough. From now on, you live in a world beyond tolerance.

ACKNOWLEDGMENTS

THIS BOOK AROSE FROM DISCUSSIONS that took place over a period of several years with my friend and literary agent Rob Weisbach. I'm grateful for his enormous drive, his passion about important issues, and his encouragement. Rob's editorial colleague David Groff, a gifted poet and writer, and also a longtime friend, was instrumental to this project as well. Many thanks to him for offering his keen eye and his activist spirit.

I'm indebted to the listeners of my radio program on SiriusXM, many of whose thoughts and experiences are reflected in these pages. I'm thankful as well to the great many LGBT, progressive, and conservative activists, authors, scholars, bloggers, educators, medical professionals, journalists, psychotherapists, politicians, parents, researchers, students, attorneys, and so many others who have been guests on my show and who informed me and this book, even when we disagreed. Thanks to SiriusXM's Scott Greenstein and Dave Gorab for believing in me and in the show for these nearly twelve years. The program director of SiriusXM Progress and my former producer, David Guggenheim; my producer, Sean Bertollo; my associate producer, Matthew McDonough; my former associate producer, Morgan Hahn; and my former producer, Anthony Veneziano have, over the years, all been crucial to this project, bringing in many of the show guests and inspiring many of the topics of discussion on the program that came to be highlighted in this book.

Arianna Huffington gave me an amazing platform to facilitate on-line discussions vital to LGBT people when she brought me on board as editor at large of *Huffington Post* Gay Voices in 2011, for which I'll forever be grateful. Those important discussions from Gay Voices are reflected in these pages. Gay Voices' executive editor, Noah Michelson, has been a great and supportive friend, and an inspiration. Our daily chats and his editorial brilliance energized me in writing on many issues, and I thank him for that. Thanks as well to the entire Gay Voices team, including editor Curtis Wong, reporter Lila Shapiro, and associate editor James Nichols. And a special thanks to deputy blog editor Clay Chiles, who edited my essays for *HuffPost*, many ideas from which are reflected in *It's Not Over*.

I'm grateful to have had a very talented editor at Houghton Mifflin Harcourt, Ben Hyman. He worked with me closely from early on in shaping *It's Not Over*, remaining passionate about this endeavor and meticulously helping me to express my ideas and tell the many important stories that appear in the book. Many thanks to Andrea Schulz, Houghton Mifflin Harcourt's editor in chief, who immediately saw why the issues and themes in this book were critical to focus on right now, and who guided the process. My copy editor on this book, Tammy Zambo, went above and beyond, and I'm thankful for her work and her input.

A big thank-you to my friend Andy Towle, founder of the LGBT news and culture blog *Towleroad*, with whom I've spent many hours, online and over drinks, chatting about ideas and events we both focus on daily, many of which are recounted in these pages. Similarly, thanks to my friends Joe Sudbay and Mike Rogers, not only for always being available to run an idea by or to read over some material; they both also guest-hosted my show while I took time off to write this book. My friend Sally Milner sparked a moment of clarity for me on the book, and I thank her for that and for her support. I'm grateful, too, to J. P. Cheuvront, Sandy Girard, and Mario Ruiz, who helped in other ways on this project.

And so much thanks to David, now my husband, who is always there for me, going on an amazing twenty years.

NOTES

Author's Note

page

x *become more informed of the ongoing conversation:* For more on the personal and political issues faced by transgender people regarding being open about gender identity, see Jamison Green, *Becoming a Visible Man* (Nashville: Vanderbilt University Press, 2004); Janet Mock, *Redefining Realness: My Path to Womanhood, Identity, Love, and So Much More* (New York: Atria Books, 2014); and Laura Erickson-Schroth, ed., *Trans Bodies, Trans Selves: A Resource for the Transgender Community* (Oxford: Oxford University Press, 2014).

1. Victory Blindness

2 *"proud to be gay":* Tim Cook, "Tim Cook Speaks Up," *Bloomberg Business Week,* October 30, 2014, http://www.businessweek.com /articles/2014-10-30/tim-cook-im-proud-to-be-gay.

3 *spiking 27% in New York City:* Sharon Stapel, "Are We a Stone's Throw from an Epidemic of Anti-LGBTQ Violence?," *Huffington Post,* June 12, 2014, http://www.huffingtonpost.com/sharon-stapel /anti-lgbtq-violence_b_5489853.html.
   In Seattle: Gene Balk, "Data: Seattle Has Third-Highest Rate of Anti-LGBT Hate Crimes," *FYI Guy* (blog), *Seattle Times,* June 6, 2014, http://blogs.seattletimes.com/fyi-guy/2014/06/06/data-seattle

-has-third-highest-rate-of-anti-lgbt-hate-crimes/; Hana Kim, "Hate
Crime Increasing Against LGBT Community, Group Says," Q13
FOX News (Seattle), August 30, 2013, http://q13fox.com/2013/08/30
/group-says-hate-crime-is-increasing-against-lgbt-community/.

a man pleaded guilty: Mike Carter, "Man Pleads Guilty to Arson at
Seattle Gay Nightclub," *The Today File* (blog), *Seattle Times,* May 2,
2014, http://blogs.seattletimes.com/today/2014/05/suspect-in-arson
-at-seattle-gay-nightclub-to-enter-plea/.

In Philadelphia: Kelly Bayliss, "Group Attacks Gay Couple in Center
City: Police," NBC10.com (Philadelphia), September 13, 2014, http://
www.nbcphiladelphia.com/news/local/2-Gay-Men-Attacked-by
-Group-Center-City-274964621.html.

4   *Three people were later arrested:* "Hearing for Center City Gay
Bashing Suspects," NBC10.com (Philadelphia), September 30, 2014,
http://www.nbcphiladelphia.com/news/local/Center-City-Gay
-Couple-Beating-Court-277617881.html.

The video shows: Cavin Sieczkowski, "Watch: Family Has Horrifying,
Violent Reaction to Son's Coming Out as Gay," *Huffington Post,*
August 28, 2014, http://www.huffingtonpost.com/2014/08/28/family
-son-coming-out-gay-video_n_5731462.html.

between 30% and 40% of teen suicides: Suicide Prevention Resource
Center, *Suicide Risk and Prevention for Lesbian, Gay, Bisexual, and
Transgender Youth* (Newton, Mass.: Education Development Center,
2008), http://www.sprc.org/sites/sprc.org/files/library/SPRC_LGBT
_Youth.pdf.

Christian therapists wouldn't accept her: Gillian Mohney, "Leelah
Alcorn: Transgender Teen's Reported Suicide Note Makes Dramatic
Appeal," ABC News, December 31, 2014, http://abcnews.go.com
/US/leelah-alcorn-transgender-teens-reported-suicide-note-makes
/story?id=27912326.

victim's eyes were rejected: Ryan Weber, "After Suicide, Gay Teens
Eye Donation Rejected," *Washington Post,* August 15, 2014, http://
www.washingtonpost.com/news/morning-mix/wp/2014/08/15/gay
-teens-organ-donation-rejected/.

5   *individual's sexual orientation:* Sabrina Tevernise, "F.D.A. Easing Ban
on Gays, to Let Some Give Blood," *New York Times,* December 23,
2014, http://www.nytimes.com/2014/12/24/health/fda-lifting-ban-on
-gay-blood-donors.html?_r=0.

A Texas gay couple: Michelangelo Signorile, "Jason Hanna and Joe Riggs, Texas Gay Fathers, Denied Legal Parenthood of Twin Sons," *Huffington Post,* June 18, 2014, http://www.huffingtonpost .com/2014/06/18/jason-hanna-and-joe-riggs_n_5506720.html.

6 *the one laid out by Susan Faludi:* Susan Faludi, preface to *Backlash: The Undeclared War Against American Women* (New York: Three Rivers Press, 2006).

one of the prominent recent histories: Linda R. Hirshman, *Victory: The Triumphant Gay Revolution* (New York: Harper, 2012).

7 *ignited a firestorm on Twitter:* Deborah Netburn, "Brendan Eich's Prop. 8 Contribution Gets Twittersphere Buzzing," *Los Angeles Times,* April 4, 2012, http://articles.latimes.com/2012/apr/04 /business/la-fi-tn-brendan-eich-prop-8-contribution-20120404.

three Mozilla board members resigned: Alistair Barr, "Three Mozilla Board Members Resign over Choice of New CEO," *Digits* (blog), *Wall Street Journal,* March 28, 2014, http://blogs.wsj.com /digits/2014/03/28/three-mozilla-board-members-resign over -choice-of-new-ceo/

8 *As* The New Yorker's *James Surowiecki explained it:* James Surowiecki, "How Mozilla Lost Its C.E.O.," *The New Yorker,* April 4, 2014, http://www.newyorker.com/business/currency/how-mozilla -lost-its-c-e-o.

The high-tech company Rarebit: "Goodbye, Firefox Marketplace," *Rarebit* (blog), March 24, 2014, http://www.teamrarebit.com/blog /2014/03/24/goodbye_firefox_marketplace.

"People think we were upset": "A Sad 'Victory,'" *Rarebit* (blog), April 3, 2104, http://www.teamrarebit.com/blog/2014/04/03/a-sad -victory.

Next, CREDO Mobile: "Mozilla Stands Up for Equality," *CREDO Action,* accessed October 16, 2014, http://credoaction.com/mozilla _equality/. Credo removed its original petition and now lauds Mozilla.

people navigating to the dating site OkCupid: Mario Aguilar, "OKCupid Website Blocks Firefox Because of Mozilla CEO's Anti-gay Beliefs," *Gizmodo* (blog), Kinja, March 3, 2014, http://gizmodo. com/okcupid-tells-users-not-to-use-firefox-because-of-ceos-1555616237.

Mozilla defended the decision: "Mozilla Supports LGBT Equality,"

The Mozilla Blog, March 29, 2014, https://blog.mozilla.org/blog
/2014/03/29/mozilla-supports-lgbt-equality/.

Eich was adamant: James Ball, "Mozilla CEO Insists He Won't
Resign over 'Private' Support for Gay Marriage Ban" (editorial),
The Guardian, April 2, 2014, http://www.theguardian.com
/technology/2014/apr/01/mozilla-ceo-brendan-eich-refuses-to-quit.

9   *he donated $1,000 to Pat Buchanan:* Alex Hern and James Ball,
"Mozilla CEO Donated to Rightwing Candidates, Records
Show," *The Guardian,* April 2, 2014, http://www.theguardian.
com/technology/2014/apr/02/controversial-mozilla-ceo-made
-donations-right-wing-candidates-brendan-eich.

"The poor homosexuals": Patrick J. Buchanan, "Is Catholicism Now
'Unacceptable'?," The American Cause, June 6, 2006, http://www
.theamericancause.org/print/062006_print.htm.

In 2008 it was revealed: Jamie Kirchick, "Angry White Man," *The
New Republic,* January 8, 2008, http://www.newrepublic.com/article
/politics/angry-white-man.

"morally unfit inclination": Linda Smith, "United States House of
Representatives: History, Art & Archives" (fact sheet), accessed
October 16, 2014, http://history.house.gov/People/Detail/21861.

10   *" 'If you call a tail a leg' ":* Patrick McGreevy, "Tom McClintock
Speaks Out on Farm Animal, Gay Marriage Measures," *L.A. Now*
(blog), *Los Angeles Times,* October 21, 2008, http://latimesblogs.
latimes.com/lanow/2008/10/mcclintock----n.html.

On my radio show and following: *The Michelangelo Signorile Show,*
SiriusXM Progress 127, April 3, 2014.

11   *"We must do better":* Mitchell Baker, "Brendan Eich Steps Down as
Mozilla CEO," *The Mozilla Blog,* April 3, 2014, https://blog.mozilla.
org/blog/2014/04/03/brendan-eich-steps-down-as-mozilla-ceo/.

"Brendan Eich is a tech legend": Markos Moulitsas, "Brandon Eich
Was a Victim of Market Forces, Conservatives Should Applaud,"
Daily Kos (blog), April 4, 2014, http://www.dailykos.com/story
/2014/04/04/1289639/-Brandon-Eich-was-a-victim-of-market
-forces-conservatives-should-applaud.

12   *only four Republican U.S. senators:* Igor Volsky, "Susan Collins
Becomes Fourth Republican Senator to Support Same-Sex
Marriage," *Think Progress,* June 25, 2014, http://thinkprogress.org

/lgbt/2014/06/25/3453486/susan-collins-becomes-fourth
-republican-senator-to-support-same-sex-marriage/.
Only fifteen Republican House members: "House Vote 638 — Repeals
'Don't Ask, Don't Tell,'" *New York Times,* December 15, 2010, http://
politics.nytimes.com/congress/votes/111/house/2/638.
only ten Republicans joined: Burgess Everett, "Senate Passes Gay
Rights Bill in Historic Vote," *Politico,* November 7, 2013, http://www
.politico.com/story/2013/11/enda-vote-senate-99538.html.
oil giant Exxon Mobil: Associated Press, "Exxon Mobil Says It'll
Follow New Anti-bias Rules," July 22, 2014, *Yahoo! News,* http://
news.yahoo.com/exxon-mobil-says-itll-anti-bias-rules-200433392
.html.

13   *"The guy who had the gall":* Andrew Sullivan, "The Hounding of a
Heretic," *The Dish* (blog), April 3, 2014, http://dish.andrewsullivan
.com/2014/04/03/the-hounding-of-brendan-eich/.
an avalanche of criticism: Andrew Sullivan, "The Hounding
of a Heretic, Ctd," The Dish (blog), April 3, 2014, http://dish.
andrewsullivan.com/2014/04/03/the-hounding-of-a-heretic-ctd/.
"broader" than that: Andrew Sullivan, "Dissents of the Day,"
The Dish (blog), April 4, 2014, http://dish.andrewsullivan.
com/2014/04/04/dissents-of-the-day-63/.
one headline blared: Warner Todd Huston, "Andrew Sullivan:
Brendan Eich's Ouster as Mozilla CEO 'Disgusts Me,'"
Breitbart.com, April 3, 2014, http://www.breitbart.com/Big
-Journalism/2014/04/03/Andrew-Sullivan-Brendan-Eich-s-Ouster
-from-Mozilla-Disgusts-Me.
The website Daily Caller: Brendan Bordelon, "Gay Journalist
Andrew Sullivan 'Disgusted' by Gay Rights 'Fanaticism' After
Mozilla CEO Resigns," *The Daily Caller,* April 4, 2014, http://
dailycaller.com/2014/04/04/andrew-sullivan-disgusted-by-gay
-rights-fanaticism-mozilla/.

14   *"the new fascism":* Kate Tummarello, "Mozilla CEO Faced 'New
Fascism,' Gingrich Says," *The Hill,* April 6, 2014, http://thehill
.com/policy/technology/202764-mozilla-ceo-faced-new-fascism
-gingrich-says.
"effeminazis": "Will Effeminazis Demand the Pope Resign?," *The
Rush Limbaugh Show* (audio blog), RushLimbaugh.com, April

8, 2014, http://www.rushlimbaugh.com/daily/2014/04/08/will
_effeminazis_demand_the_pope_resign.

"leftist fascists": "Leftist Fascists Force Out Mozilla CEO for Holding
Same Opinion Obama Held in 2008," *The Rush Limbaugh Show*
(audio blog), RushLimbaugh.com, April 4, 2014, http://www
.rushlimbaugh.com/daily/2014/04/04/leftist_fascists_force_out
_mozilla_ceo_for_holding_same_opinion_obama_held_in_2008.

"[Eich is] the victim of intolerance here": Penny Starr, "Talk Radio
Hosts: Intolerant Gays See Traditional Marriage Support as Gay
Hate," *CNS News*, April 8, 2014, http://cnsnews.com/news/article
/penny-starr/talk-radio-hosts-intolerant-gays-see-traditional
-marriage-support-gay-hate.

"the gay mafia": Chiderah Monde, "Bill Maher Thinks 'Gay Mafia'
Went After Mozilla Firefox CEO: If You Cross Them 'You Get
Whacked,'" *New York Daily News*, April 6, 2014, http://www.
nydailynews.com/entertainment/tv-movies/bill-maher-gay-mafia-
article-1.1747421.

"an ugly, illiberal footnote": Conor Friedersdorf, "Mozilla's Gay-
Marriage Litmus Test Violates Liberal Values," *The Atlantic*, April 4,
2014, http://www.theatlantic.com/politics/archive/2014/04/mozillas-
gay-marriage-litmus-test-violates-liberal-values/360156/2/.

Sullivan gladly paraded his message: Matt Wilstein, "Andrew Sullivan
Blows Colbert's Mind with Defense of Brendan Eich," *Mediaite*,
April 10, 2014, http://www.mediaite.com/tv/andrew-sullivan-blows-
colberts-mind-with-defense-of-brendan-eich/.

15   *"What is the statute of limitations"*: Jim Burroway, "Eich Resigned.
That's Not Good," *Box Turtle Bulletin* (blog), April 4, 2014, http://
www.boxturtlebulletin.com/2014/04/04/63741.

"QUICK QUESTION": David Mixner, "QUICK QUESTION: AM I
THE ONLY ONE THAT IS CONCERNED . . . .," David Mixner's
Facebook page, April 4, 2014, https://www.facebook.com/permalink
.php?story_fbid=10154057995170372&id=802800371.

16   *"dragged in a truly bizarre point"*: Kara Swisher, "Mozilla Co-founder
Brendan Eich Resigns as CEO, Leaves Foundation Board," *Re/code*,
April 3, 2014, http://recode.net/2014/04/03/mozilla-co-founder
-brendan-eich-resigns-as-ceo-and-also-from-foundation-board/.

his own open letter to Andrew Sullivan: John Becker, "No, Andrew

Sullivan, Calling Out Bigotry Is Not 'Intolerance,'" *The Bilerico Project* (blog), April 4, 2014, http://www.bilerico.com/2014/04/no _andrew_sullivan_calling_out_bigotry_intolerance.php.

"When we talk about Eich's anti-gay stance": Mark Joseph Stern, "Just a Reminder: The Campaign for Prop 8 Was Unprecedentedly Cruel," *Outward* (blog), *Slate,* April 4, 2014, http://www.slate.com /blogs/outward/2014/04/04/brendan_eich_supported_prop_8 _which_was_worse_than_you_remember.html.

"I would watch Firing Line*" and following*: Dan Savage, "Episode 389: "Hearing About Dad's Dick Makes Me Uncomfortable," *Savage Lovecast* (audio blog), April 8, 2014, http://www.savagelovecast.com /episodes/389#.VDBgPyldUwI.

17 *He was criticized*: Reive Doig, "Why Dan Savage Is Wrong to Boycott Stoli," *Huffington Post,* April 2, 2013, http://www .huffingtonpost.ca/reive-doig/dan-savage-stoli-vancouver -pride-russia-boycott_b_3694259.html; Louis Peitzman, "Why the Stoli Boycott Is Misguided and Dangerous," *BuzzFeed LGBT,* July 29, 2013, http://www.buzzfeed.com/louispeitzman /why-the-stoli-boycott-is-misguided-and-dangerous#12y58sh; Mark Adomanis, "Boycotting Russian Vodka Is an Irrelevant Sideshow," *Forbes,* August 23, 2014, http://www.forbes.com/sites /markadomanis/2013/08/22/boycotting-russian-vodka-is-an -irrelevant-sideshow/.

opposition to the Russian antigay law: Michelangelo Signorile, "Val Mendeleev, Stoli CEO, Speaks Out on Gay Community's Vodka Boycott," *Huffington Post,* July 31, 2013, http://www.huffingtonpost .com/2013/07/31/stoli-vodka-gay-boycott_n_3682365.html.

18 *according to Stolichnaya itself*: Andrew Higgins, "Facing Fury over Antigay Law, Stoli Says 'Russian? Not Really,'" *New York Times,* September 7, 2013, http://www.nytimes.com/2013/09/08/world /europe/facing-fury-over-antigay-law-stoli-says-russian-not-really .html?pagewanted=all&_r=0.

"Sullivan is right": Frank Bruni, "The New Gay Orthodoxy," *New York Times,* April 05, 2014, http://www.nytimes.com/2014/04/06 /opinion/sunday/bruni-the-new-gay-orthodoxy.html.

19 *almost universally discredited*: Michelangelo Signorile, "The Worst Problem with Jo Becker's Book on 'The Fight for

Marriage Equality,'" *Huffington Post,* April 21, 2014, http://www
.huffingtonpost.com/michelangelo-signorile/the-worst-problem
with-jo_b_5185688.html; Andrew Sullivan, "Jo Becker's Troubling
Travesty of Gay History," *The Dish* (blog), April 16, 2014, http://dish
.andrewsullivan.com/2014/04/16/jo-beckers-troubling-travesty-of
-gay-history/.

vigorous protests and shaming: "Gay Marriage Supporters Take
to California Streets," CNN, November 8, 2008, http://www.cnn
.com/2008/US/11/08/same.sex.protests/index.html.

There were massive protests: Colin Moynihan, "At Mormon Temple,
a Protest over Prop 8," *New York Times,* November 13, 2008, http://
cityroom.blogs.nytimes.com/2008/11/13/at-mormon-temple
-thousands-protest-prop-8/.

when ACT UP held "die-ins": "ACT UP Accomplishments and
Partial Chronology," ACT UP New York, accessed October 16, 2014,
http://actupny.com/actions/index.php/the-community.

when GetEQUAL activists disrupted: Kip Williams, "President
Obama Our Only Target to Repeal Don't Ask, Don't Tell This
Year," *The Bilerico Project* (blog), April 21, 2010, http://www.bilerico
.com/2010/04/president_obama_our_only_target_to_repeal_dont
_ask.php.

20   *a petition to support Eich:* "Freedom to Marry, Freedom to Dissent:
Why We Must Have Both," RealClearPolitics.com, April 22, 2014,
http://www.realclearpolitics.com/articles/2014/04/22/freedom_to
_marry_freedom_to_dissent_why_we_must_have_both_122376
.html#ixzz2zilD3d4T.

21   *"After almost 20 years":* Jonathan Rauch, "Opposing Gay Marriage
Doesn't Make You a Crypto-racist," *The Daily Beast,* April 24, 2014,
http://www.thedailybeast.com/articles/2014/04/24/opposing-gay
-marriage-doesn-t-make-you-a-crypto-racist.html.

22   *Writing as a gay Asian American* and following: Kenji Yoshino, "Gay
Covering," in *Covering: The Hidden Assault on Our Civil Rights*
(New York: Random House, 2006).

23   *who supposedly took down Eich:* Matt Willstein, "Fox's George Will:
Gay Rights Activists Are Acting Like 'Sore Winners,'" *Mediaite,*
April 4, 2014, http://www.mediaite.com/tv/foxs-george-will-gay
-rights-activists-are-acting-like-sore-winners/.

2. "We Don't Serve Fags Here"

25   *came on my show the following month:* Jennifer Tipton and Olivier
Odom, interview on *The Michelangelo Signorile Show,* SiriusXM
OutQ, August 3, 2011.
     told the women they couldn't enter the park: "Dollywood to Lesbian:
Change Gay-Marriage Tee," *CBSNews,* July 20, 2011, http://www
.cbsnews.com/news/dollywood-to-lesbian-change-gay-marriage-tee/.
27   *a landmark case in 2012:* Dana Beyer et al., "New Title VII and
EEOC Rulings Protect Transgender Employees," Transgender Law
Center, accessed September 25, 2014, http://transgenderlawcenter
.org/wp-content/uploads/2014/01/TitleVII-Report-Final012414.pdf.
28   *denied a pool pass:* Tanisha Mallet, "Same-Sex Couple Denied
'Family-Pass' at Galion Pool," WBNS-10TV (Columbus, Ohio), July
9, 2014, http://www.10tv.com/content/stories/2014/07/09/galion
-ohio-same-sex-couple-denied-family-pass-at-galion-pool.html.
     a gay male couple paying their check. Cavan Sieczkowski, "Gay
Couple Says Waitress Told Them 'We Don't Serve Fags Here,'"
Huffington Post, May 29, 2014, http://www.huffingtonpost.com
/2014/05/29/gay-couple-texas-restaurant-fags_n_5410664.html.
     told to leave a health club: Gregg McDonald, "Centreville Spa
Openly Rejects Homosexual, Transgendered Customers," *Fairfax
(Va.) Times,* February 28, 2013, http://www.fairfaxtimes.com/
article/20130222/NEWS/130228867/1064/centreville-spa-openly
-rejects-homosexual-transgendered-customers%26template%3D
fairfaxTimes.
29   *told to leave the changing room:* "Transgender Man Claims He
Was Booted from Men's Locker Room at Staten Island Pool," *CBS
New York,* June 3, 2014, http://newyork.cbslocal.com/2014/06/03/
transgender-man-claims-he-was-booted-from-mens-locker-room
-at-staten-island-pool/.
     "gay bitches" written on their receipt: Lou Chibbaro Jr.,
"Restaurant Manager Says He Fired Server for Writing Slur on
Check," *Washington (D.C.) Blade,* June 14, 2014, http://www
.washingtonblade.com/2014/06/14/restaurant-manager-says-fired
-server-writing-slur-check/.

In Pennsylvania a bridal shop: Carol Kuruvilla, "Pennsylvania Bridal Shop Turns Away Lesbian Couple to Avoid Breaking 'God's Law,'" *New York Daily News,* August 9, 2014, http://nydailynews .com/news/national/pennsylvania-bridal-shop-don-serve-lesbians- article-1.1898001.

an Elvis impersonator performs the unions: Gail Sullivan, "Despite Gay Marriage Rulings, Some Elvis-Themed Vegas Chapels Doing It Their Way," *Washington Post,* October 20, 2014, http://www .washingtonpost.com/news/morning-mix/wp/2014/10/20/born -again-owner-of-vegas-wedding-chapel-refuses-to-perform-same -sex-marriages/.

florist who refused to sell flowers: Steven Nelson, "Washington State Sues Florist Who Refused Flowers for Same-Sex Wedding," U.S. News & World Report, April 10, 2013, http://www.usnews.com/ news/newsgram/articles/2013/04/10/washington-state-sues-florist -who-refused-flowers-for-gay-marriage.

"We still stand by what we believe[d]": Emily Sinovic, "Sweet Cakes Owner: 'The State Is Hostile Toward Christian Businesses,'" KATU. com (Portland, Ore.), January 9, 2014, http://www.katu.com/news/ local/Sweet-Cakes-by-Melissa-owners-vow-to-fight-state-241026131 .html.

Melissa and Aaron Klein were celebrated: James Nichols, "Melissa Klein, Anti-gay Baker, Cries at Values Voter Summit over Business Closing," *Huffington Post,* September 29, 2014, http://www .huffingtonpost.com/2014/09/29/melissa-klein-anti-gay_n_5901036 .html.

30 *a bakery in Lakewood:* Chuck Hickey, "Civil Rights Commission Says Lakewood Bakery Discriminated Against Gay Couple," FOX31 Denver KDVR-TV, May 30, 2014, http://kdvr.com/2014/05/30/civil -rights-commission-says-lakewood-bakery-discriminated-against -gay-couple/.

cabdriver hurled antigay slurs: "Were These Women Kicked Out of a Cab for Being Gay?," KATU.com (Portland, Ore.), July 27, 2013, http://www.katu.com/news/local/Kicked-out-of-a-cab-for-being -gay-217197781.html; "Kicked Out of a Cab: Driver Discriminated Against Gay Couple, Investigation Finds," KATU.com (Portland, Ore.), March 4, 2014. http://www.katu.com/news/local/Kicked-out

-of-a-cab-Driver-discriminated-against-gay-couple-investigation
-finds-248418861.html.

31 *they filed a lawsuit:* Michele Manchir, "Lawsuit: Men Were Kicked
Out of Cab After Kiss," *Chicago Tribune,* August 26, 2014, http://
www.chicagotribune.com/news/ct-cab-driver-lawsuit-met
-20140827-story.html.
"You're two men": James Lynch, "Iraq War Vet Says He Was Forced
Out of Yellow Cab for Kissing Boyfriend," Q13 FOX News (Seattle,
Wash.), July 8, 2014, http://q13fox.com/2014/07/08/iraq-war-vet
-says-he-was-forced-out-of-ycllow-cab-for-being-gay/.

32 *give "federal agencies explicit enforcement powers":* Ian Thompson,
e-mail interview by the author, June 13, 2014. Thompson is the
legislative representative of the American Civil Liberties Union
Washington Legislative Office.

33 *21% of LGBT respondents:* "A Survey of LGBT Americans' Attitudes,
Experiences, and Values in Changing Times," Pew Research,
"Social and Demographic Trends," June 13, 2013, http://www
.pewsocialtrends.org/2013/06/13/a-survey-of-lgbt-americans/.
78% of transgender respondents: "Employment Discrimination
Against LGBT Workers," Williams Institute, accessed October 2014,
http://williamsinstitute.law.ucla.edu/headlines/research-on-lgbt
-workplace-protections/.
"One minute, I was a trusted, reliable employee": Rebecca Juro,
"Working While Trans," *The Advocate,* July 17, 2014, http://www
.advocate.com/print-issue/current-issue/2014/07/17/working-while
-trans.

34 *"being fired, denied promotion, or harassed":* Marina Villeneuve,
"Gay Rights Activists Cheer Workplace Discrimination Bill," *Los
Angeles Times,* July 10, 2013, http://articles.latimes.com/2013/jul/10/
nation/la-na-gay-discrimination-20130711.
track coach at the University of Texas: Glennisha Morgan, "Bev
Kearney, University of Texas Track Coach, Claims She Was
Discriminated Against for Being Gay," *Huffington Post,* March 20,
2013, http://www.huffingtonpost.com/2013/03/20/bev-kearney
-lesbian-track-coach_n_2917745.html.
openly gay 7-Eleven employee: Curtis M. Wong, "Bradley Kindrick,
7-Eleven Employee, Allegedly Fired for Being Gay After Being

Assaulted by a Man," *Huffington Post,* April 12, 2013, http://www
.huffingtonpost.com/2013/04/12/bradley-kindrick-7-11-fired-gay
-assault-_n_3070811.html.

gym teacher in Columbus, Ohio: Denise Yost, "Fired Bishop
Watterson Teacher Carla Hale Reaches Agreement with Diocese,"
NBC4I-TV (Columbus, Ohio), August 15, 2014, http://www.nbc4i
.com/story/23148165/fired-bishop-watterson-teacher-carla-hale
-reaches-agreement-with-diocese.

35   *"I'm gay, I'm in a relationship with a woman":* Curtis M. Wong,
"Kristen Ostendorf, Minnesota Catholic School Teacher, Allegedly
Fired for Being Gay," *Huffington Post,* September 11, 2013, http://
www.huffingtonpost.com/2013/09/11/minnesota-catholic-school
-gay-_n_3908748.html.

theology professor in California: Carol Kuruvilla, "California
Theology Professor Booted from Christian College After Coming
Out as Transgender," *New York Daily News,* September 25,
2013, http://www.nydailynews.com/welcome?rd=http://www
.nydailynews.com/news/national/transgender-theology-professor
-booted-christian-college-article-1.1467363.

man who worked in a children's home: Stevie Poole, "Lubbock Man
Says He Was Fired for Being Gay; Law Says It's OK," *Lubbock (Tex.)
Avalanche-Journal,* July 25, 2014, http://lubbockonline.com/filed
-online/2014-07-25/lubbock-man-says-he-was-fired-being-gay-law
-says-its-ok.

vice principal at a Catholic high school: Lornet Turnbull and John
Higgins, "Eastside Catholic Students Rally Around Ousted Vice
Principal," *Seattle Times,* December 19, 2013, http://seattletimes
.com/html/localnews/2022494004_gayprincipalprotestxml.html.

subject of a pending lawsuit: Katherine Weber, "Vice Principal Sues
Catholic School, Archdiocese for Firing After Gay Marriage," *The
Christian Post,* March 14, 2014, http://www.christianpost.com/news
/vice-principal-sues-catholic-school-archdiocese-for-firing-after
-gay-marriage-115822/.

Michael Griffin, a Philadelphia teacher: Gillian Mohney, "Gay
Catholic School Teacher Fired for Wedding Plans," *ABCNews,*
December 8, 2013, http://abcnews.go.com/US/gay-catholic-school
-teacher-fired-married/story?id=21141075.

36   *"I applied for a marriage license":* Clare Kim, "Gay Teacher Fired

After Applying for Marriage License," *MSNBC.com*, December 12, 2013, http://www.msnbc.com/the-last-word/gay-teacher-fired-after-applying-marriage-license.

"ENDA's religious exemption": "Why ENDA's Religious Exemption Must Be Narrowed," American Civil Liberties Union, https://www.aclu.org/blog/lgbt-rights-religion-belief-womens-rights/why-endas-religious-exemption-must-be-narrowed.

37 *the 1964 Civil Rights Act's Title VII*: Title VII allows religious institutions and some of the businesses affiliated with them — those whose "purpose and character are primarily religious" — to be exempt from the law's prohibitions on religious discrimination in hiring, allowing them a preference for members of their own faith. But it does not allow them to discriminate on the basis of other categories, such as race, age, or disability. Under ENDA's religious exemption, however, nothing stops that same institution from firing an employee after learning he or she is gay or transgender, regardless of whether the individual belongs to that institution's religious faith. See ibid. and "Text of the Employment Non-Discrimination Act of 2013," GovTrack.us, November 12, 2013, https://www.govtrack.us/congress/bills/113/s815/text.

"impact of social stigma": Carmen Cruz, "CDC Health Study Shows Doctors Discriminate Against Gays," *EDGE*, Health/Fitness, September 8, 2014, http://www.edgeonthenet.com/health_fitness/health/Features/165291/cdc_health_study_shows_doctors_discriminate_against_gays.

"chronic homosexual behavior": Sunnive Brydum, "WATCH: Man Sues After Being Diagnosed as 'Chronic' Homosexual," *The Advocate*, August 15, 2014, http://www.advocate.com/health/2014/08/15/watch-man-sues-after-being-diagnosed-chronic-homosexual.

38 *The term* transgender *encompasses a wide array*: "FAQ on Access to Transition-Related Care," Lambda Legal, accessed September 12, 2014, http://www.lambdalegal.org//know-your-rights/transgender/transition-related-care-faq.

The Affordable Care Act holds: Michele Andrews, "HHS Takes Steps Toward Protecting Transgender People Under Health-Care Law," *Washington Post*, September 3, 2012, http://www.washingtonpost.com/national/health-science/hhs-takes-steps-toward-protecting

-transgender-people-under-health-care-law/2012/08/31/83fef586
-6a2c-11e1-acc6-32fefc7ccd67_story.html; Ariana Eunjung Cha, "Ban
Lifted on Medicare Coverage for Sex Change Surgery, *Washington
Post,* May 30, 2014, http://www.washingtonpost.com/national/
health-science/ban-lifted-on-medicare-coverage-for-sex-change
-surgery/2014/05/30/28bcd122-e818-11e3-a86b-362fd5443d19_story
.html; Anemona Hartocollis, "Insurers in New York Must Cover
Gender Reassignment Surgery, Cuomo Says," *New York Times,*
December 10, 2014, http://www.nytimes.com/2014/12/11/nyregion/
in-new-york-insurance-must-cover-sex-changes-cuomo-says.html;
"New York State Acts to Remove Medicaid Ban on Transgender
Health Care," Transgender Legal Defense and Education Network,
accessed December 22, 2014, http://www.transgenderlegal.org/
headline_show.php?id=554.

"does not have to treat people like you": "Lambda Legal Sues Doctor
and Clinic for Denying Medical Care to Transgender Woman,"
Lambda Legal, April 16, 2014, http://www.lambdalegal.org/
blog/20140416_sues-doctor-clinic-for-denying-care-to-transgender
-woman.

39 *47% of gay men:* Christine S. Moyer, "LGBT Patients: Reluctant
and Underserved," *Amednews.com,* September 5, 2011, http://www
.amednews.com/article/20110905/profession/309059942/4/.

56% of gay men: Josh Barro, "More Than Half of Gay and Bisexual
Men Say a Doctor Has Never Suggested H.I.V. Testing," *New York
Times,* September 25, 2014, http://www.nytimes.com/2014/09/26/
upshot/more-than-half-of-gay-and-bisexual-men-say-a-doctor-has
-never-suggested-hiv-testing.html?abt=0002&abg=0.

bring viral loads to undetectable levels: Gus Cairns, "No-One with
an Undetectable Viral Load, Gay or Heterosexual, Transmits HIV
in First Two Years of PARTNER Study," NAM AIDSmap, February
4, 2014, http://www.aidsmap.com/No-one-with-an-undetectable
-viral-load-gay-or-heterosexual-transmits-HIV-in-first-two-years
-of-PARTNER-study/page/2832748/.

are unaware of their status: Liz Szabo, "Most Young People with
HIV Don't Know They're Infected," *USA Today,* November
27, 2012, http://www.usatoday.com/story/news/health/
menshealth/2012/11/27/most-young-people-with-hiv-dont-know
-theyre-infected/1728049/.

27% of transgender women: Leela Genelle, "Why the CDC's Latest HIV Report Is So Alarming" (op-ed), *The Advocate,* January 8, 2014, http://www.advocate.com/commentary/2014/01/08/op-ed-why -cdc%25E2%2580%2599s-latest-hiv-report-so-alarming.

an alarming 132% rise: Sunnive Brydum, "Shocking Increase in HIV Infection Rate Among Young Gay, Bi Men," *The Advocate,* July 22, 2014, http://www.advocate.com/health/2014/07/22/shocking-increase-hiv-infection-rate-among-young-gay-bi-men.

The CDC has cut its HIV-prevention budget: Rebecca Haag, "HIV Budget Cuts Show Why U.S. Health Care Is Broken," *The Atlantic,* August 16, 2011, http://www.theatlantic.com/health/archive/2011/08/ hiv-budget-cuts-show-why-us-health-care-is-broken/243695/.

pre-exposure prophylaxis: For significant research on PrEP, see Jared M. Baeten et al., "Antiretroviral Prophylaxis for HIV Prevention in Heterosexual Men and Women," *New England Journal of Medicine* 367 (August 2, 2012). 399–410, http://www.nejm.org/doi/ full/10.1056/NEJMoa1108524; and Robert Grant et al., "Preexposure Chemoprophylaxis for HIV Prevention in Men Who Have Sex with Men," *New England Journal of Medicine* 363 (December 30, 2010): 2587–99, http://www.nejm.org/doi/full/10.1056/NEJMoa1011205.

40 *it does not inhibit condom use:* Albert Y. Liu et al., "Sexual Risk Behavior Among HIV Uninfected Men," *Journal of Acquired Immune Deficiency Syndrome* 64, no. 1 (2013): 87–94, http:// www.natap.org/2013/HIV/Sexual_Risk_Behavior_Among_HIV_ Uninfected_Men_Who.14.pdf; Robert Grant et al., "Uptake of Pre-exposure Prophylaxis, Sexual Practices, and HIV Incidence in Men and Transgender Women Who Have Sex with Men: A Cohort Study," *The Lancet Infectious Diseases* 14, no. 9 (September 2014): 820–29, http://www.thelancet.com/journals/laninf/article/PIIS1473-3099(14)70847-3/fulltext; "Insurers and Medicaid Cover It. So What's Behind the Slow Adoption of Truvada PrEP?," *Healthline News,* accessed September 12, 2014, http://www.healthline.com /health-news/hiv-prevention-truvada-prep-covered-by-most -insurers-050814.

two days after the sexual activity: Mark S. King, "'PrEP on Demand' Study Halted Because It Was So Successful," *HIV Plus,* November 5, 2014, http://www.hivplusmag.com/research/2014/11/05/prep-demand-study-halted-because-it-was-so-successful.

"extraordinarily effective intervention" and following: Chris Beyrer, "The Global HIV Epidemic Among Gay, Bisexual Men and Other MSM: Time to Act" (lecture at the HIV Center for Clinical and Behavioral Studies, New York State Psychiatric Institute and Columbia University, New York, N.Y., May 22, 2014), http:// gendersexualityhealth.org/lectures/May_2014_index.html. For more on the "end of AIDS" rhetoric and discussion, see also Benjamin Ryan, "Selling the End of AIDS," *POZ*, October 1, 2014, http://www. poz.com/articles/end_of_AIDS_401_26251.shtml; and Mark S. King, "The End of AIDS Is a Cynical Lie," *The Body*, November 15, 2014.

41   *the history of the epidemic:* For more on CDC inaction and pressure from activists, see Jim Eigo, "The Neverending Epidemic: And How We Can End It," *Huffington Post,* June 9, 2014, http://www.huffingtonpost.com/jim-eigo/the-neverending-epidemic-_b_5467437.html.
"We're so caught up in the giddiness": Peter Staley, "Gay Marriage Is Great, but How About Some Love for the AIDS Fight?," *Washington Post,* June 28, 2013, http://www.washingtonpost.com/opinions/ gay-marriage-is-great-but-how-about-some-love-for-the-aids-fightlove-will-tear-us-apart/2013/06/28/5b18c50c-ddd0-11e2-948c-d644453cf169_story.html.

For more on HIV-criminalization laws, see the Sero Project, http:// seroproject.com/; and Sean Strub, "Think Having HIV Is Not a Crime? Think Again," October 29, 2014, http://www.huffingtonpost .com/sean-strub/lgbt-hiv-criminalization_b_2039539.html.
Nick Rhodes, an HIV-positive Iowa man: Alison Gowans, "Iowa Supreme Court Throws Out Criminal Transmission of HIV Conviction," *Cedar Rapids (Iowa) Gazette,* June 13, 2014, http:// thegazette.com/subject/news/public-safety/iowa-supreme-court-throws-out-criminal-transmission-of-hiv-conviction-20140613.
Activists, working with the legislature: "Iowa Modernizes HIV Criminalization Law," *AIDS.gov* (blog), June 2, 2014, http://blog .aids.gov/2014/06/iowa-modernizes-hiv-criminalization-law.html.

42   *"I've been spending the last two years"* and following: Seth Stephens-Davidowitz, interview on *The Michelangelo Signorile Show,* SiriusXM Progress, December 13, 2013.

43   *"One of the things that was so clear"* and following: Seth Stephens-Davidowitz, telephone interview by author, June 19, 2014.

roughly 5% of men are gay: Seth Stephens-Davidowitz, "How Many American Men Are Gay?," *New York Times,* December 7, 2013, http://www.nytimes.com/2013/12/08/opinion/sunday/how-many -american-men-are-gay.html?pagewanted=all&_r=0.

Gates showed the percentage: Gary J. Gates, "How Many Lesbian, Gay, Bisexual, and Transgender?," Williams Institute, UCLA School of Law, April 2011, http://williamsinstitute.law.ucla.edu/wp-content/ uploads/Gates-How-Many-People-LGBT-Apr-2011.pdf.

46 *"identify themselves as gay":* Neil Steinberg, "True Gay Stats Hidden in the Closet," *Chicago Sun-Times,* January 14, 2014, http://www .suntimes.com/news/steinberg/24337489-452/true-gay-stats-still -hidden-in-the-closet.html#.VG__eVXF9ew.

Canada's most recent national survey: Kathryn Blaze Carlson, "The True North LGBT: New Poll Reveals Landscape of Gay Canada," *The National Post,* July 6, 2012, http://news.nationalpost .com/2012/07/06/the-true-north-lgbt-new-poll-reveals-landscape -of-gay-canada/#anchor.

47 *"While life gets better"* and following: Alex Morris, "The Forsaken: A Rising Number of Homeless Gay Teens Are Being Cast Out by Religious Families," *Rolling Stone,* September 3, 2014, http:// www.rollingstone.com/culture/features/the-forsaken-a-rising -number-of-homeless-gay-teens-are-being-cast-out-by-religious -families-20140903.

The number of homeless youth: Bernadine Watson, "The Number of Homeless Youth Is Growing, but Funding to Help Them Is Not," *Washington Post,* September 20, 2013, http://www.washingtonpost. com/blogs/she-the-people/wp/2013/12/20/the-number-of-homeles s-youth-is-growing-but-funding-to-help-them-is-not/.

40% or more of homeless teens: Blake Ellis, "Student Homelessness Hits Record High," *CNNMoney,* October 24, 2013, http://money. cnn.com/2013/10/24/pf/homeless-students/. For more information on the problem of LGBT teen homelessness, see Guy Shilo and Riki Savaya, "Effects of Family and Friend Support on LGB Youths' Mental Health and Sexual Orientation Milestones," *Family Relations: Interdisciplinary Journal of Applied Family Studies* 60, no. 3 (June 15, 2011): 316–30, http://onlinelibrary.wiley.com/doi/10.1111/ j.1741-3729.2011.00648.x/abstract;jsessionid=105867060A0B002474 A168D4F8DE9639.f03t02; Caitlin Ryan et al., "Family Acceptance in Adolescence and the Health of LGBT Young Adults," *Journal of Child and Adolescent Psychiatric Nursing* 23, no. 4 (November 2010), http://familyproject.sfsu.edu/files/FAP_Family%20Acceptance _JCAPN.pdf; and Adrienne L. Fernandes-Alcantara, *Runaway and Homeless Youth: Demographics and Programs,* Congressional Research Service report no. 7-5700, Washington, D.C., 2013, http://www.nchcw.org/uploads/7/5/3/3/7533556/crs_2013_rhya_history _and_lit_review.pdf.

48   *one widely reported 2013 poll:* "Gay Marriage: Key Data Points from Pew Research," Pew Research Center, June 13, 2013, http://www .pewresearch.org/key-data-points/gay-marriage-key-data-points -from-pew-research/.
     change in underlying biases and following: Rachel Riskind, telephone interview by author, February 19 and June 12, 2014.
     Project Implicit: https://implicit.harvard.edu/implicit/.
     Project Implicit has amassed data: "About Project Implicit," Project Implicit, https://www.projectimplicit.net/about.html.

50   *published the results of four studies:* David J. Lick, Kerri L. Johnson, and Rachel G. Riskind, "Haven't I Seen You Before? Straight Men Who Are Insecure of Their Masculinity Remember Gender-Atypical Faces," *Group Processes and Intergroup Relations,* June 30, 2014, http://gpi.sagepub.com/content/ea rly/2014/06/30/1368430214538324.abstract.

52   *highest number of anti-LGBT murders* and following: Lila Shapiro, "Highest Number of Anti-gay Murders Ever Reported in 2011: The National Coalition of Anti-violence Programs," *Huffington Post,* June 2, 2012, http://www.huffingtonpost.com/2012/06/02/ anti-gay-hate-crimes-murders-national-coalition-of-anti-violence -programs_n_1564885.html.

53   *"I think that hate violence":* Ibid.
     gay-friendly Seattle: Gene Balk, "Data: Seattle Has Third-Highest Rate of Anti-LGBT Hate Crimes," *FYI Guy* (blog), *Seattle Times,* http://blogs.seattletimes.com/fyi-guy/2014/06/06/data-seattle-has- third-highest-rate-of-anti-lgbt-hate-crimes/.
     violent attacks were reported: Erinn Cawthon and Sarah Aarthun, "Anti-gay Crime Up in New York as City Prepares for Pride Events," *CNN,* May 22, 2013, http://www.cnn.com/2013/05/22/us/new-york- hate-crimes/.

Mark Carson, an African American gay man: Dennis Slattery, Eric Badia, and Joe Kemp, "Gunman Shoots 32-year-old Mark Carson Dead in Greenwich Village Bias Attack: Officials," *New York Daily News,* May 18, 2013, http://www.nydailynews.com/new-york/ gunman-shoots-32-year-old-man-dead-greenwich-village-bias -attack-officials-article-1.1347776.

In September of the same year: Lila Shapiro, "Charges Dropped in Beating Death of Transgender Woman, but Family and Advocates Hopeful," *Huffington Post,* November 20, 2013, http://www .huffingtonpost.com/2013/11/20/islan-nettles_n_4311344.html.

a transgender woman was viciously beaten: "Rally Held After Transgender Woman Attacked in Bushwick, Brooklyn," ABC7 New York, October 15, 2014, http://7online.com/news/transgender -woman-attacked-in-bushwick/349516/.

54 *gay Brooklyn man was shot:* Jan Ransom, Rocco Parascandola, and Barry Paddock, "Man Chased, Shot in Anti-gay Attack in Brooklyn: Cops," *New York Daily News,* September 27, 2013, http://www .nydailynews.com/new-york/nyc-crime/man-chased-shot-anti-gay -attack-brooklyn-cops-article-1.1955422.

attacked with a hammer: "Man Hit with Hammer, Robbed in Anti-gay Attack: NYPD," NBC New York, accessed October 22, 2014, http://www.nbcnewyork.com/news/local/Man-Robbed- Struck-With-Hammer-in-Brooklyn-Anti-Gay-Attack-279180661 .html.

The New York City Police Department: Tina Moore, "Gay-Bashing Attacks on the Rise in City, Could Double Last Year's Total," *New York Daily News,* August 18, 2014, http://www.nydailynews.com/ new-york/gay-bashing-attacks-rise-city-article-1.1430370.

called it a "surge" and following: Sharon Stapel, "Are We a Stone's Throw from an Epidemic of Anti-LGBTQ Violence?," *Huffington Post,* June 12, 2014, http://www.huffingtonpost.com/sharon-stapel/ anti-lgbtq-violence_b_5489853.html.

55 *"After she hit me with the glass" and following:* Michelangelo Signorile, "CeCe McDonald, Transgender Activist, Recalls Hate Attack, Manslaughter Case," *Huffington Post,* February 22, 2014, http://www.huffingtonpost.com/2014/02/22/cece-mcdonald- manslaughter-case_n_4831677.html?utm_hp_ref=gay-voices.

"the disproportionate rate of LGBT people": Catherine Hanssens et

al., *A Roadmap for Change: Federal Policy Recommendations for Addressing the Criminalization of LGBT People and People Living with HIV* (New York: Columbia Law School, 2014), http://web.law .columbia.edu/sites/default/files/microsites/gender-sexuality/files/ roadmap_for_change_full_report.pdf.

3. Bias and Backlash

58 *50% of GOP primary voters:* Phil Hirschkorn and Jennifer Pinto, "White Evangelicals Are Half of GOP Primary Voters," *CBSNews,* March 15, 2012, http://www.cbsnews.com/news/white-evangelicals -are-half-of-gop-primary-voters/.

59 *"What concrete factual arguments do you have?":* Ian Millhiser, "Federal Appeals Court Judge: Ban on Same-Sex Marriage Is 'Based on Hate,'" August 26, 2014, *Think Progress,* http://thinkprogress .org/justice/2014/08/26/3476116/federal-appeals-court-judge-ban -on-same-sex-marriage-is-based-on-hate/.

60 *"Heterosexuals get drunk and pregnant":* Baskin v. Bogan and *Wolf v. Walker,* nos. 14-2386 to 14-2388, 14-2526, pp. 19–20 (7th Cir., 2014), http://media.ca7.uscourts.gov/cgi-bin/rssExec .pl?Submit=Display&Path=Y2014%2FD09-04%2FC%3A14 -2526%3AJ%3APosner%3Aaut%3AT%3AfnOp%3AN%3A1412339 %3AS%3A0.

"My understanding": Michelangelo Signorile, "Stacey Campfield, Tennessee Senator Behind 'Don't Say Gay' Bill, on Bullying, AIDS, and Homosexual 'Glorification,'" *Huffington Post,* January 26, 2012, http://www.huffingtonpost.com/2012/01/26/stacey-campfield -tennessee-senator-dont-say-gay-bill_n_1233697.html.

61 *the interview drew national attention:* Coleen Curry, "Senator Booted from Restaurant over 'Homophobic' Views," *ABCNews,* January 30, 2012, http://abcnews.go.com/blogs/headlines/2012/01/ senator-booted-from-restaurant-over-homophobic-views/.

"I was incensed": Michelangelo Signorile, "Martha Boggs, Tennessee Restaurant Owner Who Kicked Out Senator Stacey Campfield for Anti-gay Remarks, Describes Encounter," *Huffington Post,* January 31, 2012, http://www.huffingtonpost.com/2012/01/31/martha-boggs -stacey-campfield-restaurant-removal-_n_1243967.html.

Campfield would go on to lose: "State Sen. Stacey Campfield Loses
Seat in Primary," *Memphis (Tenn.) Commercial Appeal,* August 7,
2014, http://www.commercialappeal.com/news/local-news/politics/
state-sen-stacey-campfield-loses-seat-in-primary.
The bill, though, reared its head again: Zack Ford, " 'Don't Say Gay'
Bill Could Prevent Counselors from Providing Mental Health
Support," *Think Progress,* March 14, 2013, http://thinkprogress
.org/lgbt/2013/03/14/1719701/dont-say-gay-bill-could-even-prevent
-counselors-from-providing-mental-health-support/.
This version, thankfully, failed: Katie McDonough, "Tennessee 'Don't
Say Gay' Bill Dies, Again," *Salon,* March 27, 2013, http://www.salon
.com/2013/03/27/tennessee_dont_say_gay_bill_dies_again/.

62 *Reformer of the Year award:* Katie McDonough, "StudentsFirst Dubs
'Don't Say Gay' Bill Sponsor 'Reformer of the Year,' " *Salon,* April
29, 2013, http://www.salon.com/2013/04/29/studentsfirst_dubs_dont
say_gay_bill_co_sponsor_education_reformer_of_the_year/.
The group claims to speak: Daniel Denvir, "Michelle Rhee's Right
Turn," *Salon,* November 17, 2012, http://www.salon.com/2012/11/17/
michele_rhees_right_turn/.
"spent nearly $2 million": Michael J. Mishak and Howard Blume,
"Taking a Crack at California's Education System," *Los Angeles
Times,* March 26, 2013, http://articles.latimes.com/2013/mar/26/
local/la-me-michelle-rhee-20130327.
"I am Marcel Neergaard": Marcel Neergaard, "Taking a Stand
Against Anti-gay Bullying (VIDEO)," *Huffington Post,* June 1, 2013,
http://www.huffingtonpost.com/marcel-neergaard/taking-a-stand
-against-anti-gay-bullying_b_3368922.html.

63 *StudentsFirst withdrew the award:* Cavin Sieczkowski, "Gay 11-Year-
Old's Petition Against Homophobic Politician Succeeds," *Huffington
Post,* June 5, 2013, http://www.huffingtonpost.com/2013/06/05/gay
-11-year-old-petition-john-ragan-_n_3391599.html.
"no district shall include in its course of study": Zack Ford, "9 States
with Anti-gay Laws That Aren't That Different from Russia's,"
Think Progress, February 3, 2014, http://thinkprogress.org/
lgbt/2014/02/03/3241421/9-state-gay-propaganda-laws/.

64 *"On one level, we hear clearly":* Ian Haney López, interview
by Amy Goodman, *Democracy Now!,* January 14, 2014, http://
www.democracynow.org/2014/1/14/dog_whistle_politics_how

_politicians_use. Haney López's book is *Dog Whistle Politics: How Coded Racial Appeals Have Reinvented Racism and Wrecked the Middle Class* (New York: Oxford University Press, 2014).

65   *"I did not hear that":* Michelangelo Signorile, "James Inhofe, GOP Senator, Stunned at CPAC over Learning of Rob Portman's Gay Marriage Support," *Huffington Post,* March 15, 2013, http://www .huffingtonpost.com/2013/03/15/james-inhofe-cpac-gay-marriage -rob-portman_n_2884724.html.

66   *now talked of "reclaiming" marriage:* Andrew Kaczynski, "Rick Santorum Says Gay Marriage Is Like Marrying Your Brother or Niece, Sexual Abuse Higher in Gay Families," *BuzzFeed*, February 22, 2012, http://www.buzzfeed.com/andrewkaczynski/rick -santorum-says-gay-marriage-is-like-marrying-y.
      comparing gays to pedophiles: Andrew Kirell, "Blitzer Grills Ben Carson over His Gays/Pedophile Remark: 'You Understand How Offensive That Might Be?,'" *Mediaite*, March 28, 2013, http://www .mediaite.com/tv/blitzer-grills-ben-carson-over-his-gayspedophile -remark-you-understand-how-offensive-that-might-be/.
      a rebranding to reach millennials: Adele Stan, interview on *The Michelangelo Signorile Show*, SiriusXM Progress, September 29, 2014.

67   *there was a main-ballroom event:* Michelangelo Signorile, "CPAC 2012: Are the Republican Party's Views on Gay Marriage Shifting?," *Huffington Post,* February 12, 2012, http://www .huffingtonpost.com/2012/02/12/cpac-2012-republican-party-gay -marriage_n_1271709.html?ref=gay-voices.
      Attendance was sparse: Chris Geidner, "At CPAC, the Marriage Fight Is Over," Gay Voices, *Huffington Post,* March 17, 2013, http://www .huffingtonpost.com/2012/02/12/cpac-2012-republican-party-gay -marriage_n_1271709.html?ref=gay-voices.
      a panel in support of gay marriage: Chris Good, "Gay Republicans Find a Venue at CPAC," *ABCNews,* March 14, 2013, http://abcnews .go.com/blogs/politics/2013/03/gay-republicans-find-a-venue-at -cpac/.
      So, in 2014, it wasn't surprising and following: Michelangelo Signorile, "How the National Organization for Marriage Was Banished to the Basement at CPAC 2014," *Huffington Post,* March 12, 2014, http://www.huffingtonpost.com/michelangelo

-signorile/national-organization-for-marriage-cpac-2014-basement
_b_4941514.html.

showed young Republicans supporting gay marriage by 61%: "Young
Voters Supported Obama Less, but May Have Mattered More,"
Pew Research, November 26, 2012, http://www.people-press.
org/2012/11/26/young-voters-supported-obama-less-but-may-have-
mattered-more/.

The candidacy of David Brat: Kristina Peterson and Janet Hook,
"Eric Cantor Loses to Tea Party's David Brat in Virginia Primary,"
Wall Street Journal, June 10, 2014, http://online.wsj.com/articles/
no-2-house-republican-eric-cantor-defeated-in-virginia-primary
-upset-1402445714.

69 *"theocratic libertarianism":* Michael J. McVicar, "The Libertarian
Theocrats: The Long, Strange History of R. J. Rushdoony and
Christian Reconstructionism," *The Public Eye,* Political Research
Associates, Fall 2007, http://www.publiceye.org/magazine/v22n3/
libertarian.html. See also Julie Ingersoll, "David Brat: Catholic,
Calvinist, and Libertarian, Oh My!," *Religion Dispatches,* University
of Southern California Annenberg School for Communication and
Journalism, June 11, 2014, http://religiondispatches.org/david-brat
-catholic-calvinist-and-libertarian-oh-my/.

Brat and others like him: Jack Jenkins, "David Brat: Embrace
Christian Capitalism, or Hitler Will Come Back," *Think Progress,*
June 11, 2014, http://thinkprogress.org/election/2014/06/11/3447712/
david-brat-embrace-christian-capitalism-or-hitler-will-come-back/.

a twenty-three-year-old, Zachary Werrell: "Meet the Young
Campaign Whiz Who Helped Oust Eric Cantor," *CBSNews,* June
20, 2014, http://www.cbsnews.com/news/dave-brats-23-year-old-
campaign-manager-zachary-werrell/.

scrubbed comments on his social-media accounts: Garance Franke-
Ruta, "David Brat Campaign Manager Scrubs Facebook Page After
Election," *Yahoo! News,* June 11, 2014, http://news.yahoo.com/brat
-campaign-manager-scrubs-facebook-page-after-election-173536113
.html.

"protect" the "sanctity of marriage": "Protecting Values," Dave Brat
for Congress — 7th District of Virginia, accessed June 30, 2014,
http://davebrat.com/protecting-values/.

Among white men ages eighteen to twenty-nine: "Young Voters Supported Obama Less."

70   *a large majority of millennial independents:* Justin McCarthy, "Same-Sex Marriage Support Reaches New High at 55%," Gallup, May 21, 2014, http://www.gallup.com/poll/169640/sex-marriage-support -reaches-new-high.aspx.

a drop in turnout among all young voters: "Low Midterm Turnout Likely, Conservatives More Enthusiastic, Harvard Youth Poll Finds," Harvard University Institute of Politics, http://www.iop.harvard .edu/Spring-2014-HarvardIOP-Survey.

which hurts Democrats and progressive causes: Rock the Vote, "What We Know About Young Voters," Winning Campaigns, accessed October 12, 2014, http://www.winningcampaigns.org/Winning -Campaigns-Archive-Articles/What-We-Know-About-Young-Voter .html.

young Republican turnout has been on the rise: Ronald Brownstein, "Why Republicans Can Get Away with Ignoring Their Problems," *The National Journal,* June 6, 2013, http://www.nationaljournal. com/columns/political-connections/why-republicans-can-get-away -with-ignoring-their-problems-20130606.

"participating in the upcoming midterms": Harvard University Institute of Politics, "Low Midterm Turnout Likely, Conservatives More Enthusiastic, Harvard Youth Poll Finds," April 29, 2014, http:// www.iop.harvard.edu/Spring-2014-HarvardIOP-Survey.

"the Democrats' advantage with young voters": Jennifer De Pinto, "The Young Voter Turnout in 2014," *CBSNews,* November 13, 2014, http://www.cbsnews.com/news/the-young-voter-turnout-in-2014/.

more Republicans were elected: Associated Press, "Election Brings New GOP Power to State Capitols," *Huffington Post,* November 6, 2014, http://www.huffingtonpost.com/2014/11/06/state-elections -2014_n_6113942.html.

"not-so-subtle makeover": Josh Vorhees, "Joni Makes 'Em Squeal," *Slate,* November 5, 2014, http://www.slate.com/articles/news_and _politics/politics/2014/11/joni_ernst_iowa_senate_the_country_s _most_conservative_senate_candidate.html.

71   *evangelical voters in the GOP base:* Thomas Edsall, "The Demise of the White Democratic Voter," *New York Times,* November 11, 2014,

http://www.nytimes.com/2014/11/12/opinion/thomas-edsall-the
-demise-of-the-white-democratic-voter.html.
In 2013 a New Mexico lesbian couple: Sherry F. Colb, "The New
Mexico Supreme Court Applies Anti-discrimination Law to
Wedding Photographer Refusing to Photograph Same-Sex
Commitment Ceremonies," *Verdict,* Justia.com, September 4, 2013,
http://verdict.justia.com/2013/09/04/new-mexico-supreme-court
-anti-discrimination-law-to-wedding-photographer.

72   *the justices declined to hear it:* Robert Barnes, "Supreme
Court Declines Case of Photographer Who Denied Service
to Gay Couple," *Washington Post,* April 7, 2014, http://www
.washingtonpost.com/politics/supreme-court-wont-review-new
-mexico-gay-commitment-ceremony-photo-case/2014/04/07/
f9246cb2-bc3a-11e3-9a05-c739f29ccb08_story.html.
passed a law that would protect: Ray Sanchez and Miguel Marquez,
"Arizona Lawmakers Pass Controversial Anti-gay Bill," CNN,
February 21, 2014, http://www.cnn.com/2014/02/21/us/arizona-anti
-gay-bill/.

73   *activists had time in the national spotlight:* Cindy Carcamo, "Gay
Rights Activists in Uproar over Arizona 'Religious Freedom' Bill," *Los
Angeles Times,* February 20, 2014, http://articles.latimes.com/2014/
feb/20/nation/la-na-nn-ff-gay-rights-arizona-bill-20140220.
LGBT groups in Washington: Joe Jervis, "Major LGBT Orgs Silent
on Arizona," *JoeMyGod* (blog), February 21, 2014, http://joemygod
.blogspot.com/2014/02/major-lgbt-orgs-silent-on-arizona.html.
The delay encouraged major corporations: Jillian Berman, "Apple,
Delta, PetSmart Join Fight Against Arizona's Anti-gay Bill,"
Huffington Post, February 26, 2014, http://www.huffingtonpost
.com/2014/02/26/companies-arizona-gay-bill_n_4857964.html.
threatening to pull the 2015 Super Bowl: Barry Petchesky, "Anti-gay
Bill Could Cost Arizona the Super Bowl," *Deadspin* (blog), Kinja,
February 26, 2014, http://deadspin.com/anti-gay-bill-could-cost
-arizona-the-super-bowl-1531409894.
she vetoed the bill: Catherine E. Shoichet and Halimah Abdullah,
"Arizona Gov. Jan Brewer Vetoes Controversial Anti-gay Bill, SB
1062," CNN, February 26, 2014, http://www.cnn.com/2014/02/26/
politics/arizona-brewer-bill/.

In all but a few cities: Dylan Smith, "Tempe Joins AZ Cities Barring
Discrimination Against Gays," *Tucson (Ariz.) Sentinel,* February 28,
2014, http://www.tucsonsentinel.com/local/report/022814_tempe
_discrimination/tempe-joins-az-cities-barring-discrimination
-against-gays/.

74   *Mississippi Religious Freedom Restoration Act:* Mississippi
     Religious Freedom Restoration Act, Miss. Reg. Sess. 2014, S.B.
     No. 2681, accessed August 10, 2014, http://billstatus.ls.state.ms.us/
     documents/2014/html/SB/2600-2699/SB2681SG.htm.
     the ACLU and other legal analysts believe: Sarah Posner, "Is Supreme
     Court Jurisprudence Making State Religious Freedom Bills More
     Dangerous?," *Religion Dispatches,* University of Southern California
     Annenberg School for Communication and Journalism, March 11,
     2014, http://religiondispatches.org/is-supreme-court-jurisprudence
     -making-state-religious-freedom-bills-more-dangerous/.
     "Religious right activists clearly envision": Adam Serwer, "Anti-gay
     Activists Celebrate Mississippi 'Religious Freedom' Law," *MSNBC,*
     April 1, 2014, http://www.msnbc.com/msnbc/mississippis-religious
     -freedom-law.
     Tony Perkins of the antigay Family Research Council: "FRC
     Commends Mississippi Legislature for Approving Religious
     Freedom Legislation" (press release), Family Research Council,
     April 1, 2014, http://www.frc.org/pressrelease/frc-commends-
     mississippi-legislature-for-approving-religious-freedom-legislation.
     plan to continue this movement in other states: Reid Wilson,
     "Mississippi Passes Arizona-Style Religious Freedom Bill,"
     Washington Post, April 1, 2014, http://www.washingtonpost.com/
     blogs/govbeat/wp/2014/04/01/mississippi-passes-arizona-style
     -religious-freedom-bill/.

75   Burwell v. Hobby Lobby Stores: *Burwell, Secretary of Health and
     Human Services et al. v. Hobby Lobby Stores, Inc., et al.,* 573 U.S.
     (2014), http://www.supremecourt.gov/opinions/13pdf/13-354_olp1
     .pdf.
     it has already been cited by lower courts: Jeffrey Toobin, "On Hobby
     Lobby, Ginsburg Was Right," *The New Yorker,* September 30, 2014,
     http://www.newyorker.com/news/daily-comment/hobby-lobbys
     -troubling-aftermath.

LGBT groups were so concerned: Caitlin MacNeal, "LGBT Groups Pull Support for ENDA in Wake of Hobby Lobby Ruling," *Talking Points Memo,* October 22, 2014, http://talkingpointsmemo.com/livewire/aclu-drops-support-enda-hobby-lobby.

Passed by a large majority of both parties: William L. Glankler, "Religious Freedom Restoration Act (RFRA)," in *Encyclopedia of American History: Contemporary United States, 1969 to the Present,* ed. Donald T. Critchlow and Gary B. Nash, rev. ed., vol. 10 (New York: Facts on File, 2010).

76   *the* Washington Post *ran a front-page story:* Juliet Eilperin, "After Veto in Arizona, Conservatives Vow to Fight for Religious Liberties," *Washington Post,* February 27, 2014, http://www.washingtonpost.com/politics/after-veto-in-arizona-conservatives-vow-to-fight-for-religious-liberties/2014/02/27/4c0f877a-9fcb-11e3-b8d8-94577ff66b28_story.html.

Sprigg himself is an extremist: Kyle Mantyla, "FRC's Sprigg Wants to See Homosexuality Criminalized," *Right Wing Watch,* People for the American Way, February 3, 2010, http://www.rightwingwatch.org/content/frcs-sprigg-wants-see-homosexuality-criminalized.

77   *"The Christian Right campaign"* and following: Jay Michaelson, *Redefining Religious Liberty: The Covert Campaign Against Civil Rights* (Somerville, Mass.: Political Research Associates, 2013), http://www.politicalresearch.org/wp-content/uploads/downloads/2013/04/PRA_Redefining-Religious-Liberty_March2013_PUBLISH.pdf.

78   *letting court rulings stand in three circuits:* Robert Barnes, "Supreme Court Declines to Review Same-Sex Marriage Cases, Allowing Unions in 5 States," *Washington Post,* October 6, 2014, http://www.washingtonpost.com/politics/courts_law/supreme-court-declines-to-review-same-sex-marriage-cases/2014/10/06/ee822848-4d5e-11e4-babe-e91da079cb8a_story.html.

I later asked Schubert: Michelangelo Signorile, "The Right's New Strategy After Gay Marriage Loss: Finding the Gay 'Partial Birth Abortion,'" *Huffington Post,* October 7, 2014, http://www.huffingtonpost.com/michelangelo-signorile/the-rights-new-strategy-a_b_5944894.html.

"license to discriminate" bill: Zack Ford, "New Bill Would

Create 'License to Discriminate' for Religious Adoption
Agencies," *Think Progress,* July 31, 2014, http://thinkprogress.org/
lgbt/2014/07/31/3466152/adoption-license-to-discriminate/.

4. Hiding in Plain Sight

81 *"tone down a disfavored identity":* Kenji Yoshino, preface to
Covering: The Hidden Assault on Our Civil Rights (New York:
Random House, 2006).

elderly, obese, or disabled: Erving Goffman, *Stigma: Notes on the
Management of a Spoiled Identity* (New York: Simon & Schuster,
1963).

82 *distinguishes covering from conversion and passing* and following:
Kenji Yoshino, "Gay Covering," in *Covering.*

The two most important governing bodies: APA Task Force on
Appropriate Therapeutic Responses to Sexual Orientation,
*Report of the Task Force on Appropriate Therapeutic Responses to
Sexual Orientation* (Washington, D.C.: American Psychological
Association, 2009), http://www.apa.org/pi/lgbc/publications/;
American Psychiatric Association, "Position Statement on Therapies
Focused on Attempts to Change Sexual Orientation (Reparative or
Conversion Therapies)," 2000, APA Official Actions, http://www
.psychiatry.org/.

administering such therapy to minors: Aaron C. Davis, "D.C. Bans
Gay Conversion Therapy of Minors," *Washington Post,* December
2, 2014, http://www.washingtonpost.com/local/dc-politics/dc-bans
-gay-conversion-therapy/2014/12/02/58e6aae4-7a67-11e4-84d4
-7c896b90abdc_story.html.

apologized for the harm he'd done: Ed Payne, "Group Apologizes
to Gay Community, Shuts Down 'Cure' Ministry," CNN, July 8,
2013, http://www.cnn.com/2013/06/20/us/exodus-international
-shutdown/; Michelangelo Signorile, "Alan Chambers,
Exodus International's Former President, on Sexual Labels,
'Ex-Gay' Therapy," *Huffington Post,* August 4, 2013, http://
www.huffingtonpost.com/2013/08/04/alan-chambers-exodus
-international-_n_3696750.html.

84 *Sam came under attack:* Holly Yan and Dave Alsup, "NFL Draft:

Reactions Heat Up after Michael Sam Kisses Boyfriend on TV,"
CNN, May 13, 2014, http://www.cnn.com/2014/05/12/us/michael
-sam-nfl-kiss-reaction/.
it "looked pretty out there to me": Katherine Fung, "Donald
Trump Thought Michael Sam Was 'Pretty Out There' for Kissing
His Boyfriend," *Huffington Post,* May 12, 2014, http://www
.huffingtonpost.com/2014/05/12/donald-trump-michael-sam-kiss
-out-there_n_5309229.html.
a salient short piece: Mark Joseph Stern, "Michael Sam Proves It:
Gay People Need to Kiss in Public Much, Much More," *Slate,* May
12, 2014, http://www.slate.com/blogs/outward/2014/05/12/michael
_sam_gay_kiss_proves_we_need_more_gay_kissing.html.
"The Great Facebook Kiss-In": Michelangelo Signorile, "How
Michael Sam Inspired the Great Facebook Kiss-In," *Huffington
Post,* May 14, 2014, http://www.huffingtonpost.com/michelangelo
-signorile/michael-sam-facebook-kiss-in b 5320085.html.

85   *my own work in years past:* For a report and analysis of the closet
in media, Washington, Hollywood, and American society, see
Michelangelo Signorile, *Queer in America: Sex, the Media, and the
Closets of Power* (New York: Random House, 1993).
the "glass closet": For a foundational analysis of the closet and its
politics, see Eve Kosofsky Sedgwick, *Epistemology of the Closet*
(Berkeley: University of California Press, 1990).

86   *"described as lesbian, gay or bisexual":* Associated Press, "Label of
Gay Is No Longer Defamatory, Court Rules," *New York Times,* May
31, 2012, http://www.nytimes.com/2012/06/01/nyregion/court-rules
-calling-someone-gay-is-not-defamatory.html; Associated Press,
"Some Courts Are Ruling Gay Is Not Slanderous," *Fox News,* June 1,
2014, http://www.foxnews.com/us/2012/06/01/some-judges-say-gay
-is-no-longer-slanderous/.
the politician who votes antigay: Shailagh Murray, "The Open and
Closeted Lives of a Gay Congressman," *Washington Post,* October
4, 2006, http://www.washingtonpost.com/wp-dyn/content/
article/2006/10/03/AR2006100301492.html.
GOP congressman Mark Foley: Michelangelo Signorile, "Media
Should've Outed Foley," *Los Angeles Times,* October 13, 2006, http://
articles.latimes.com/2006/oct/13/opinion/oe-signorile13.

87   *congressman David Dreier of California:* Doug Ireland, "The

Outing," *Los Angeles Weekly,* September 23, 2004, http://www
.laweekly.com/2004-09-23/news/the-outing/.
Dreier lived with his chief of staff and following: Brian Brooks,
"First Look: Kirby Dick's "Outrage"; New Tribeca Doc Names
Names," *Indiewire,* April 3, 2009, http://www.indiewire.com/article/
first_look_kirby_dicks_outrage_tribeca_premiere_names_names/;
John Diaz, "The Real Outrage Is in the 'Outing,'" *SFGate,* May 10,
2009, http://www.sfgate.com/opinion/article/The-real-outrage-is
-in-the-outing-3242518.php; Patrick Goldstein and James Rainey,
"'Outrage': Kirby Dick Kicks Open Washington's Closet Door," *Los
Angeles Times,* April 23, 2009, http://latimesblogs.latimes.com/the
_big_picture/2009/04/outraged-kirby-dick-kicks-open-washingtons
-closet-door-.html.

88   *hadn't "really thought too much about it":* Chris Geidner, "Rep.
Aaron Schock Hedges on Federal Marriage Amendment," *BuzzFeed,*
August 27, 2012, http://www.buzzfeed.com/chrisgeidner/rep-aaron
-schock-hedges-on-federal-marriage-amend.

89   *"Schock is hoping his romantic prospects will improve":* Jason
Zengerle, "Aaron Schock: The Freshman," *Details,* May 2009, http://
www.details.com/culture-trends/news-and-politics/200904/aaron
-schock-is-the-youngest-member-of-congress.
a photo of Schock: Andy Towle, "Rep. Aaron Schock 'Burned
the Belt' That Made Him Look Gay," *Towleroad: A Site with
Homosexual Tendencies* (blog), June 14, 2010, http://www.towleroad
.com/2010/06/rep-aaron-schock-burned-the-belt-that-made-him
-look-gay.html; Jim Newell, "Congressman's Outfit Making Gay
Staffer Rounds on Capitol Hill," *Gawker,* June 11, 2010, http://
gawker.com/5561462/congressmans-outfit-making-gay-staffer
-rounds-on-capitol-hill; Aaron Schock's tweet on Twitter, June 14,
2010, https://twitter.com/aaronschock/status/16179557697.

90   *coming from a media event:* "Rep. Aaron Schock: Paul Ryan
Needs to Flaunt His Bod," *TMZ,* August 30, 2012, http://www.tmz
.com/2012/08/30/paul-ryan-republican-national-convention-rnc
-aaron-schock-tampa/#ixzz3Jp9VEflt.
I caught up with Schock: Michelangelo Signorile, "Aaron
Schock, Republican Congressman, Responds to Gay Rumors,
Anti-gay Voting Record," *Huffington Post,* September 3, 2012,

http://www.huffingtonpost.com/2012/09/03/aaron-schock-gay
-rumors_n_1851827.html.

91   *"Are we still not allowed to out him?"*: Itay Hod's Facebook
page, January 3, 2014, https://www.facebook.com/iamitayhod/
posts/10153719602440624.
Hod's status update itself went viral: For example, see "Aaron Schock
Outed as Gay by Itay Hod, Journalist, on Facebook?," *Huffington
Post,* January 4, 2014, http://www.huffingtonpost.com/2014/01/04/
aaron-schock-outed_n_4542133.html.
He gave an interview to the New York Times: Jacob Bernstein,
"Pointing a Finger on Facebook," *New York Times,* January 15,
2014, http://www.nytimes.com/2014/01/16/fashion/Facebook-gay
-congressman-Itay-Hod.html.
did discuss Schock by name: Jonathan Capehart, "No Schock
in Gay Gossip," *Washington Post,* January 7, 2014, http://www
.washingtonpost.com/blogs/post-partisan/wp/2014/01/07/no
schock in gay gossip/.

92   *"progress we often forget we've made":* Brandon Ambrosino, "Outing
the Hypocrisy of Outing," *Time,* January 7, 2014, http://time
.com/171/outing-the-hypocrisy-of-outing/.
The term assumed too much: Nathaniel Frank, "Should the AP
Have Banned Homophobia?," *Slate,* November 27, 2012, http://
www.slate.com/articles/double_x/doublex/2012/11/the_ap_bans
_homophobia_is_the_word_really_inaccurate.html.
akin to sexism or racism: Trudy Ring, "AP Denounces Homophobia
— the Word, That Is," *The Advocate,* November 26, 2012, http://
www.advocate.com/politics/media/2012/11/26/ap-says-homophobia
-mark-describing-antigay-bigotry

93   *Fox News anchor Shepard Smith:* J. K. Trotter, "Shepard Smith Tells
Waitress: 'Get My Fucking Drink!,'" *Gawker,* October 22, 2013,
http://gawker.com/shepard-smith-tells-waitress-get-my-fucking
-drink-1449482969.
the boyfriend is a Fox staffer: J. K. Trotter, "Shepard Smith's Office
Romance: A 26-Year-Old Fox Staffer," *Gawker,* October 25, 2013,
http://gawker.com/shepard-smith-s-office-romance-a-26-year-old
-fox-staff-1451438005.
a piece critical of Gawker and following: David Carr, "Gawker Kicks

Open the Closet, but Its Disclosure Barely Reverberates," *New York Times,* October 27, 2013, http://www.nytimes.com/2013/10/28/ business/media/gawker-kicks-open-the-closet-but-its-disclosure -barely-reverberates.html?pagewanted=all.

Time magazine dreamed up the word: William A. Henry III, "Ethics: Forcing Gays Out of the Closet," *Time,* January 29, 1990, http:// content.time.com/time/magazine/article/0,9171,969264,00.html.

I'd written a cover piece: Michelangelo Signorile, "The Secret Gay Life of Malcolm Forbes," *OutWeek,* March 18, 1990, http://www .outweek.net/pdfs/ow_38.pdf.

94   *a fact his widow confirmed:* Gail M. Henry, letter to the editor, *Gay City News,* November 6, 2003, http://gaycitynews.nyc/gcn_245/ letterstotheeditor.html.

In its 2014 Studio Responsibility Index: GLAAD, "2014 Studio Responsibility Index," 2014, http://www.glaad.org/sri/2014.

96   *"it made no sense to us":* Tim Malloy, "Steven Soderbergh: Every Studio Rejected Liberace Film as 'Too Gay,'" *The Wrap,* January 13, 2013, http://www.thewrap.com/tv/column-post/steven-soderbergh -every-studio-rejected-liberace-film-too-gay-71506/.

97   *less "scarce and regressive":* GLAAD, "Network Responsibility Index 2013," 2013, http://www.glaad.org/nri2013.

"Is TV too gay?": Erin Skarda, "FOX Affiliate: Is 'Glee' Gay Teen Propaganda?," *TIME.com,* May 23, 2011, http://newsfeed.time .com/2011/05/08/fox-affiliate-is-glee-gay-teen-propaganda/.

98   *same-sex public displays of affection:* Massoud Hayoun, "US Straights Want to See Gay Rights but Not Kissing, Study Shows," *Al Jazeera America*, November 20, 2014, http://america.aljazeera.com/ articles/2014/11/20/us-straights-wanttoseegayrightsbutnotkissingstu dyshows.html.

"vehicles to show how tolerant straight people are": Daniel D'Addario, "When It Comes to Gay Characters, TV's Not That Much Better Than Movies," *Salon,* July 23, 2014, http://www.salon .com/2014/07/23/when_it_comes_to_gay_characters_tvs_not_that _much_better_than_movies/.

"two gay men who don't even seem to like each other": Louis Peitzman, "Television May Be Embracing Gay Characters, but Where Is the Same-Sex Intimacy?," *BuzzFeed,* December 10,

2013, http://www.buzzfeed.com/louispeitzman/television-may-be
-embracing-gay-characters-but-where-is-the#12y58sh.

99 *she counted jab after jab:* Sue Kerr, "CBS Program *Mike and
Molly* Says 'F*ck You' to the LGBT Community," *Huffington Post,*
November 18, 2013, http://www.huffingtonpost.com/sue-kerr/mike
-and-molly-transphobic-jokes_b_4287778.html.
Most of the depictions were abysmal: GLAAD, "Victims or Villains:
Examining Ten Years of Transgender Images on Television," 2013,
http://www.glaad.org/publications/victims-or-villains-examining
-ten-years-transgender-images-television.
infection rates hold steady: United States Centers for Disease Control
and Prevention, "HIV Among Gay and Bisexual Men," May 14,
2014, http://www.cdc.gov/hiv/risk/gender/msm/facts/.

100 *popular culture helps fuel* and following: Peter Staley, telephone
interview by author, January 27, 2014.
"that fractional .002 percent": Todd Holland, "The Gatekeepers at
Hollywood's Closet Door," *The Wrap,* July 20, 2009, http://www
.thewrap.com/movies/article/gatekeepers-hollywoods-closet-door
-4435/.
in a 2012 survey: David Robb, "Study Suggests Hollywood Is
Not So Gay-Friendly," *Deadline,* September 10, 2014, http://
deadline.com/2014/09/hollywood-gay-friendly-study-ucla-lgbt
-performers-832504/.

101 *and his agent told* The Backlot: Michael Jenson, "Is Luke Evans Gay?
Publicist Tries to Get His Story Straight," *Thebacklot.com,* August 8,
2011, http://www.thebacklot.com/is-luke-evans-gay-publicist-tries
-to-get-his-story-straight/08/2011/.
Evans came out again, delicately: Erik Maza, "Luke Evans: Slaying
Them Softly," October 9, 2014, *Women's Wear Daily,* http://www
.wwd.com/menswear-news/lifestyle/slaying-them-softly-7973152;
Daniel D'Addario, "Luke Evans Has Been Out for Years, but He's
Finally Stopped Hiding," *Time,* October 10, 2014, http://time
.com/3491050/luke-evans-dracula-untold-coming-out/.

102 *came out as a lesbian* and following: Seth Abramovitch, "Ellen
Page Comes Out as Gay: 'I Am Tired of Lying by Omission'
(Exclusive)," *Hollywood Reporter,* February 14, 2014, http://www
.hollywoodreporter.com/news/ellen-page-comes-as-gay-680563.

103 *this character was important for him as a gay man:* Laura Prudom, "'How to Get Away with Murder' Creator Peter Nowalk on Working with Shonda Rhimes, Diversity on TV," *Variety,* September 25, 2014, http://variety.com/2014/tv/news/how-to-get-away-with -murder-creator-peter-nowalk-shonda-rhimes-viola-davis -diversity-1201313779/.
"push the envelope": Krystin Dos Santos, "Why There Will Be Plenty of Gay Sex on *How to Get Away with Murder,*" *E! Online,* September 25, 2014, http://www.eonline.com/news/582954/why-there-will-be -lots-of-gay-sex-on-how-to-get-away-with-murder.
winning rights is only one part of the battle: Kenji Yoshino, "Gay Covering," in *Covering: The Hidden Assault on Our Civil Rights* (New York: Random House, 2006).

104 *a law that was passed in 2011:* "California Governor Signs Bill Requiring Schools to Teach Gay History," CNN, July 15, 2011, http:// www.cnn.com/2011/US/07/14/california.lgbt.education/.
"That this is a page in history" and following: "Interview with Mark Leno," *The Michelangelo Signorile Show,* SiriusXM OutQ, December 22, 2010, and July 21, 2011.

105 *only 11% of students reported being bullied:* S. T. Russell et al., *LGBT Issues in the Curriculum Promotes School Safety,* California Safe Schools Coalition Research Brief 4 (San Francisco: California Safe Schools Coalition, 2006).
this law promoted "propaganda": Chelsea Rudman, "Fox Attacks LGBT History Bill as 'Propaganda' from 'Pro-Gay Agenda,'" Media Matters for America, December 20, 2010, http://mediamatters.org/ research/2010/12/20/fox-attacks-lgbt-history-bill-as-propaganda -fro/174519.

106 *"We don't want to interrupt":* Hailey Branson-Potts, "New LGBT-Specific History Lessons Planned for L.A. County Schools," *Los Angeles Times,* October 1, 2013, http://www.latimes.com/local/ lanow/la-me-ln-gay-curriculum-20131001-story.html.

5. Worthy of Defending

107 *Alex, sixteen at the time:* "Alex" is a pseudonym.
108 *74% of LGBT students surveyed were harassed:* Gay, Lesbian, Straight

Education Network (GLSEN), "The 2013 National School Climate Survey: The Experiences of Lesbian, Bisexual, and Transgender Youth in Our Nation's Schools," October 2014, http://www.glsen .org/sites/default/files/2013%20National%20School%20Climate%20 Survey%20Full%20Report.pdf.

109   *"Progress is being made"*: "GLSEN Releases New National School Climate Survey," GLSEN, October 22, 2014, http://glsen.org/article/ glsen-releases-new-national-school-climate-survey.

former antibullying czar: "The Arcus Foundation Names Kevin Jennings Executive Director," *The Advocate*, July 13, 2012, http:// www.advocate.com/politics/2012/07/13/arcus-foundation-names -kevin-jennings-executive-director.

a founder of GLSEN: "Improving Education, Creating a Better World," GLSEN, http://glsen.org/learn/about-glsen.

a self-defense course called "Model Mugging": "Why Model Mugging?," Model Mugging, http://modelmugging.org/why-model -mugging/.

"a huge difference in my personal life" and following: Kevin Jennings, telephone interview by author, January 3, 2014.

110   *between 30% and 40% of LGBT youth*: Effie Malley et al., "Suicide Risk and Prevention for Lesbian, Gay, Bisexual, and Transgender Youth," Suicide Prevention Resource Center, Prepared for the Center for Mental Health Services Substance Abuse and Mental Health Services, U.S. Department of Health and Human Services, 2008, http://www.sprc.org/sites/sprc.org/files/library/SPRC_LGBT _Youth.pdf.

four times as likely to attempt suicide: Centers for Disease Control and Prevention, "Sexual Identity, Sex of Sexual Contacts, and Health-Risk Behaviors Among Students in Grades 9–12 — Youth Risk Behavior Surveillance, Selected Sites, United States, 2001– 2009," June 2011, http://www.cdc.gov/healthyyouth/disparities/pdf/ smybackgrounder.pdf.

111   *"I definitely felt like there was a lot of bravado"*: Michelangelo Signorile, "James Clementi Remembers Tyler: On Younger Brother's Suicide, Coming Out as Gay, and Media Barrage," *Huffington Post*, February 3, 2012, http://www.huffingtonpost.com/2012/02/03/tyler -clementi-brother-gay-suicide_n_1252568.html.

"He played football, basketball, soccer": Sirdeaner Walker,

interview on *The Michelangelo Signorile Show,* SiriusXM OutQ, July 7, 2009.

112   *"Jamie was a very sensitive boy"* and following: Tim Rodemeyer, interview on *The Michelangelo Signorile Show,* SiriusXM OutQ, September 30, 2011.
      The It Gets Better Project: "It Gets Better Project — Give Hope to LGBT Youth," It Gets Better, http://www.itgetsbetter.org/.

113   *I wrote about knowing I was gay* and following: Michelangelo Signorile, *Queer in America: Sex, the Media, and the Closets of Power* (New York: Random House, 1993).

116   *Matt, another listener:* "Matt" is a pseudonym.
      the individual has as he or she grows up: For more information about intersex people, see Intersex Society of North America, "What Is Intersex?," accessed December 4, 2014, http://www.isna.org/faq/what_is_intersex.

117   *a landmark case won by Jamie Nasbosny:* Don Terry, "Suit Says Schools Failed to Protect a Gay Student," *New York Times,* March 28, 1996, http://www.nytimes.com/1996/03/29/us/suit-says-schools-failed-to-protect-a-gay-student.html.

118   *1979 book:* Linda Tschirhart Sanford and Ann Fetter, *In Defense of Ourselves: A Rape Prevention Handbook for Women* (Garden City, N.Y.: Doubleday, 1979).
      "The common thread" and following: Center for Anti-violence Education (CAE), "Our Mission," accessed December 23, 2013, http://caeny.org/who-we-are/mission/.

119   *"It was a time"* and following: Annie Ellman, telephone interview by author, February 2 and October 20, 2014.

121   *"I carry myself completely differently":* Kevin Jennings, telephone interview by author, January 3, 2014.
      young people who stand up to their bullies: Benedict Carey, "Can an Enemy Be a Child's Friend?," *New York Times,* May 17, 2010, http://www.nytimes.com/2010/05/18/health/18mind.html?pagewanted=all. For an in-depth study of bullying, see also Emily Bazelon, *Sticks and Stones: Defeating the Culture of Bullying and Rediscovering the Power of Character and Empathy* (New York; Random House, 2013).

122   *"The children who are not disliked by anybody":* "Witkow Researches Role Peer Groups Play in How Kids Respond to Bullying,"

Willamette University, News, October 16, 2013, http://willamette
.edu/news/library/2013/10/bullying_research.html.
"You have several options, as I see it": Carey, "Can an Enemy Be a
Child's Friend?"
"a significant part of the bully–victim dynamic": Ruth Peters, "Q &
A — How Can My Child Cope Best with Bullying?," RuthPeters.
com, accessed December 19, 2013, http://www.ruthpeters.com/
articles/q%20and%20a-how%20can%20my%20child%20cope%20
with%20bullying.pdf.

123 *"This type of 'superior force' advice"*: Carrie Goldman, "Why
Telling Bullying Victims to 'Just Fight Back' Doesn't Work," CNN,
October 31, 2012, http://www.cnn.com/2012/10/31/living/bullying
-fight-back/.
teens still report greater stress: Danah Boyd, *It's Complicated. The
Social Lives of Networked Teens* (New Haven, Conn.: Yale University
Press, 2014).

124 *"I found something really surprising"* and following: Danah Boyd,
interview on *The Michelangelo Signorile Show*, SiriusXM Progress,
May 30, 2014.

6. Not Up for Debate

127 *compared gay marriage to slavery:* Tim Grieve, "James Dobson: Gay
Marriage Is Like Slavery, Only Worse," *Salon,* June 28, 2006, http://
www.salon.com/2006/06/28/dobson_8/.
"group marriage": James C. Dobson, "Dobson: Media Provides
Cover for Assault on Traditional Marriage," CNN, October 20,
2006, http://www.cnn.com/2006/US/06/28/dobson.gaymarriage/
index.html; *"marriage between daddies and little girls"*: "Dobson:
Same-Sex Marriage Would Lead to 'Marriage Between Daddies and
Little Girls . . . Between a Man and His Donkey,'" Media Matters for
America, http://mediamatters.org/video/2005/10/07/dobson-same
-sex-marriage-would-lead-to-marriage/133967.
gays "are intolerant": Kyle Mantyla, "Perkins: Gay Activists Are
Intolerant, Hateful, Vile, Spiteful Pawns of the Devil," *Right Wing
Watch,* People for the American Way, May 3, 2011, http://www

.rightwingwatch.org/content/perkins-gay-activists-are-intolerant
-hateful-vile-spiteful-pawns-devil.

gay young people "have a higher propensity to depression": Tony
Perkins, "Christian Compassion Requires the Truth About Harms of
Homosexuality," *OnFaith,* FaithStreet, October 11, 2010, http://www
.faithstreet.com/onfaith/2010/10/11/christian-compassion-requires
-the-truth-about-harms-of-homosexuality/324.

An FRC official, Peter Sprigg: Kyle Mantyla, "FRC's Sprigg Wants to
See Homosexuality Criminalized," *Right Wing Watch,* People for the
American Way, February 3, 2010, http://www.rightwingwatch.org/
content/frcs-sprigg-wants-see-homosexuality-criminalized.

the FRC contributed $25,000: Brian Montopoli, "Family Research
Council Lobbied Congress on Resolution Denouncing Ugandan
Anti-gay Bill," *CBSNews,* June 4, 2010, http://www.cbsnews.com/
news/family-research-council-lobbied-congress-on-resolution
-denouncing-ugandan-anti-gay-bill/.

128   *added the FRC to its list of hate groups:* "Family Research Council,"
Southern Poverty Law Center Extremist Files, http://www.splcenter
.org/get-informed/intelligence-files/groups/family-research-council.

A group doesn't need to be violent: "Hate and Extremism," Southern
Poverty Law Center: What We Do, http://www.splcenter.org/what
-we-do/hate-and-extremism.

a deranged gunman: Tal Kopan, "Floyd Lee Corkins, the Family
Research Center Shooter, Sentenced to 25 Years," *Politico,*
September 9, 2013, http://www.politico.com/story/2013/09/frc
-shooter-sentenced-to-25-years-97069.html.

argued the FRC's hate-group label: Dana Milbank, "Dana Milbank:
Hateful Speech on Hate Groups," *Washington Post,* August 16, 2012,
http://www.washingtonpost.com/opinions/dana-milbank-hateful
-speech-on-hate-groups/2012/08/16/70a60ac6-e7e8-11e1-8487
-64e4b2a79ba8_story.html.

Milbank received a fair amount of criticism: See, for example, Zack
Ford, "*Washington Post* Columnists Argue Family Research Council
Shouldn't be Called a 'Hate Group,'" *Think Progress,* August 17,
2012, http://thinkprogress.org/lgbt/2012/08/17/705331/washington
-post-columnists-argue-family-research-council-shouldnt-be
-called-a-hate-group/; and Peter Rosenstein, "Memo to Dana
Milbank: FRC Is a Hate Group," *Washington Blade,* August 21,

2012, http://www.washingtonblade.com/2012/08/21/memo-to-dana-milbank-frc-is-a-hate-group/.

129 *"not a group that puts on sheets"*: Michelangelo Signorile, "Dana Milbank, *Washington Post* Writer, Slams LGBT Activists, SPLC for FRC's 'Hate Group' Label," *Huffington Post,* August 22, 2012, http://www.huffingtonpost.com/2012/08/22/dana-milbank-washington-post-family-research-council-hate-group_n_1822805.html.
calling the criticism "idiotic": Scott Wooledge, *"Washington Post's* Deputy Editorial Page Editor Jackson Diehl Calls His Readers 'Idiotic,'" *Daily Kos* (blog), August 21, 2012, http://www.dailykos.com/story/2012/08/21/1122489/-Washington-Post-s-Deputy-Editorial-Page-Editor-Editor-Jackson-Diehl-calls-his-readers-idiotic#.
ABC News announced: Hadas Gold, "Laura Ingraham Joins ABC News," *Politico,* April 4, 2014, http://www.politico.com/blogs/media/2014/04/laura-ingraham-joins-abc-news-186819.html.
reminding opponents that she has a gay brother: Margaret Carlson, "A Pundit's Conversion," *Time,* April 21, 1997, http://www.cnn.com/ALLPOLITICS/1997/04/14/time/carlson.html; Mike Daniels, "Laura Ingraham: Being Gay 'Absolutely Not a Choice,'" *Secular Daily News,* October 18, 2010, http://www.secularnewsdaily.com/2010/10/laura-ingraham-being-gay-absolutely-not-a-choice/; Eddie Scarry, "Laura Ingraham, Who Has 'a Lot of Close' Gay Friends, Has No Opinion on the Repeal of DADT," *The Blaze,* May 28, 2013, http://www.theblaze.com/blog/2013/05/28/laura-ingraham-dadt-military-gay-larry-king/.
"Welcome to the new totalitarianism": Emily Arrowood and Olivia Kittel, "Right-Wing Media Denounce Guinness for Protesting Parade's Homophobia," Media Matters for America, March 17, 2014, http://mediamatters.org/research/2014/03/17/right-wing-media-denounce-guinness-for-protesti/198508.
the "gender-bending phenomenon": Carlos Maza, "Laura Ingraham Dispenses Dangerous Advice for Raising Transgender Youth," Media Matters for America, May 31, 2013, http://mediamatters.org/blog/2013/05/31/laura-ingraham-dispenses-dangerous-advice-for-r/194286.

130 *"child abuse"*: Elias Isquith, "Laura Ingraham Says Hormone Therapy for Transgender Kids Is 'Child Abuse,'" *Salon,* August

6, 2014, http://www.salon.com/2014/08/06/laura_ingraham_says
_hormone_therapy_for_trangender_kids_is_child_abuse/.

she lambasted Michigan's governor: Heather Digby Parton, "ABC's
New Right-Wing Hack: Why a Network Is Paying for Laura
Ingraham's Vile Racism," *Salon,* April 15, 2014, http://www.salon.
com/2014/04/15/abcs_new_right_wing_hack_why_a_network_is
_paying_for_laura_ingrahams_vile_racism/.

"the Catholic perspective": "Laura Ingraham Says Decision to
Strike Down DOMA May Make Catholics 'Persona Non Grata'
in America," Media Matters for America, June 26, 2013, http://
mediamatters.org/video/2013/06/26/laura-ingraham-says-decision
-to-strike-down-dom/194621.

"I want the law to discriminate": David Badash, "Bill Donohue to
Piers Morgan: 'I Want the Law to Discriminate,'" New Civil Rights
Movement, May 10, 2012, http://www.thenewcivilrightsmovement
.com/bill-donohue-to-piers-morgan-i-want-the-law-to-
discriminate-against-gays/politics/2012/05/10/39300.

131 *among all Catholics, 60% support gay marriage:* "U.S. Catholics Back
Pope on Changing Church Focus, Quinnipiac University National
Poll Finds; Catholics Support Gay Marriage, Women Priests 2–1,"
Quinnipiac University, October 4, 2013, http://www.quinnipiac.edu/
images/polling/us/us10042013_er9hjp.pdf.

"Overall, the religious spokespeople used": "Skewed Perception:
Religious Voices on President Obama and Marriage Equality,"
GLAAD, accessed July 30, 2014, http://www.glaad.org/publications/
skewed-perception-religious-voices-president-obama-and-
marriage-equality.

132 *"Media outlets persistently quoted":* Debra L. Mason and Cathy Ellen
Rosenholtz, *Missing Voices: A Study of Religious Voices in Mainstream
Media Reports about LGBT Equality* (Columbia: University of
Missouri Center on Religion and the Professions, 2012), http://www
.glaad.org/sites/default/files/GLAAD_MissingVoices_2012.pdf.

133 *a young, inexperienced writer:* Luke Brinker, "Meet Brandon
Ambrosino, Homophobes' Favorite Gay Writer and Vox's
Newest Hire," Media Matters for America, March 12, 2014, http://
mediamatters.org/blog/2014/03/12/meet-brandon-ambrosino
-homophobes-favorite-gay/198461.

came under fire from many LGBT critics: See, for example, Noah

Michelson, "Ezra Klein, I'm Calling Bullsh*t on Your Defense of Hiring Brandon Ambrosino, and Here's Why," *Huffington Post,* March 14, 2014, http://www.huffingtonpost.com/noah-michelson/ ezra-klein-im-calling-bul_b_4965557.html; Gabriel Arana, "Ezra Klein's Queer New Hire," *The American Prospect,* March 13, 2014, http://prospect.org/article/ezra-kleins-queer-new-hire; and Rich Juzwiak, "Ezra Klein Hired Contrarian Gay Without Having Read His Work," *Gawker,* March 13, 2014, http://gawker.com/ezra-klein hired-contrarian-gay-without-having-read-his-1543320286.

"handled this hire a lot better": Ezra Klein's Facebook page, March 14, 2014, https://www.facebook.com/ezraklein/ posts/10152347488818410.

134 *Dana Loesch, who was a Tea Party organizer:* Eric Hananoki, "CNN's Loesch: CNN Has 'Blatant Disregard for Objectivity,' 'Biggest Bunch of Idiot Blockheads,'" Media Matters for America, February 17, 2011, http://mediamatters.org/research/2011/02/17/ cnns-loesch-cnn-has-blatant-disregard-for-objec/176579.

she applauded U.S. Marines: "Dana Loesch, CNN Contributor, Says She'd Urinate on Taliban Soldiers Too (AUDIO)," *Huffington Post,* January 13, 2012, http://www.huffingtonpost.com/2012/01/13/dana -loesch-urinate-taliban-soldiers_n_1204727.html.

defended a fourteen-year-old radio host: Lucas Grindley, "CNN Contributor Defends Radio Host Who Said Obama Turns Kids Gay," *The Advocate,* June 7, 2012, http://www.advocate.com/politics/ media/2012/06/07/cnn-contributor-defends-radio-host-who-said -obama-turns-kids-gay.

"You only prescribe to certain aspects of Christianity": "CNN's Dana Loesch to Chick-Fil-A Critic: 'I Know You Hate Christ,'" Equality Matters, July 25, 2012, http://equalitymatters.org/ emtv/201207250006.

railed against allowing transgender women: "CNN's Dana Loesch Attacks Trans-Inclusive Bathrooms: It's a 'Safety Issue' Because 'Men Are Stronger Than Women,'" Equality Matters, May 25, 2012, http://equalitymatters.org/emtv/201205250001.

castigated Dan Savage: "CNN's Loesch Agrees with Caller Who Accuses Dan Savage of Trying to 'Take Out Homosexual Rage on Children,'" Equality Matters, May 1, 2012, http://equalitymatters. org/emtv/201205010005.

called marriage "a covenant": Dana Loesch, "The Argument for 'Marriage Equality' Is Not a Conservative One," *Red State*, March 26, 2013, http://www.redstate.com/diary/dloesch/2013/03/26/the-argument-for-marriage-equality-is-not-a-conservative-one/.

135   *"ABC's* The View *reportedly plans"*: Justin Berrier, "ABC's *The View* to Mainstream Conservative Demagogue Dana Loesch," Media Matters for America, January 31, 2014, http://mediamatters .org/blog/2014/01/31/abcs-the-view-to-mainstream-conservative -demago/197866.

gay people "must repent" and "not act": Jeremy Hooper, "Red State's Erick Erickson Goes Full on Anti-gay; Gay Boy Scouts Must 'Repent,'" GLAAD, May 24, 2013, http://www.glaad.org/blog/red -states-erick-erickson-goes-full-anti-gay.

"comparing gay rights activists to the Nazis": Erick Erickson, "Gay Rights Proponents Act Like the Third Reich," *The Erick Erickson Show* Daily Notes, December 4, 2008, http://www.erickerickson.org/ blog/2008/12/04/gay-rights-proponents-act-like-the-third-reich/.

"enormous energy is being expended": Erick Erickson, "Tolerate or Be Stamped Out," *Town Hall*, August 7, 2014, http://townhall .com/columnists/erickerickson/2014/08/07/tolerate-or-be-stamped -out-n1875995/page/full.

"a psychotic delusion": Zack Ford, "Following Criticism, FOX News Removes Transphobic Commentary on Chaz Bono's Transition," *Think Progress*, May 18, 2011, http://thinkprogress.org/ lgbt/2011/05/18/177426/fox-news-transphobia-wipe/.

136   *Christian evangelical leader Randy Thomasson*: Katherine T. Phan, "Randy Thomasson Launches Campaign for Children and Families," *The Christian Post*, November 30, 2004, http://www .christianpost.com/news/randy-thomasson-launches-campaign-for -children-and-families-20745/.

also lists as a hate group: Josh Israel, "Newly Designated Anti-gay Hate Groups Earned That Distinction," *Think Progress*, March 9, 2012, http://thinkprogress.org/lgbt/2012/03/09/441448/anti-gay -hate-groups-earned-that-distinction/.

"tsunami of perversity": Becky Yeh, "Parental Rights, Decency Out the Window," *OneNewsNow*, June 7, 2011, http://web.archive.org/ web/20110815080730/http://www.onenewsnow.com/Education/ Default.aspx?id=1363306.

stop using Tony Perkins: "REPORT: Hate Group Leader's
Appearances Plummet on CNN and MSNBC, Hold Steady on FOX
News," Equality Matters, July 30, 2014, http://equalitymatters.org/
factcheck/201407300001.

7. Winning True Equality

138   *Winning an apology:* Wayne Bledsoe, "Dolly Parton Responds to
      Dollywood Splash Country T-Shirt Controversy," August 2, 2011,
      Knoxville (Tenn.) News Sentinel, http://www.knoxnews.com/news/
      local-news/dolly-parton-responds-to-dollywood-splash-t.
      didn't initially get the kind of response: Jennifer Tipton and Olivier
      Odom, interview on *The Michelangelo Signorile Show,* SiriusXM
      OutQ, August 3, 2011.

139   (*REPEAL) HIV Discrimination Act:* Dan Roberts, "New Bill Seeks to
      Repeal Outdated State HIV Discrimination Laws," *The Guardian,*
      December 10, 2013, http://www.theguardian.com/world/2013/
      dec/10/us-house-hiv-bill-discrimination; *Barbara Lee in the House:*
      Josh Richman, "Barbara Lee Bill Would Push States to Roll Back
      Criminal HIV Laws," *San Jose (Calif.) Mercury News,* May 9,
      2013, http://www.mercurynews.com/ci_23201838/barbara-lee-bill
      -would-push-states-roll-back; Human Rights Campaign, "Repeal
      Existing Policies That Encourage and Allow Legal (REPEAL) HIV
      Discrimination Act," accessed November 20, 2014, http://www.hrc
      .org/resources/entry/repeal-existing-policies-that-encourage-and
      -allow-legal-repeal-hiv-discrimi.
      died in three subcommittees: REPEAL Act, H.R. 3053, 112th Cong.
      (2011–2012), https://www.congress.gov/bill/112th-congress/house
      bill/3053/all-actions-with-amendments.

140   *failed to get a Republican cosponsor:* Dan Roberts, "New Bill Seeks
      to Repeal Outdated State HIV Discrimination Laws," *The Guardian,*
      December 10, 2014, http://www.theguardian.com/world/2013/
      dec/10/us-house-hiv-bill-discrimination.
      HIV-prevention campaigns: National Alliance of State and Territorial
      AIDS Directors, *National HIV Prevention Inventory: 2013 Funding
      Survey Report,* (Washington, D.C.: NASTAD, 2013), http://www
      .nastad.org/Docs/NHPI-2013-Funding-Report-Final.pdf; "HIV

and the LGBT Community," Human Rights Campaign, accessed
September 20, 2014, http://www.hrc.org/resources/entry/hrc-issue
-brief-hiv-aids-and-the-lgbt-community.

"no compelling medical rationale": Joseph Straw, "Panel Chaired
by Joycelyn Elders Urges Lifting of Ban on Transgender Troops,"
New York Daily News, March 14, 2014, http://www.nydailynews
.com/news/politics/lift-ban-transgender-troops-panel-report
-article-1.1721650; Joycelyn Elders and Alan M. Steinman, *Report
of the Transgender Military Service Commission* (Palm Center,
March 2014), http://www.palmcenter.org/files/Transgender%20
Military%20Service%20Report_0.pdf; "Secretary of Defense
Chuck Hagel: Military's Transgender Policy 'Continually Should
Be Reviewed,'" ABCNews, May 11, 2014, http://abcnews.go.com/
blogs/politics/2014/05/secretary-of-defense-chuck-hagel-militarys
-transgender-policy-continually-should-be-reviewed/.

The policy could be ended: "Transgender Military Service,"
OutServe-SLDN, accessed October 1, 2014, http://www.sldn.org/
pages/transgender-issues.

he was "open" to reviewing it: Helene Cooper, "Hagel 'Open' to
Reviewing Military's Ban on Transgender People," *New York Times*,
May 11, 2014, http://www.nytimes.com/2014/05/12/us/hagel-open
-to-review-of-military-policy-on-transgender-people.html?_r=1.

Wilson served: Michelangelo Signorile, "Landon Wilson,
Transgender Navy Sailor, on Being Discharged and His
Documentary Project," *Huffington Post*, May 3, 2014, http://www
.huffingtonpost.com/2014/05/03/landon-wilson-transgender
-navy-_n_5253439.html.

141   *Safe Schools Improvement Act:* "Safe Schools Improvement Act,"
Human Rights Campaign, Resources, http://www.hrc.org/resources/
entry/safe-schools-improvement-act.

"We get her like we get our moms": Amy Chozick, "Hillary Clinton's
Gay Rights Evolution," *New York Times*, August 29, 2014, http://
www.nytimes.com/2014/08/31/fashion/hillary-clinton-gay-rights
-evolution.html.

142   *"put its weight behind"*: Chad Griffin, "Why HRC Supports a
Comprehensive LGBT Civil Rights Bill," *BuzzFeed*, July 9, 2014,
http://www.buzzfeed.com/chadhgriffin/why-hrc-supports-a
-comprehensive-lgbt-civil-rights-bill#12y58sh.

a report calling for such a bill: Human Rights Campaign, *Beyond Marriage Equality: A Blueprint for Federal Non-discrimination Protections,* accessed December 4, 2014, http://hrc-assets.s3-website-us-east-1.amazonaws.com//files/images/campaign/ HRC_BeyondMarriageEquality.pdf; Sheryl Gay Stolberg, "Rights Bill Sought for Lesbian, Gay, Bisexual and Transgender Americans," *New York Times,* December 4, 2014, http://www.nytimes. com/2014/12/05/us/advocates-seek-civil-rights-bill-for-lesbian-gay -bisexual-and-transgender-americans.html?hp&action=click&p gtype=Homepage&module=second-column-region&region=top -news&WT.nav=top-news.

143 *Only after the Supreme Court's* Hobby Lobby *decision:* Jennifer Bendery and Amanda Terkel, "Gay Rights Groups Pull Support for ENDA over Sweeping Religious Exemption," *Huffington Post,* July 8, 2014, http://www.huffingtonpost.com/2014/07/08/enda-religious -exemption_n_5568736.html.
   "ENDA is not as new" and following: Michael Crawford, interview on *The Michelangelo Signorile Show,* SiriusXM OutQ, "Netroots Nation," June 21, 2013.

145 *couples in Hawaii who sued:* "*Baehr v. Miike,*" Lambda Legal, accessed March 3, 2014, http://www.lambdalegal.org/in-court/cases/ baehr-v-miike.
   the group Freedom to Marry: "Evan Wolfson, Founder and President," Freedom to Marry, accessed March 3, 2014, http://www .freedomtomarry.org/pages/evan-wolfson-founder-and-president.
   conservatives responded with the Defense of Marriage Act: "Defense of Marriage Act," American Civil Liberties Union, accessed March 5, 2014, https://www.aclu.org/blog/tag/defense-marriage-act.
   and there will surely be more: For a recent book on the battle for marriage equality in key states, see Mark Solomon, *Winning Marriage: The Inside Story of How Same-Sex Couples Took On the Politicians and Pundits — and Won* (Hanover, N.H.: ForeEdge, 2014).

146 *pioneering attorney Mary Bonauto:* Sheryl Gay Stolberg, "In Fight for Marriage Rights, 'She's Our Thurgood Marshall,'" *New York Times,* March 27, 2013, http://www.nytimes.com/2013/03/28/ us/maine-lawyer-credited-in-fight-for-gay-marriage.html ?pagewanted=all.
   the American Foundation for Equal Rights: Bill Higgins, "How

Rob Reiner, Bruce Cohen, and Dustin Lance Black helped defeat Prop. 8," *Hollywood Reporter,* February 16, 2012, http://www .hollywoodreporter.com/news/prop-8-defeated-rob-reiner-bruce -cohen-dustin-lance-black-292021.

Jo Becker's book: Jo Becker, *Forcing the Spring: Inside the Fight for Marriage Equality* (New York: Penguin, 2014).

it overplayed the Prop 8 case: Michelangelo Signorile, "The Worst Problem with Jo Becker's Book on 'the Fight for Marriage Equality,'" *Huffington Post,* April 21, 2014, http://www .huffingtonpost.com/michelangelo-signorile/the-worst-problem -with-jo_b_5185688.html.

147   *one initial slap:* Joe Solmonese, "Obama's Inaugural Mistake," *Washington Post,* December 19, 2008, http://www.washingtonpost .com/wp-dyn/content/article/2008/12/18/AR2008121802788.html.

"People wrongly assume": Philip Elliott, "Obama Promises to Push on Gay Rights Agenda," *Salon,* June 22, 2010, http://www.salon .com/2010/06/22/obama_pushes_on_gay_rights/.

actually defending DOMA in court: John Aravosis, "Obama Defends DOMA in Federal Court: Says Banning Gay Marriage Is Good for the Federal Budget; Invokes Incest and Marrying Children," *AMERICAblog* (blog), June 12, 2009, http://americablog .com/2009/06/obama-defends-doma-in-federal-court-says -banning-gay-marriage-is-good-for-the-federal-budget-invokes -incest-and-marrying-children.html.

148   *"written by Pat Robertson":* David Mixner, "A Personal Statement: DOMA brief brings shame to Obama team!," DavidMixner.com, June 15, 2009, http://www.davidmixner.com/2009/06/a-personal -statement-doma-brief-brings-shame-to-obama-team.html.

bloggers inspired some LGBT donors to boycott: Huma Khan, "Outraged by Obama Legal Brief, Gay Democratic Donors Boycotting DNC Bash," *ABCNews,* June 16, 2009, http://abcnews .go.com/blogs/politics/2009/06/outraged-by-obama-legal-brief-gay -democratic-donors-boycotting-dnc-bash/.

the "Democratic effort to milk money": John Aravosis, "DNC Fundraiser Starting to Fall Apart over Rupture Between Obama and Gay Community," *AMERICAblog* (blog), June 15, 2009, http:// americablog.com/2009/06/dnc-gay-fundraiser-starting-to-fall -apart-over-rupture-between-obama-and-gay-community.html.

an obligation "to defend federal statutes": "Obama Says He Still Wants to Repeal Marriage Law," *USA Today,* August 17, 2009, http://usatoday30.usatoday.com/news/washington/2009-08-17-gay -marriage_N.htm.

former Clinton-administration officials: Richard Socarides, "The Choice to Defend DOMA, and its Consequences," *AMERICAblog* (blog), June 14, 2009, http://americablog.com/2009/06/choice -to-defend-doma-and-its.html. (Former Clinton administration solicitor general Walter Dellinger would also later write a memo supporting the Obama administration's decision to stop defending DOMA. See Jan Crawford, "Obama Administration Decision to Not Defend Defense of Marriage Act Will Trigger Heated Political Battle," *CBSNews,* February 24, 2011, http://www.cbsnews.com /news/obama-administration-decision-to-not-defend-defense-of -marriage-act-will-trigger-heated-political-battle.)

Both President George W. Bush. John Aravosis, "Obama DOJ Lies to Politico in Defending Hate Brief Against Gays," *AMERICAblog* (blog), June 12, 2009, http://americablog.com/2009/06/obama-doj -lies-to-politico-in-defending-hate-brief-against-gays.html.

took on what Joe Sudbay later called "apologists": Joe Sudbay, "Boehner: House GOP Will Decide This Week Whether to Defend DOMA," *AMERICAblog* (blog), February 28, 2011, http:// americablog.com/2011/02/boehner-house-gopers-will-decide-this -week-whether-to-defend-doma.html.

defended DOMA in court in yet another case: Igor Volsky, "Obama DOJ Files Brief in Defense of DOMA: Congress Established 'Federal Uniformity' as States Tackle Marriage Question," *Think Progress,* January 13, 2011, http://thinkprogress.org/lgbt/2011/01/13/177215/ doma-brief/.

149 *it believed DOMA to be unconstitutional:* Brian Montopoli, "Obama Administration Will No Longer Defend DOMA," *CBSNews,* February 24, 2011, http://www.cbsnews.com/news/obama -administration-will-no-longer-defend-doma/.

"Attitudes evolve, including mine": Joe Sudbay, "BREAKING: President Obama Supports Marriage Equality," *AMERICAblog* (blog), May 9, 2012, http://americablog.com/2012/05/breaking -president-obama-supports-marriage-equality.html.

mention his "evolving": Peter Wallsten and Scott Wilson, "For

Obama, Gay Marriage Stance Born of a Long Evolution,"
Washington Post, May 10, 2012, http://www.washingtonpost.
com/politics/for-obama-gay-marriage-stance-borne-of-a-long
-evolution/2012/05/10/gIQAIDIlGU_story.html.

"EVOLVE ALREADY!": Joe Sudbay, "Thanks for Bending the 'Arc
of History,' Mr. President," *Huffington Post,* May 10, 2012, http://
www.huffingtonpost.com/joe-sudbay/obama-gay-marriage-arc-of
-history_b_1508036.html.

"I think the gay community": Erica Werner, "Obama Stops Short
of Endorsing Gay Marriage; 'Evolve Already' Reads Button Worn
by Dan Savage," *Miami Herald,* June 30, 2011, http://miamiherald
.typepad.com/gaysouthflorida/2011/06/obama-stops-short-of
-endorsing-gay-marriage-evolve-already-reads-button-worn-by
-dan-savage.html.

Even HRC had, by this point, urged: "HRC Urges President Obama
to Support Marriage Equality for All Americans" (press release),
Human Rights Campaign, January 13, 2011, http://www.hrc.org/
press-releases/entry/hrc-urges-president-obama-to-support
-marriage-equality-for-all-americans.

Obama needed to energize his base: Michelangelo Signorile, "Why
Obama Must Come Out of the Closet on Gay Marriage," *Huffington
Post,* April 6, 2012, http://www.huffingtonpost.com/michelangelo
-signorile/obama-gay-marriage_b_1407991.html.

Joe Biden made his infamous slip-up: Igor Volsky, "BREAKING:
Joe Biden Endorses Same-Sex Marriage," *Think Progress,* May
6, 2012, http://thinkprogress.org/lgbt/2012/05/06/478786/biden
-marriage/.

the president announced his support: Rick Klein, "Obama: 'I Think
Same-Sex Couples Should Be Able to Get Married,'" *ABCNews,*
May 9, 2012, http://abcnews.go.com/blogs/politics/2012/05/obama
-comes-out-i-think-same-sex-couples-should-be-able-to-get
-married/.

it helped in four states: Erik Eckholm, "As Victories Pile Up, Gay
Rights Advocates Cheer 'Milestone Year,'" *New York Times,*
November 7, 2012, http://www.nytimes.com/2012/11/08/us/same
-sex-marriage-gains-cheer-gay-rights-advocates.html.

150   *comes to mind:* University of Pennsylvania Law School, "A Front
Row Seat to History: Tobias Barrington Wolff on the Repeal

of DADT," December 23, 2014, https://www.law.upenn.edu/
live/news/1896-a-front-row-seat-to-history-tobias-barrington#
.VHrSsqTF9ew.

Hate Crimes Prevention Act was passed: "Obama Signs Hate Crimes
Bill into Law," CNN, October 28, 2009, http://www.cnn.com/2009/
POLITICS/10/28/hate.crimes/index.html?iref=nextin.

"Where's our 'fierce advocate'?": Richard Socarides, "A Chance for
Barack Obama to Take Bold Action on Behalf of Gay Americans,"
Washington Post, May 2, 2009, http://www.washingtonpost.com/wp
-dyn/content/article/2009/05/01/AR2009050103401.html.

David Mixner asked, "How much longer": Sheryl Gay Stolberg,
"As Gay Issues Arise, Obama Is Pressed to Engage," *New York
Times,* May 6, 2009, http://www.nytimes.com/2009/05/07/us/
politics/07obama.html.

151   *"They have a vision":* Ibid.

called for a march on Washington: David Mixner, "March on
Washington for Marriage Equality 2009," DavidMixner.com,
May 20, 2009, http://www.davidmixner.com/2009/05/march-on
-washington-for-marriage-equality-2009.html.

led by organizers: Kip Williams and Robin McGehee, "Let's
Stop Talking About Failure and Go Win," The Bilerico Project,
September 17, 2009, http://www.bilerico.com/2009/09/lets_stop
_talking_about_failure_and_go_win.php.

Almost two hundred thousand people: John Cloud, "The Gay March:
A New Generation of Protesters," *Time,* October 12, 2009, http://
content.time.com/time/magazine/article/0,9171,1930526,00.html.

"Let us be clear to America": "The Text of David Mixner's Speech,"
The Advocate, October 11, 2009, http://www.advocate.com/news/
news-features/2009/10/11/text-david-mixners-speech.

scheduled Obama to speak: Joe Sudbay, "Obama Will Speak at HRC
Dinner This Weekend," *AMERICAblog* (blog), October 5, 2009,
http://americablog.com/2009/10/obama-will-speak-at-hrc-dinner
-this-weekend.html.

"continue to pressure me": "Presidential Remarks at Human Rights
Campaign Dinner," C-SPAN, October 10, 2009, http://www.c-span
.org/video/?289399-1/presidential-remarks-human-rights-campaign
-dinner.

152   *in his State of the Union address:* "Obama Calls for 'Don't Ask, Don't

Tell' Repeal," CNN, January 27, 2010, http://www.cnn.com/2010/
POLITICS/01/27/obama.gays.military/.

Gates announced that the Pentagon: Rachel Slajda, "Mullen and
Gates Announce Study of DADT, Which May Take a Year," *Talking
Points Memo,* February 2, 2010, http://talkingpointsmemo.com/
news/mullen-and-gates-announce-study-of-dadt-which-may-take
-a-year.

gays served with distinction: Nathaniel Frank, "What Does the
Empirical Research Say About the Impact of Openly Gay Service on
the Military?," Palm Center, March 3, 2010, http://www.palmcenter
.org/publications/dadt/what_does_empirical_research_say_about
_impact_openly_gay_service_military.

"counseled the president against acting": Kerry Eleveld, "White
House Sends Mixed Messages on DADT," *The Advocate,* April 21,
2010, http://www.advocate.com/news/daily-news/2010/04/21/white
-house-sends-mixed-messages-dadt.

sprang into action: See Get Equal, "Frequently Asked Questions,"
accessed November 20, 2014, http://getequal.org/faqs/.

153   *arrested for chaining themselves:* Brian Montopoli, "Dan Choi, Other
Gay Rights Protesters Arrested After Chaining Selves to White
House Fence," *CBSNews,* April 20, 2010, http://www.cbsnews.com/
news/dan-choi-other-gay-rights-protesters-arrested-after-chaining
-selves-to-white-house-fence/.

Choi had even gotten a public promise: Stephanie Condon,
"Netroots Nation 2010: Harry Reid Makes Promise to Dan Choi
to Repeal 'Don't Ask, Don't Tell,'" *Huffington Post,* July 24, 2010,
http://www.huffingtonpost.com/2010/07/24/netroots-nation-2010
-harr_n_658364.html.

The Net roots kept up the pressure: For an in-depth narrative account
of the repeal of "don't ask, don't tell," see Michelangelo Signorile,
"Rewriting History," *The Advocate,* February 7, 2011, http://www
.advocate.com/arts-entertainment/features/2011/02/07/rewriting
-history.

Republicans surprised Democrats: Sam Stein, "Harry Reid Pulls
Omnibus, but Announces Votes on DADT and DREAM Act,"
Huffington Post, December 16, 2010, http://www.huffingtonpost
.com/2010/12/16/senate-plans-dont-ask-don_n_798016.html.

White House still wasn't pushing hard enough: Igor Volsky, "Carl

Levin: Obama Lacks 'a Willingness to Fight Hard' and Keep Senate in Town to Pass Priorities," *Think Progress,* December 13, 2010, http://thinkprogress.org/politics/2010/12/13/134718/levin-obama -priorities/.

154   *activists were invited:* William Branigin, Debbi Wilgoren, and Perry Bacon Jr., "Obama Signs DADT Repeal Before Big, Emotional Crowd," *Washington Post,* December 22, 2010, http:// www.washingtonpost.com/wp-dyn/content/article/2010/12/22/ AR2010122201888.html.
       a sweeping bill: Jerome Hunt, "A History of the Employment Non-Discrimination Act," Center for American Progress, July 19, 2011, http://www.americanprogress.org/issues/lgbt/ news/2011/07/19/10006/a-history-of-the-employment-non -discrimination-act/.

155   *the narrow version of ENDA:* Ibid.
       I asked Senator Tammy Baldwin: Tammy Baldwin, interview on *The Michelangelo Signorile Show,* SiriusXM Progress, July 23, 2013.

157   *"hazy, crystal ball question":* Stolberg, "Rights Bill Sought."
       possible the Equal Employment Opportunity Commission will rule: Chris Geidner, "Federal Judge Rules Existing Civil Rights Law Can Protect Gay People from Job Bias," *BuzzFeed,* April 2, 2014, http:// www.buzzfeed.com/chrisgeidner/federal-judge-existing-civil-rights -law-can-protect-gay-peop#12y58sh.
       "This is a point in time": Maggie Haberman, "Gay Donor: Gay Rights Not 'Inevitable,'" *Politico,* May 2, 2014, http://www.politico. com/story/2014/05/tim-gill-a-top-gay-donor-talks-strategy-106265. html.
       it is opening up field offices: Jay Reeves, "Human Rights Campaign Plans LGBT Equality Push in the South," *Huffington Post,* April 26, 2014, http://www.huffingtonpost.com/2014/04/26/human-rights -campaign-south_n_5219089.html.

158   *reviews on Yelp describing Big Earl's:* Caroline Moss, "Yelp Reviewers Had the Perfect Response After a Restaurant Kicked Two Men Out for Being Gay," *Business Insider,* June 2, 2014, http://www .businessinsider.com/big-earls-bait-and-tackle-yelp-reviews-2014-6.
       Yelp eventually removed these reviews: Mark Joseph Stern, "Why Did Yelp Delete Critical Reviews of the Texas Restaurant That Wouldn't Serve 'Fags'?," *Slate,* June 4, 2014, http://www.slate.com/blogs/

outward/2014/06/04/yelp_took_down_reviews_of_anti_gay_big
_earl_s.html.

a queer eat-in: Cavan Sieczkowski, "Texas Restaurant That Refused
'Fag' Customers Touted as Gay Bar Online," *Huffington Post,*
May 31, 2014, http://www.huffingtonpost.com/2014/05/31/texas
-restaurant-fag-customers-gay-bar_n_5423727.html.

Then there was Pamela Raintree and following: Michelangelo
Signorile, "Pamela Raintree, Transgender Woman Who Dared
Councilman to Stone Her, Speaks Out," *Huffington Post,* February
1, 2014, http://www.huffingtonpost.com/2014/02/01/pamela-raintree
-rob-webb-_n_4699226.html.

8. Fields of Combat

160 *the International Olympic Committee:* Cyd Zeigler, "Moment
#22: International Olympic Committee Allows Transgender
Athletes to Compete," *Outsports,* September 11, 2011, http://www
.outsports.com/2011/9/12/4051806/moment-22-international
-olympic-committee-allows-transgender-athletes; *the National
Collegiate Athletic Association:* "NCAA Inclusion of Transgender
Student-Athletes," NCAA, http://www.ncaa.org/sites/default/files/
Transgender_Handbook_2011_Final.pdf.

Renée Richards fought to compete: Mitch Abramson, "Renee
Richards, First Transgender Tennis Player to Compete in U.S.
Open, Subject of New Documentary," *New York Daily News,*
July 22, 2011, http://www.nydailynews.com/sports/more-sports/
renee-richards-transgender-tennis-player-compete-u-s-open
-subject-new-documentary-article-1.158359; *Fallon Fox in recent
years:* Steven Rondina, "Fox Putting Promoters in Awkward Spot,"
Bleacher Report, October 20, 2014, http://bleacherreport.com/
articles/2208997-fallon-fox-transgender-fighters-success-putting
-promoters-in-awkward-spot.

openly gay current diving champion: Cavan Sieczkowski, "Tom
Daley: 'I Am a Gay Man Now,'" *Huffington Post,* April 3, 2014,
http://www.huffingtonpost.com/2014/04/03/tom-daley-gay-man
-now_n_5083865.html.

Sheryl Swoopes came out as gay: Sheryl Swoopes, as told to LZ Granderson, "Outside the Arc," *ESPN: The Magazine,* updated April 12, 2006, http://sports.espn.go.com/wnba/news/story?id=2204322/. *engaged to a man:* "WNBA Player Sheryl Swoopes Is Now Engaged to a Man," *Autostraddle,* July 15, 2011, http://www.autostraddle .com/lesbian-wnba-player-sheryl-swoopes-is-now-engaged-to -a-man-99696/; *not identifying herself as straight:* Maya Rupert, "What Sheryl Swoopes' Engagement Means: Understanding the Role of Identity and Combo Guards," *Huffington Post,* August 1, 2011, http://www.huffingtonpost.com/maya-rupert/sheryl-swoopes -marriage_b_909288.html.

Brittney Griner came out and following: "Brittney Griner Discusses Being Gay," *ESPN,* April 21, 2013, http://espn.go.com/wnba/story/_/ id/9185633/brittney-griner-comes-says-just-are; *"a collective shrug":* Jessica Luther, "The WNBA Can Teach Male Athletes About Coming Out and Being Allies," *The Atlantic,* April 30, 2013, http:// www.theatlantic.com/sexes/archive/2013/04/the-wnba-can-teach -male-athletes-about-coming-out-and-being-allies/275414/.

161   *the first openly gay NBA executive:* Jim Buzinkski, "A Year After Coming Out as Gay, Warriors President Rick Welts at Peace," *Outsports,* April 10, 2012, http://www.outsports. com/2012/4/10/4052920/a-year-after-coming-out-as-gay-warriors -president-rick-welts-at-peace.

162   *in the big four major sports leagues:* Jason Collins, "Parting Shot: Jason Collins Announces NBA Retirement in His Own Words," *Sports Illustrated,* November 24, 2014, http://www.si.com/ nba/2014/11/19/jason-collins-retirement-nba. *could inhibit other players from coming out:* Michelangelo Signorile, "Michael Sam and the NFL's Virulent Homophobia," *Huffington Post,* September 22, 2014, http://www.huffingtonpost.com/ michelangelo-signorile/michael-sam-and-the-nfls_b_5751632 .html; ESPN's Adam Schefter, post on Twitter, September 1, 2014, https://twitter.com/AdamSchefter/status/506513600044101632; Mike Freeman, "Michael Sam Not Being Signed: On the Media, Excuse-Making, and Homophobia," *Bleacher Report,* September 2, 2014, http://bleacherreport.com/articles/2183720-michael-sam -not-being-signed-on-the-media-excuse-making-and-homophobia;

Jim Buzinski, "Michael Sam Being Cut Will Give Other Gay Pro Athletes Pause," *Outsports*, October 22, 2014, http://www.outsports .com/2014/10/22/7037797/michael-sam-cut-dallas-cowboys-gay -players-nfl-future; Cyd Zeigler, "Michael Sam's NFL Snub Already at Historic Level," *Outsports*, November 4, 2014, http://www .outsports.com/2014/11/4/7152717/michael-sam-nfl-draft-snub-gay. *"It is the working relationship":* Josh Katzowitz, "Giants Hiring of Former WR David Tyree Already Causing Controversy," *CBSSports,* July 22, 2014, http://www.cbssports.com/nfl/eye-on- football/24633397/giants-hiring-of-former-wr-david-tyree-already- causing-controversy.

163   *"Honestly, I would":* Kenneth Lovett, "David Tyree, Hero of Giants' Super Bowl Upset of Patriots, Said He'd Trade Win to Block Gay Marriage," *New York Daily News,* June 20, 2011, http:// www.nydailynews.com/news/politics/david-tyree-hero-giants -super-bowl-upset-patriots-trade-win-block-gay-marriage -article-1.129720.

164   *"If this does pass":* "Champion of Marriage: David Tyree," YouTube, https://www.youtube.com/watch?v=i6lwIx9f5uk.
a strongly worded press release: "When Did David Tyree Decide to be Straight?" (press release), Human Rights Campaign, July 22, 2014, http://www.hrc.org/press-releases/entry/when-did-david -tyree-decide-to-be-straight. HRC sent out a second press release the next day: "NY Giants Defend David Tyree After Heinous Anti- gay Comments Come to Light" (press release), Human Rights Campaign, July 23, 2014, http://www.hrc.org/press-releases/entry/ ny-giants-defend-david-tyree-after-heinous-anti-gay-comments -come-to-light.
"We don't got no gay people": Gary Myers, "Backup Cornerback Chris Culliver Makes Anti-gay Comments, Issues Half-hearted Apology Through San Francisco 49ers," *New York Daily News,* January 30, 2013, http://www.nydailynews.com/sports/football/ culliver-anti-gay-remarks-issues-apology-49ers-article-1.1251764.
GLAAD, in fact, appeared satisfied: Aaron McQuade, "GLAAD, Athlete Ally, and You Can Play Respond to Anti-gay Remarks from San Francisco 49er Player Chris Culliver," GLAAD, January 30, 2013, http://www.glaad.org/blog/glaad-athlete-ally-and-you-can -play-respond-anti-gay-remarks-san-francisco-49er-player-chris;

"sensitivity training": Tyson Langland, "Chris Culliver Takes the Initiative to Learn More About LGTBQ," *Bleacher Report,* February 2, 2013, http://bleacherreport.com/articles/1512683-chris-culliver -takes-the-initiative-to-learn-more-about-lgtbq.

"Sometimes you say some things": Dan Benton, "Giants' Jerry Reese Stands by Decision to Hire David Tyree; Human Rights Campaign Not Happy," Giants 101, July 23, 2014, http://www.giants101 .com/2014/07/23/giants-jerry-reese-stands-by-decision-to-hire -david-tyree-human-rights-campaign-not-happy/.

165   *wouldn't have drafted Sam:* Ryan Parker, "Tony Dungy's Comments on Openly Gay NFL Player Michael Sam Draw Ire," *Los Angeles Times,* July 21, 2014, http://www.latimes.com/sports/sportsnow/la -sp-sn-tony-dungy-michael-sam-20140721-story.html.

Dungy's clarification: "Dungy: Sam Deserves NFL Chance," *ESPN,* July 23, 2014, http://espn.go.com/nfl/story/_/id/11248177/tony- dungy-clarifies-comments-michael-sam-st-louis-rams.

a "distraction" of any kind: Cyd Zeigler, "Tony Dungy Says He Would Welcome Ray Rice, Doesn't Want Michael Sam," *Outsports,* November 30, 2014, http://www.outsports.com/2014/11/30/7311813/ tony-dungy-ray-rice-michael-sam-gay-nfl.

the Giants were given cover: Michael O'Keeffe, "You Can Play Founder Says Executive Director Wade Davis Will Talk to NY Giants Director of Player Development David Tyree," *New York Daily News,* July 24, 2014, http://www.nydailynews.com/sports/ football/giants/giants-gm-jerry-reese-defends-david-tyree-gay -rights-group-rips-hiring-article-1.1877792.

166   *Patrick Burke, a straight ally:* "Welcome from the Founders," You Can Play Project, http://youcanplayproject.org/pages/welcome -from-the-founders.

"He approached me" and following: Wade Davis, "Only Love Drives Out Hate," Monday Morning Quarterback, *Sports Illustrated,* July 24, 2014, http://mmqb.si.com/2014/07/24/new-york-giants-david -tyree-gay-comments-wade-davis/?utm_source=fantasyleaguegm .com.

"While I don't think wrongheaded views": Dan Graziano, "David Tyree Hire a Bad Move for Giants," *NFL Nation* (blog), ESPN, July 22, 2014, http://espn.go.com/blog/new-york-giants/post/_/id/37199/ david-tyree-hire-a-bad-move-for-giants.

167 *"doesn't even know what conversion therapy is"*: Cyd Zeigler, "After Speaking with David Tyree, I'm Convinced He Doesn't Support Gay Conversion Therapy and the Giants Aren't Anti-gay," *Outsports*, July 28, 2014, http://www.outsports.com/2014/7/28/5945557/david-tyree-gay-giants-conversion-therapy.
too many men are "effeminate": Screen capture of tweet by author, July 24, 2014, https://twitter.com/MSignorile/status/492501497855619074.
He also had retweeted: Screen capture of tweet by author, July 31, 2014, https://www.facebook.com/108028277819/photos/pb .108028277819.-2207520000.1406899355./10152144355447820/ ?type=1.
"What would you do": Post on Meg Meeker's Facebook page, March 24, 2014, https://www.facebook.com/megmeekermd/photos/a.15737 3247627878.32089.116913701673833/743169905714873/?type=1.
his "spiritual mother" and following: Rachel Tabachnick,. "Anti-gay Gatekeepers of the NFL: The NY Giants' David Tyree Controversy," Political Research Associates, July 25, 2014, http:// www.politicalresearch.org/2014/07/25/anti-gay-gatekeepers-of-the -nfl-the-ny-giants-david-tyree-controversy/#.

168 *Amar'e Stoudemire of the New York Knicks*: David Whitley, "Amar'e Stoudemire's Gay Slur Tweet Is His Fault, Not Twitter's," *Sporting News*, June 29, 2012, http://www.sportingnews.com/nba/ story/2012-06-29/amare-stoudemire-tweet-gay-slur-twitter-fine -50k-new-york-knicks.
a five-year, $100 million contract: Ian Begley, "Amar'e Stoudemire to Miss 6 Weeks," *ESPN*, March 10, 2013, http://espn.go.com/new -york/nba/story/_/id/9035257/amare-stoudemire-six-weeks-left -knee-procedure.
Matt Barnes of the Los Angeles Clippers: Cesar Brioso, "NBA Player Used Gay Slur During Arrest," *USA Today*, October 2, 2012, http:// www.usatoday.com/story/gameon/2012/10/02/matt-barnes-uses -gay-slur-when-getting-arrested/1609049/.
A gay caterer in 2014: Tom Ley, "Lawsuit: Rockets Players Called Gay Caterer a 'Faggot,'" *Deadspin* (blog), Kinja, April 3, 2014, http:// deadspin.com/lawsuit-rockets-players-called-homosexual-caterer -a-f-1557697719.
Roy Hibbert of the Indiana Pacers: Mitch Lawrence, "Pacers Center

Roy Hibbert Apologizes for Gay Slur, Reaches Out to Jason Collins," *New York Daily News,* June 2, 2013, http://www.nydailynews.com/sports/basketball/hibbert-apologizes-gay-slur-article-1.1361086.

169   *"The NBA had an opportunity":* Dave Zirin, "No Homo? No Way: Suspend Roy Hibbert for Game 7," *The Nation,* June 2, 2013, http://www.thenation.com/blog/174612/no-homo-no-way-suspend-roy-hibbert-game-7.

openly gay former player Billy Bean: Michelle Garcia, "Major League Baseball Hires Billy Bean, Honors Gay Legend," *The Advocate,* July 15, 2014, http://www.advocate.com/sports/2014/07/15/major-league-baseball-hires-billy-bean-honors-gay-legend; *taking a stand against "homophobia":* Haley Miller, "Major League Baseball Pledges to Fight Homophobia and Transphobia," Human Rights Campaign blog, July 15, 2014, http://www.hrc.org/blog/entry/major-league-baseball-pledges-to-fight-homophobia-and-transphobia.

sponsoring LGBT Pride Night. Cyd Zeigler, "Chicago White Sox LGBT Pride Night Brings Out the Whiners, Some Claim They Will Boycott Team," *Outsports,* August 5, 2014, http://www.outsports.com/2014/8/5/5968839/chicago-white-sox-gay-night-homophobia.

was supported by the league: Jim Buzinski, "Dale Scott Gets Tons of Support After Coming Out," *Outsports,* December 2, 2014, http://www.outsports.com/2014/12/2/7325207/major-league-baseball-umpire-dale-scott-gay-reactions-coming-out.

When Ray Rice brutally pummeled: Louis Bien, "A Complete Timeline of the Ray Rice Assault Case," SBNation.com, September 15, 2014, http://www.sbnation.com/nfl/2014/5/23/5744964/ray-rice-arrest-assault-statement-apology-ravens.

flew a banner over MetLife Stadium: Renee Lewis, "Women's Group Flies Banners over NFL Games, Demands Goodell Step Down," *Al Jazeera America,* September 14, 2014, http://america.aljazeera.com/articles/2014/9/14/ultraviolet-nfl-rice.html.

170   *A black women's coalition:* Mary C. Curtis, "NFL Meeting with Black Women's Groups on Domestic Violence a 'Productive' Beginning," *Washington Post,* October 2, 2014, http://www.washingtonpost.com/blogs/she-the-people/wp/2014/10/02/nfl-meeting-with-black-womens-groups-on-domestic-violence-a-productive-beginning/.

NFL sponsors: Ira Boudway, "NFL Scandals Reveal the Power of

Corporate Sponsors," *Business Week,* September 17, 2014, http://
www.businessweek.com/articles/2014-09-17/ray-rice-adrian
-peterson-scandals-reveal-the-power-of-nfl-sponsors.

lambasted the league: Rob Gloster, "Senators Criticize NFL over
Ray Rice Episode," NorthJersey.com, September 15, 2014, http://
www.northjersey.com/sports/football/senators-pan-nfl-over-rice
-1.1088055.

ending massive tax breaks: Bruce Alpert, "Congressional
Unhappiness with NFL Grows, with Some Threatening End to Tax
Breaks," *New Orleans Times-Picayune,* NOLA.com, September
22, 2014, http://www.nola.com/politics/index.ssf/2014/09/
congressional_unhappiness_with.html.

Goodell made more than $44 million: Frank Schwab, "Roger Goodell
Made More Than $44 Million Last Year. Wait, What?," *Yahoo!
Sports,* February 14, 2014, http://sports.yahoo.com/blogs/shutdown
-corner/roger-goodell-made-more-44-million-last-wait-211537621
--nfl.html.

an arbitrator reinstated Rice: Amanda Taub, "Ray Rice's Arbitration
Win Proves the NFL Never Took Domestic Violence Seriously," *Vox,*
November 29, 2014, http://www.vox.com/2014/11/29/7304885/ray
-rice-arbitration.

Hundreds of people protested in November 2013: Jeff Baenen,
"Hundreds Rally in Minn. Against Redskins' Name," The Big Story,
Associated Press, November 7, 2013, http://bigstory.ap.org/article/
minn-politicians-criticize-redskins-name.

fifty U.S. senators signed a letter: Erik Brady, "50 Senators Sign Letter
Urging Redskins to Change Team Name," *USA Today,* May 22, 2014,
http://www.usatoday.com/story/sports/nfl/redskins/2014/05/22/
washington-redskins-senate-nickname-american-indians-daniel
-snyder/9439613/.

inspired California legislators: Hunter Schwarz, "California Bill
Inspired by Donald Sterling Bans Pro Sports Owners from Tax
Write Offs for League Fines," *Washington Post,* September 30, 2014,
http://www.washingtonpost.com/blogs/govbeat/wp/2014/09/30/
california-bill-inspired-by-donald-sterling-bans-pro-sports-owners
-from-tax-write-offs-for-league-fines/.

171   *seventeen state lawmakers in Minnesota* and following: Michelangelo
Signorile, "17 Minnesota Lawmakers Demand Vikings Impose

Harsher Penalty on Coach for Anti-gay Comments," *Huffington Post,* August 7, 2014, http://www.huffingtonpost.com/2014/08/07/scott-dibble-gay-minnesota-vikings_n_5657784.html.

given a three-game suspension: Josh Katzowitz, "Vikes Suspend Special Teams Coach Mike Priefer over Kluwe Allegations," *CBSSports,* July 18, 2014, http://www.cbssports.com/nfl/eye-on-football/24627358/vikes-suspend-special-teams-coach-mike-priefer-over-kluwe-allegations.

172 *Kluwe settled with the Vikings:* Amy Forliti, "Chris Kluwe, Minnesota Vikings Reach Settlement to Avert Lawsuit," *Huffington Post,* August 19, 2014, http://www.huffingtonpost.com/2014/08/19/chris-kluwe-vikings-settle_n_5692560.html.

"Mike Priefer said something": Signorile, "17 Minnesota Lawmakers."

INDEX